THE DON

THE DON

The Story of Toronto's Infamous Jail

" Remember the Don "

LORNA POPLAK

To Norma + Gail
Merry Christmas!

DUNDURN
TORONTO

Lorna

Dec 2020

Publisher: Scott Fraser | Acquiring editor: Kathryn Lane | Editor: Dominic Farrell
Cover designer: Sophie Paas-Lang
Cover image: Gary Cross
Printer: Marquis Book Printing Inc.

Library and Archives Canada Cataloguing in Publication

Title: The Don : the story of Toronto's infamous jail / Lorna Poplak.
Names: Poplak, Lorna, author.
Description: Includes bibliographical references and index.
Identifiers: Canadiana (print) 9781459745964 | Canadiana (ebook) 20200333135 | ISBN 9781459745964 (softcover) | ISBN 9781459745971 (PDF) | ISBN 9781459745988 (EPUB)
Subjects: LCSH: Don Jail (Toronto, Ont.)—History. | LCSH: Jails—Ontario—Toronto—History.
Classification: LCC HV8746.C32 T67 2021 | DDC 365/.9713541—dc23

We acknowledge the support of the Canada Council for the Arts and the Ontario Arts Council for our publishing program. We also acknowledge the financial support of the Government of Ontario, through the Ontario Book Publishing Tax Credit and Ontario Creates, and the Government of Canada.

Printed and bound in Canada.

VISIT US AT

dundurn.com | @dundurnpress | dundurnpress | dundurnpress

Dundurn
3 Church Street, Suite 500
Toronto, Ontario, Canada
M5E 1M2

For my family

No one truly knows a nation until one has been inside its jails. A nation should not be judged by how it treats its highest citizens but its lowest ones.

— Nelson Mandela

Prison is essentially a shortage of space made up for by a surplus of time; to an inmate, both are palpable.

— Joseph Brodsky

CONTENTS

AUTHOR'S NOTE

Throughout this book, I usually refer to the historic building that forms its focus as the Don Jail. However, as will be seen from direct quotes included in the text, early sources more often than not called it a gaol, which is a variant and now archaic word for jail. For other correctional institutions, I have followed the generally accepted usage: whereas Chatham, Ontario, had a jail, for example, there were gaols in both Ottawa and Goderich.

All sources agree that construction of the Don Jail started in 1858; there is less consensus on when it ended. Over time, conventional wisdom has suggested that the building was completed and opened in 1865. However, archival newspaper reports point to 1864 as the completion date. As this has been corroborated by several authoritative modern sources, I have accepted 1864 as the year when the Don "welcomed" its first occupants.

It will be noticed that news items from the nineteenth century sometimes quote prices in pounds and sometimes in dollars. The British pound was the official unit of currency in British North America from as early as 1763. In 1853, legislation in the Province of Canada (now Ontario and Quebec) provided that official accounts could be kept in both pounds and dollars. From 1857 the dollar became the official currency in Canada, although merchants continued to use whichever currency they preferred until well into the 1870s. Throughout the whole period, the pound was worth four dollars. When pounds are used in archival news reports, I have provided the dollar equivalent in square brackets.

The Toronto city council was instrumental in the establishment of the jail in the 1850s. Over the years, it also played a vital role in its funding and supervision. Members of the city council were initially called aldermen; only in 1989 did they become known as councillors — not in the interests of gender neutrality, as might be expected, but to comply with changes introduced in the provincial Municipal Act.

Early European travellers and settlers in what is now known as Toronto fearfully documented a silent disease characterized by "agues [shivering fits] and intermittent fevers" that ravaged the population each year. One writer in the early 1800s claimed that possibly five-sevenths of the populace was afflicted. Although these agues and fevers were originally attributed to a foul-smelling and poisonous vapour called a miasma that was released, mainly at night, it is now accepted that the cause was malaria, which was prevalent in Ontario at the time. As I write, another silent and exceptionally deadly airborne killer is wreaking havoc on communities around the globe. It is my fervent hope that viable therapies will soon be developed, as well as a vaccine to stop the spread of this lethal pandemic. In the meantime, I salute all those who risk their lives to keep ours safe.

INTRODUCTION

On December 31, 1977, the correctional services minister of Ontario rang out the old year with a sledgehammer blow to the cornerstone of an old building on the east side of the Don River in Toronto. He was not alone: another senior correctional services official and a well-known activist also took a crack at it. Watched by television crews, newspaper reporters, politicians, police officers, jail superintendents, and a few bemused members of the public, they finally managed to chip away a one-foot-square piece of stone from the building's façade.

The target of all this negativity was the infamous Toronto Jail, also known as the Toronto gaol, the Don Jail, the Old Don, or, simply, the Don. It was not the first time that this institution, located at the northwest corner of Gerrard Street East and Broadview Avenue, had been assailed during its 113-year lifespan, but previous attacks had been verbal rather than physical. The jail had been variously called a "lion's den," a "black hole of Calcutta," "Toronto's Bastile [*sic*]," or worse. The correctional services minister liked to call it a "monument to human misery" in the "early barbaric" style.

Very occasionally, on the other hand, the Don Jail had been lauded as a veritable "palace for prisoners," incorporating the finest and most progressive of correctional philosophies. This was certainly true in the mid-1800s, when the building was conceived and constructed.

||||||||||||

The Don, Toronto's fourth jail, opened its doors to its first reluctant residents in 1864, predating the Confederation of Canada by three years. It originally stood remote from the city on the "wrong" side of the Don River, the meandering and strategically significant waterway that spilled into Lake Ontario just east of where a tiny settlement had been established in 1793 by British colonists in what was then the newly formed province of Upper Canada.

In accordance with a Royal Proclamation of 1763 relating to the governance of Britain's territorial possessions in North America, the legal system adopted in Upper Canada was English law.

When it came to criminal justice, did British law guarantee the fair and equitable treatment of those accused of committing an offence in Upper Canada? Not at all. In those days, it was all about crime and punishment. And the crime did not have to be very significant by modern standards to earn a very harsh penalty, one that was generally administered in full public view. Cursing or refusing to go to church could lead to corporal or physical punishment — flogging, branding, or being locked in wooden stocks for hours or days were the norm. Then there were the offences that were punishable by death. The list of capital crimes in Upper Canada in the early 1800s was a long one: prior to 1833, a person could receive the death penalty for killing (or even maiming) a cow, burning a stack of corn, or impersonating a pensioner. And, as was laid down in English law, capital punishment always meant death by hanging.

While the penalties generally involved public humiliation or shaming, there were, of course, also jails. Authorities needed a secure place to confine offenders pending the execution of their sentence. Primitive lockups have existed from early times; however, the idea of detention as punishment is more recent, largely influenced by the writings in the late 1700s and early 1800s of reformers, such as the British philanthropist John Howard, who were horrified by the appalling conditions they came across in penal institutions.

In 1792, an act was passed by the first Parliament of Upper Canada that called for the construction of a court house and jail in each district of the province, and another law in 1810 provided for the use of jails as houses of correction for "idle and disorderly" persons. By the mid-1800s, two types of institution had emerged in Canada for the confinement of wrongdoers — or alleged wrongdoers.

The first, jails, were generally smaller establishments, run by local or district authorities. In addition to serving as "holding tanks" for people on remand (that is, awaiting trial or sentencing), they housed offenders with short-term sentences or those appealing their sentences, as well as individuals waiting for transfer to a provincial or federal facility. As many of these inmates might be guilty of serious crimes such as armed robbery or murder, and as some of their stays turned out much longer than anticipated, it followed that jails were viewed as maximum-security facilities.

The second type, penitentiaries, were run by provincial and federal governments to house prisoners serving longer sentences. An act in Upper Canada in 1834 paved the way for the construction of the first Canadian penitentiary, which opened the following year at Portsmouth, near Kingston, and later became known as the Kingston Penitentiary. Besides imposing hard and often unproductive labour on offenders, early penitentiaries were designed to give them time, lots of time, to repent their actions through isolation, silence, and hefty doses of religious instruction.

The Don Jail, originally a joint venture between the City of Toronto and the County of York, belonged in the first category. By 1958, nearly a century after the Don's opening, grossly inadequate conditions and chronic overcrowding in the antiquated building led to the addition of a new wing. This newer facility was officially called the Toronto Jail, but, predictably, it was nicknamed the New Don, and, eventually, the Don. Both jails were taken over by the province of Ontario in the late 1960s.

The pages that follow are not an academic treatise on penal philosophy or Canadian correctional institutions. Instead, they tell of the struggle in one small corner of the Canadian correctional system to negotiate the complicated and often contentious relations between a jail and the city that sprang up around it. The story of Toronto's infamous Don jails raises thorny questions: How and why did the Old Don deviate so radically from the enlightened reformist principles that underpinned its architecture and original correctional practices? Did the jails protect individuals on both sides of the barred doors and windows? Did they in any way meet the requirements of a rapidly expanding city in an ever-changing world? And what should be done with a toxic artifact once it has outlived its original function?

Although attention will be paid to both jails, it is the original Don that, as the book's cover so graphically illustrates, forms the main focus.

In addition to bringing to light the facts behind its location and construction, *The Don* is the intertwining saga of the historic jail and the people who have occupied it during its one-hundred-and-fifty-plus years of existence. To quote American poet Henry Wadsworth Longfellow, "all houses wherein men have lived and died are haunted houses." Many men — and women — have lived and died within the bleak precincts of the Don Jail. You will meet a large and diverse group of the spectres, both benevolent and malevolent, that haunt the unhallowed halls of this notorious place: the pitifully young and the old; the guardians and the guarded; the criminal, the innocent, and the mentally afflicted.

Ontario Corrections Minister Frank Drea was not granted his New Year's wish for 1978. The fourth Toronto jail still stands on the east bank of the Don River, in the very heart of what is now the thriving urban community of Riverdale. Today, the building seems much diminished: a small, stone centre block with two wings, dwarfed by a multi-storey health centre on its western flank. For much of its existence, however, this controversial institution dominated the news, the skyline, and the consciousness of the city.

So this, too, is a story of Toronto, seen through the prism of the infamous jail that, since its inception in the mid-1800s, has left such an indelible mark on the city it has served.

4

CHAPTER 1

Out with the Old

The year 1793 saw the establishment, on the northern shore of Lake Ontario in Upper Canada, of the garrison town of "muddy" York (now Toronto), all laid out in a neat little ten-block grid that would have made the Romans blush with pride. Some seven years later, its first jail was built on the south side of King Street, just east of Yonge Street, to accommodate a bewildering jumble of men, women, children, lunatics, debtors, and inmates awaiting trial or execution of sentence.

Henry Scadding, nineteenth-century scholar and chronicler of long-ago Toronto, describes this appallingly primitive structure in his book *Toronto of Old* as "a squat unpainted wooden building with hipped roof, concealed from persons passing in the street by a tall cedar stockade such as those which we see surrounding a Hudson's Bay post or a military wood-yard. At the outer entrance hung a billet of wood suspended by a chain communicating with a bell within." That wood-chunk-and-chain communication device was a mischief magnet for naughty boys. One "clever youth," notes Scadding, received very rough treatment from the custodian's son on being caught in the act of pulling on the billet and running away.

The basic materials used for construction were not the issue. With the exception of the first Houses of Parliament of Upper Canada, two "elegant" brick halls connected by a covered walkway at the corner of Berkeley and Palace (now Front) streets, the first hastily constructed buildings that sprang up in the new town during the last few years of the eighteenth century were all built using the only material that came readily to hand: wood.

However, none of them could possibly have been as wretched as that bleak structure at the corner of King Street and what is now Leader Lane. Consisting of ten cells, each measuring ten feet by fourteen feet, and two additional rooms with the luxury of "turn-up" beds for the jailer and the keeper, it was the jail of the Home District, one of the four huge tracts of land that constituted Upper Canada (now Ontario) at the time.

By 1811 its condition was "dilapidated and comfortless," and, clearly, hazardous to all. John Beikie, the local sheriff, sombrely reported to the city magistrates "that the sills of the east cells of the Jail of the Home District are completely rotten; that the ceilings in the debtors' rooms are insufficient; and that he cannot think himself safe, should necessity oblige him to confine any persons in said cells or debtors' rooms." In December of that year, Beikie submitted a letter to the magistrates containing a further litany of serious complaints: "The

"Muddy" York's first jail, built around 1800. The primitive log cabin surrounded by a wooden palisade was situated on the corner of what is now King Street East and Leader Lane.

Prisoners in the Cells ... suffer much from Cold and Damp, there being no method of communicating heat from the Chimnies [*sic*], nor any Bedsteads to raise the Straw from the Floors which lie nearly, if not altogether, on the ground." He suggested setting up a small stove in the lobby between each range of cells and providing rugs or blankets for the "unhappy Persons confined." And unhappy they certainly must have been, sleeping on a thin layer of straw and totally without heat in an oversized log cabin in the depths of a frigid Upper Canadian winter. Reportedly, they would sometimes escape through the roof to show their extreme disapproval of the abysmal conditions.

It wasn't as if folks back then weren't aware of best practices when it came to building jails. In August 1796, Lieutenant Peter Russell, administrator of Upper Canada, stated in a letter quoted by Edith G. Firth in *The Town of York 1793–1815: A Collection of Documents of Early Toronto* that when laying out a jail "the Scite [*sic*] ... should be chosen high & dry, for the sake of health & defence." Russell also had firm ideas on the inventory requirements for an up-to-date jail. In a letter in May 1798, this one to Alexander McDonell, sheriff of the Home District, Russell advises that McDonell "will likewise be pleased to provide Handcuffs and other Irons for binding gross Offenders, and stocks for punishing those who may deserve such Chastisement."

In addition to the regular brutal varieties of "chastisement" — flogging, branding, stocks — the threat of capital punishment always loomed large. In 1800, a certain Humphrey Sullivan, as reported in a court document in Firth's collection, was convicted in York for knowingly passing a counterfeit note. The chief justice rose, recommended the man "to the mercy of God for pardon and salvation," and sentenced him to death.

All types of punishment would generally be carried out in a place thronged with onlookers for maximum effect, such as a marketplace, and (or so the authorities hoped) would serve as a stern warning to other possible transgressors.

Scadding describes a public execution that was held in front of York's original jail — it was "ridiculous, were not the occasion so seriously tragic." Who knows what crime, grave or trivial, the condemned man had committed? One thing was for sure: he categorically refused to walk the plank placed between the cart on which he stood and the scaffold where he was to be hanged. In an attempt to help the sheriff, whose job it was to organize the hanging, and to encourage the doomed man to cooperate, the officiating clergyman gave a demonstration. He climbed onto the plank and walked toward the scaffold. "See how easy it is?" you can imagine him saying. "The condemned," writes Scadding, "demur[red] and openly remark[ed] on the obvious difference in the two cases." Eventually, the noose was placed around the neck of the "wretched culprit," and the cart was wheeled away. Instead of a quicker and presumably more humane death from a broken neck, the victim died by slow strangulation.

One source lists the number of men and women living in York in 1797 as 241. Although the population fluctuated, numbers continued to rise. In 1820, there were 1,240 residents. Three years later, the town consisted of 209 houses, twenty-seven stores, and five storehouses. Accommodating the expanding criminal element that accompanied this growth meant that a new and bigger jail was urgently required.

So, in 1824, Jail Number One was replaced by Jail Number Two, situated a few paces away on the north side of King Street near Church Street. In his *Landmarks of Toronto*, John Ross Robertson, the founder of the *Toronto Evening Telegram*, describes the jail as "a good, substantial, plain-looking two-storied red brick building." Scadding, however, was much less complimentary, saying that the jail was "of a pretentious character, but of poor architectural style." This plain, poorly styled building had an equally ugly twin on its eastern flank: the court house. A pediment like that of a Greek temple stood at the top of both buildings, and stone pilasters ran up the front and outer edges. There were gables and chimneys, and a stone staircase at the front to finish off the picture. The parish stocks took grim pride of place at the entrance to the jail.

York's second jail, built in 1824 on the corner of what is now King Street East and Toronto Street. Henry Scadding, nineteenth-century chronicler of long-ago Toronto, described it as "of poor architectural style."

The buildings were designed by multitalented doctor, lawyer, architect, and politician William Warren Baldwin, and the combined cost for the two was £3,800 [$15,200]. On April 24, as was customary, there was a stone-setting ceremony, which was attended by dignitaries including His Excellency Lieutenant Governor Maitland, members of the Executive Council, an assortment of judges, lawyers, and magistrates, and an elite group of York townsfolk.

Scadding picks up the story here with a quote from the *Canadian Review* of July 1824: "A sovereign and half-sovereign of gold, and several coins of silver and copper, of the present reign, together with some newspapers and other memorials of the present day, were deposited in a cavity of the stone, over which a plate of copper, bearing an appropriate inscription, was placed." Then His Excellency gave a whack with a hammer — although exactly what he whacked is not made clear — and the ceremony ended with "several hearty cheers."

Perhaps this second jail was a step up architecturally from the original drafty log cabin, but inmates were similarly wretchedly treated. In *Pioneer Crimes and Punishments in Toronto and the Home District*, James Edmund Jones points out that it was only in 1836 that soup was introduced into their diet — before that, in both jails, the fare had consisted of just dry bread and water, the bread supposedly distributed three times a day, but often at the whim of the jailer.

In March 1835, a grand jury noted that "they have seen the state of the prisoners with great concern; these suffer intensely from cold, as glass in the windows is broken. There is no adequate supply of straw and blankets. Many of the prisoners are necessarily entirely innocent." (Disgracefully, it would take until 1851 before inmates were provided with iron bedsteads instead of having to sleep directly on the ground.) And another grand jury in 1837 recorded this blistering criticism of the classification of inmates: the jurors were "obliged to mark with a most decided disapprobation the practice of promiscuously confining together the young, the novice in crime, the hardened felon and the unfortunate maniac."

On April 12, 1838, according to a 2003 commemorative plaque, some ten thousand people gathered in front of the jail to watch the execution of Samuel Lount and Peter Matthews. (Although the number seems high, given that the population of Toronto was 12,571 at the time, it is possible that people had flooded in from other parts of Canada and even the United States to witness the controversial hanging.)

Samuel Lount was born in Pennsylvania but moved with his family to Upper Canada in 1811. He eventually settled at Holland Landing, where he earned his living primarily as a blacksmith. By 1834, he was deeply involved in public politics in the County of Simcoe. Peter Matthews was Canadian-born, an ex-military man who had a farm near Pickering. The bond between the two men was their friendship and political association with Scottish-born William Lyon Mackenzie: newspaper man, first mayor of Toronto, and later leader of the radical element of the Reform movement. These Reformers vehemently opposed the government of the colony, which was then dominated by a conservative clique of British loyalists called the Family Compact.

In the general election of 1836, the new lieutenant governor, Sir Frances Bond Head, allied himself with the Conservative Party. Mackenzie's Reformers were utterly demolished. The Conservatives embraced loyalty to the British Crown and were opposed to reform of any nature. Their successful campaign was helped along by the violence and intimidation exercised during the election by the Orange Order, a powerful Protestant social and political organization.

With their electoral defeat, the Mackenzie Reformers despaired of changing the status quo by legitimate means, and in December 1837 they launched what has come to be known as the Upper Canada Rebellion. This failed disastrously, with the defeat of the poorly armed rebels in a series of skirmishes with loyalist troops. Mackenzie fled to the United States, although he was ultimately pardoned. He returned to Canada, and to public office, in the early 1850s. Many of his fellow rebels were not as fortunate: some were killed; others were jailed or transported to the penal colony of Van Diemen's Land (now Tasmania), Australia.

However, the authorities decided to set a stern example with two of Mackenzie's most faithful followers, Lount and Matthews — this despite the fact that Lount had attempted to get medical assistance for a loyalist officer during the rebellion and had stopped Mackenzie from burning down the sheriff's house, and Matthews had fought with British Loyalists against the Americans in the War of 1812. In the end, though, all of this counted for nothing. The two men were convicted of high treason, placed in shackles, and thrown into the Toronto jail to await their death by hanging.

Even though the jail yard was surrounded by a fifteen-foot-high palisade, the gallows were perfectly visible to both inmates and onlookers. The foreman of the team tasked with building the scaffold, a young Yorkshireman named Joseph Sheard, who later became mayor of Toronto, hotly refused to have anything to do with it. "I'll not put a hand to it. Lount and Matthews have done nothing that I might not have done myself, and I'll never help build a gallows to hang them."

The horror and pathos of their execution is captured by Robertson in a long description provided by a man who was in jail with the two Reformers. On that fine spring morning in April 1838, with government troops ("Orange militia") nervously standing by with loaded muskets to prevent any rescue, the two men were led out in chains. "Lount ... stopped at the door. We could not see him, but there were sad hearts in that room as we heard Samuel Lount's voice, without a quiver in it, give us his last greeting: 'Be of good courage, boys. I am not ashamed of anything I've done. I trust in God, and I'm going to die like a man.'"

Lount and Matthews were hanged side by side. Their bodies were buried in the Potter's Field, a non-sectarian cemetery on Bloor Street just west of Yonge Street, now long gone. They were reinterred some years later in the Toronto Necropolis, situated on Winchester Street on the west side of the Don Valley. Today, a large memorial to the two men, buried as traitors but now praised as heroes, stands in the Necropolis. Interestingly, you will also find there the tomb of William Lyon Mackenzie, to whom Lount and Matthews were so tragically linked, as well as that of our historian John Ross Robertson.

The third Toronto jail (or more correctly, the first one, as it was constructed after the city was incorporated in 1834 and its name changed from York to Toronto) made no bones about what it was. As Robertson wittily puts it, "the whole building plainly said: This is a prison." It was built on a green overlooking the harbour on the south side of Front Street between Berkeley and Parliament streets. This was the same site that had previously been occupied by both the first and second Parliament buildings, which had been destroyed by fire in 1813 and 1824 respectively. Designed by John G. Howard and constructed from grey Kingston limestone, the structure cost $80,000, a very tidy sum

The stone jail built in 1840 overlooking the harbour on Front Street East between Berkeley and Parliament streets. A forbidding structure with two wings radiating from a central core.

in 1840. It consisted of a central core, topped with a turret, and two wings. Arched windows pierced the walls on each floor. In *Toronto, No Mean City*, architect Eric Arthur unflatteringly comments that "the windows in this grim pile remind one of a columbarium, with its niches for urns [containing cremated remains]." A twelve-foot-high stone perimeter wall completed the bleak picture. When required, a scaffold was erected on top of the wall to allow the public clear view of a hanging.

The roof sported a small brass cannon for firing off salutes on the Queen's birthday and other special occasions, and the green sloping down to the lake was a favourite play area for local boys.

In stark contrast to the image of carefree boys playing on the lawns was an 1855 report in the *Globe* that highlighted the ongoing problems caused by "committing infants to the common gaol, there to be educated into finished thieves." The article posed some difficult and pertinent questions: "How shall we in future deal with the juveniles? Shall we go on for years, taking no steps to train and save them? Shall we shut our eyes to the ruin which awaits them in prison?"

The governor of the jail at the time was George Littleton Allen. Born in 1811 to a Protestant family in Sligo, Ireland, Allen immigrated to New York at the age of fifteen before heading north to settle in Toronto. In 1847, he was appointed to the position of high (or chief) constable of the Toronto Police. His subsequent stint as governor of the jail, beginning in 1852, was riddled with controversy and censure: the following year, the *Globe* expressed with deep regret in its report of proceedings in the Police Court that

> liquor-selling ha[d] been practised in the gaol for some time past. Mr. G.L. Allen, the gaoler, was accused of selling strong drink to the prisoners without a license, and the charge being fully proved, the magistrate fined him $10.... Supplying prisoners with strong drink, to gratify their base appetite, and to deaden their moral sense, was one of the worst parts of the old gaol system, and one of the first which was removed.... The excuse of keeping liquor for cases of delirium tremens is a very flimsy covering for the general sale of the article.

Allen evidently dodged this particular bullet, as he was still in a position in November 1856 to make a generous offer to the city. He was willing to give up his own apartments at the jail, with the exception of one bedroom, in exchange for a home, "free of rent and taxes," for his family. This, he noted, would make space available in the jail to house fifty more inmates. And, fortunately, he had already found a residence that would suit his purposes very well, at an annual cost of $400.

The governor had laid the groundwork for his proposal two months earlier in an ominous letter to Mayor John Beverley Robinson, in which he stressed "the urgent necessity that exists for providing immediate accommodation for city prisoners." Failing that, he warned, "it will become absolutely necessary to close the present prison against their reception; for we are unable to find even standing room for them, much less sleeping accommodation. We have now *one hundred and eighty prisoners* within our walls, just one hundred more than the gaol was ever designed to keep."

Allen's numbers did not quite add up: even with his suggested changes, the jail would still have been fifty inmates over the limit. However, the unnerved council hastily gave him the go-ahead to take the house.

Backing up the governor's bitter complaint about having to shoehorn close to two hundred prisoners into a space originally designed to hold less than half that number was this passionate plea in November 1856 from the *Globe*, in anticipation of upcoming municipal elections: "Who will take up the gaol question and make it a 'plank' at the elections? Surely no candidate could better commend himself to the moral part of the community, than by presenting a feasible scheme for relieving the city from the evils, the danger, and the expense of such an establishment as the present gaol. If the city must build a gaol for itself, let it be done at once. We shall save both money and character by expedition."

Toronto had clearly outgrown its jail — again. According to the census of 1851–52, the population had swelled to 30,775, with an associated increase in criminal activity. The current institution was straining at the seams; there was an urgent need for something bigger and better to house the inmate population.

CHAPTER 2

Location, Location, Location

The end of 1856 ushered in some good news: the city finally had plans to build a new jail. And the burning question, "Where shall we put it?" seemed to have been satisfactorily resolved in the opinion of the men who governed Toronto.

This is where the Don River flows into the picture. Toronto was rapidly expanding on the western side of the river; the jail would be built on its eastern bank, outside the city limits.

Long before the river's name became a three-letter word, the local Indigenous Peoples had their own names for it: NechengQuaKekonk, as recorded by Crown surveyor Alexander Aiken in September 1788, and Wonscotonach, as mentioned by late-eighteenth-century surveyor Augustus Jones. Jones translated it as "'back burnt grounds," perhaps as an allusion to the vulnerability of the area to sweeping forest fires. Historian Jennifer L. Bonnell prefers Anishinaabe scholar and linguist Basil Johnston's alternative translation of "burning bright point or peninsula," possibly a reference to what was once a peninsula near the mouth of the river, now the Toronto Islands.

We catch a glimpse of the pristine, meandering waters of the Don through the eyes of British artist and diarist Elizabeth Posthuma Simcoe. In July 1793, Elizabeth took up residence in the tiny, newly named town of York with her husband and family in two canvas houses, better known as tents. (According to one legend, now convincingly debunked, the tents had originally belonged to British explorer and navigator Captain James Cook.) Where these famous canvas houses were pitched is difficult to pinpoint: tradition has it that they were moved several times to different sites on the western side of town.

Elizabeth's husband was John Graves Simcoe, who, in 1791, had been appointed lieutenant governor of the newly created British colony of Upper Canada. Upon his arrival from Britain in 1792, Simcoe had intended to establish the new provincial capital in Newark (now Niagara-on-the-Lake), but, given the simmering disagreements between the English and their American neighbours to the south, he needed to find a more secure site. His next choice, an inland spot on the River La Tranche (Thames), was frustrated by a different kind of enemy: Lord Dorchester, the captain general and governor-in-chief of both Upper Canada and Lower Canada (now Quebec). Dorchester, Simcoe's commanding officer (and nemesis), coldly vetoed his suggestion.

Simcoe, ever resourceful, set off from Newark with a party of officers in May 1793 to scope out another possible location for the new provincial capital. As his wife recorded in a letter dated May 13: "Coll [*sic*] Simcoe returned from Toronto, & speaks in praise of the harbour, & a fine spot near it covered with large Oak which he intends to fix upon as a scite [*sic*] for a Town. I am going to send you some beautiful Butterflies."

After settling into the family's new canvas pad, Elizabeth Simcoe went exploring. She introduced her diary in August 1793 to "a Creek which is to be called the River Don. It falls in to the Bay near the Peninsula. After we entered we rowed some distance among Low lands covered with Rushes, abounding with wild ducks & swamp black birds with red wings. About a mile beyond the Bay the banks became high & wooded, as the River contracts its width."

The river, it seemed, was about to lose its time-honoured Indigenous names and be sucked into the colonial lexicon. As decreed by a nostalgic

Lieutenant Colonel John Graves Simcoe, it would thenceforth be called the Don River, after a river in far-off South Yorkshire, England.

Simcoe had done something very similar three months earlier with the name of the provincial capital. On May 31, Simcoe wrote the following to the acting colonial administrator and lieutenant governor of Lower Canada, Major General Alured Clarke: "It is with great pleasure that I offer to you some observations upon the Military strength and Naval convenience of Toronto (now York), which I propose immediately to occupy." In the space of just a few days and with a few simple strokes of his pen, the lieutenant governor had officially changed the name of the capital from Toronto to York.

Although strategic, renaming the town after the Duke of York, an unsuccessful military commander, in an attempt to curry favour with the king of England, the duke's father, was not exactly a successful branding exercise. This was because the settlement — a ten-block hamlet, really, at that stage — became known as "Little York," or even more pejoratively, "Muddy York" to distinguish it from other far more glamorous Yorks scattered around the globe: think New York City, for example.

Even at the time, Simcoe's practice of choosing English names above traditional ones led to protest. As mentioned by Edwin C. Guillet in *Pioneer Settlements in Upper Canada*, Irish explorer and artist Isaac Weld, who travelled through the province in 1796, soberly commented: "It is to be lamented that the Indian names, so grand and sonorous, should ever have been changed for others. Newark, Kingston, York are poor substitutes for the original names of the respective places Niagara, Cataraqui, Toronto." Weld simply refused to use the new names.

Amid widespread support, the name York was changed back to Toronto when the city was incorporated in 1834, but other early British names, like that of the Don River, have stuck.

However, in addition to Simcoe's reported distaste for Indigenous names and, probably, his jingoistic desire to put the stamp of Britain on everything he encountered, something much more basic lay at the heart of his decisions: the colonial idea of *terra nullius*, or the belief that the land belonged to no one. This is perfectly illustrated in the words of Joseph Bouchette, who made the first formal survey of Toronto's harbour in 1793, as quoted by Henry Scadding:

> I still distinctly recollect the untamed aspect which the country exhibited when first I entered the beautiful basin, which thus became the scene of my early hydrographical operations. Dense and trackless forests lined the margin of the lake and reflected their inverted images in its glassy surface. The wandering savage had constructed his ephemeral habitation beneath their luxuriant foliage — the group then consisting of two families of Mississagas, — and the bay and neighbouring marshes were the hitherto uninvaded haunts of immense coveys of wild fowl.

The country, then, was "untamed" and the habitation of the "wandering savage" was "ephemeral," with their presence on the land limited to "two families of Mississagas." As Jennifer Bonnell puts it: "Suggestions of an essentially unoccupied, 'hitherto uninvaded' landscape lent support to European territorial claims.... The area's first inhabitants 'left no trace' of their passing: by failing, in the terms of Lockean logic, to use the land to its full capacity, they had no legitimate claim to the lands they occupied. Without the investment of human labour to transform the land, its potential remained untapped, wasted."

And thus up for grabs.

However, although the Indigenous Peoples were not intensive farmers or city builders, archaeological excavations have pointed to the presence of First Nations peoples in the area since the Late Woodland period (1000–1700 CE) and perhaps even earlier. This is acknowledged on a plaque attached to the wall of the Withrow Avenue Junior

Public School on Bain Avenue, close to Riverdale Park on the east side of the Don River. It reads, in part: "As long as 4,000 years ago, this sandy knoll was the location of campsites for generations of native people. It provided an excellent lookout over the Don River Valley for observing game. Here small family groups probably lived in skin tents during hunting seasons. Lost for many years, the site was uncovered by workers digging a roadbed in 1886."

Sadly, as Bonnell points out, with the local Indigenous people, the Mississauga, relinquishing hundreds of thousands of acres to the settlers in a series of land purchases in the late 1700s and early 1800s, this became a story of dispossession. Europeans who arrived on the scene early were richly rewarded with the opportunity to snap up prime lots, both within and outside the new township.

One of the lucky beneficiaries was John Scadding, a native of Devonshire, England, who had lived just down the road from the Wolford estate of John Graves Simcoe. Scadding became Simcoe's farm manager, and the ties between the two men were close and cordial. When Simcoe received his appointment as lieutenant governor and decamped to Niagara in 1792, John Scadding followed him. After the provincial government moved to Toronto/York, Simcoe was happy to ensure that his friend and confidant would be generously recompensed. In 1796, Scadding received a Crown Grant of Lot 15 in the township of York — 253 acres stretching from the Don River in the west to Mill Street (now Broadview Avenue) in the east, and from the present-day Danforth Avenue in the north to the lakeshore in the south.

Lot No. 15, according to John Ross Robertson in his *Landmarks of Toronto*, was a jewel. Some highlights: ancient elms, basswood, butternut, and crabapple trees; lake views in the distance and river scenes in the foreground; the river leaping with salmon and brimming with perch and pike; and the banks alive with game birds such as grouse, quail, and snipe, and "numerous fur-producing animals" such as fox and muskrat, to say nothing of the occasional deer, bear, or wolf. In short, "for the enthusiast in almost every branch of natural history, it was a paradise." It was not so great for farming, but the "first patentee of lot fifteen," John Scadding, did his best.

Scadding initially built a small log cabin and barn on the site in fulfillment of what were called settlement duties. As explained by Elizabeth Simcoe, "the Law obliges persons having Lots of land to build a House upon them within the year." Scadding later constructed a more permanent farmhouse, with a barn for horses and cattle. An early bridge over the Don was named Scadding's Bridge in his honour. The life of this gentleman, described as a veritable pioneer of civilization, was brought to a sudden end in March 1824, when he was struck and mortally injured by a falling tree.

Scadding's family had been living in York since 1821, and their history is tightly woven into the original fabric of the city of Toronto. Remember much-quoted historian and writer Henry Scadding? Well, he was John's youngest son; he not only documented early Toronto but played an active role in its unfolding saga. In 1830 he became the first student enrolled in the newly minted Upper Canada College in York, and later, courtesy of Elizabeth Simcoe, he studied at St. John's College, Cambridge. He returned to Canada in 1837, and the following year he was ordained as a priest.

A deed of sale dated December 30, 1856, records that almost half of the Scadding farm was sold to the "Mayor, Aldermen and Commonalty of the city of Toronto ... for the purposes of an Industrial Farm and Gaol," as T.A. Reed notes in *The Scaddings, A Pioneer Family in York*. The plot consisted of 119 acres of land, bounded by the Don River, Broadview Avenue (then Mill Street), Gerrard Street (according to a map dated 1857, called Danforth Road on the east side of the river), and a line south of today's Danforth Avenue. One of the signatories to that deed was the Reverend Henry Scadding.

It might be thought that British penal reformer John Howard would have approved of the site chosen for the new jail, for, as he wrote in his hugely influential 1777 work, *The State of the Prisons in England and Wales*, "A county gaol, and indeed every prison, should be built on a spot that is airy, and if possible near a river, or brook. I

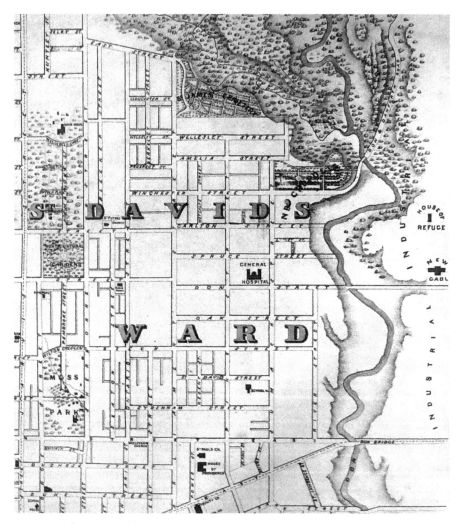

Detail from a City of Toronto map dated 1873, showing the New Gaol and the House of Refuge on the Industrial Farm lands to the east of the Don River.

have commonly found prisons situated near a river, the cleanest and most healthy." He also advised that "an eminence should be chosen: for as the walls round a prison must be so high as greatly to obstruct a free circulation of air, this inconvenience should be lessened by a rising ground." And, thirdly, he stressed that a prison should not be located within the confines of a town or city. On paper, the proposed site seemed just perfect.

However, if Howard had actually surveyed the scene from the banks of the Don River in 1856, he would have been horrified. For by then the river forming the western boundary of the site was no longer the natural paradise so glowingly described by Elizabeth Simcoe and John Ross Robertson.

CHAPTER 3

Paradise Lost

I n the 1790s, Elizabeth Simcoe could enjoy relatively easy access to the beautiful Don River. Out on the water, Elizabeth described "the spot where [the Indians] were catching maskalonge, a superior kind of pike, and pickerell." But even in those early days there were ominous warning signs: "At the mouth of the Don I fished from my carriole, but the fish are not to be caught, as they were last winter, several dozen in an hour. It is said that the noise occasioned by our driving constantly over this ice frightens away the fish."

The Simcoes' country home, Castle Frank, and the site chosen in 1856 for the new jail were on opposite banks of the Lower Don. Formed by the confluence of the east and west branches of the river, this stretch meandered along for some seven kilometres before spilling into Lake Ontario through a widespread marshy delta.

Historians and environmentalists have documented in grim detail the rapid descent of the Lower Don from pristine waterway to toxic sewer.

The original British colonialists, with the fire of Empire in their bellies, were primarily focused on security and economic development, and Toronto fitted these purposes splendidly. As recorded by Edith Firth, Lieutenant Governor Simcoe had reported in May 1793 to his counterpart in Lower Canada, Major General Clarke, that "at the Bottom of the Harbour there is a Situation admirably adapted for a Naval Arsenal and Dock Yard, and there flows into the Harbour a River [the Don] the Banks of which are covered with excellent Timber." The site had strategic importance, too. Historian J.M.S. Careless explains that Toronto's location was particularly significant, as it stood at the junction of the land and water routes through the Great Lakes region. Particularly notable were "its accessible lake harbour, low, easily traversed shoreline, and gate position on a passage through the midst of southern Ontario."

Once it had been decided that, in addition to a naval arsenal, this admirable spot at the bottom of the harbour would become the new capital of Upper Canada, Simcoe and other early settlers snapped up prime one-hundred- and two-hundred-acre lots on both sides of the river.

It did not take long for the newcomers to start chopping away at all that "excellent Timber" on the banks of the river, and within two years a sawmill was up and running on the lower reaches of the Don. Then came a gristmill for grinding grain. The area just east of the river, originally called the Don Mills and today known as Todmorden Mills, developed into a small industrial complex that included a brewery, a distillery, and, by 1827, another gristmill and a paper mill.

By 1825, as Jennifer Bonnell notes in *Imagined Futures and Unintended Consequences*, there were twenty-three saw- and gristmills along the Don River and its tributaries. Potteries and brickworks profiting from the deep clay deposits in the Lower Don Valley, an ancient lakebed, also made an early appearance. The fast-flowing river played three important roles in servicing these industries: it powered millstones, turbines, and other machinery; its water served both as a coolant and an ingredient; and it became an all-too-convenient location to dump garbage and toxic wastes. Predictably, one of the important effects of the deforestation, noise, and poisonous by-products generated by these industrial activities was the extermination of the local fish populations. By the 1860s there were more than fifty mills of various types dotted throughout the river system, and, ominously, the salmon had stopped spawning.

In addition to the growing pollution in the more northerly reaches of the Lower Don, there were from the outset ongoing problems associated with the extensive marshes where the river flowed into the lake.

Many critics well into the 1800s believed that setting up a town at the mouth of the Don River was a really rotten idea. Just why was succinctly and satirically expressed in 1825 by inventor and journalist Edward Allen Talbot:

> The situation of the town is very unhealthy; for it stands on a piece of low marshy land, which is better calculated for a frog-pond, or beaver-meadow, than for the residence of human beings. The inhabitants are, on this account, much subject, particularly in Spring and Autumn, to agues [shivering fits] and intermittent fevers; and probably five-sevenths of the people are annually afflicted with these complaints. He who first fixed upon this spot as the site of the capital of Upper Canada, whatever predilection he may have had for the roaring of frogs, or for the effluvia arising from stagnated waters and putrid vegetables, can certainly have had no very great regard for preserving the lives of his Majesty's subjects.

Was that reference to the frog- and effluvia fancier aimed directly at Lieutenant Governor Simcoe? To be fair, although Simcoe had strongly recommended York as an excellent spot for a naval arsenal, the decision to make it the capital of Upper Canada was not his. It had become the compromise choice following a spat with his hostile boss, Commander-in-chief Lord Dorchester, who strongly favoured Kingston, as opposed to Simcoe's preference for something farther west, along what is now the Thames River. And while the claim that five-sevenths of the population came down with agues and fevers each year is hardly scientific and perhaps not entirely accurate, Talbot did have a point: the place *was* unhealthy. The stagnant waters of the marshlands were fertile breeding grounds for mosquitoes. Whereas it is well understood today that those chills and fevers were symptoms of malaria, which is transmitted through mosquito bites, Talbot's words reflect the popular belief at the time that diseases were caused by a miasma, a foul-smelling vapour emanating from rotting organic matter that hung in the air, especially at night, poisoning anyone unfortunate enough to inhale it. Fears of unseen perils lurking in the east drove the city's expansion westward. As the lieutenant governor of the day explained in 1833 in a letter included in Firth's *The Town of York* collection, "the rapid increase in the population requires that the Town should be extended towards the Westward, the most salubrious and convenient site." As the gentry fled west, the less desirable areas to the east soon began to be populated with workers and working-class families, attracted by lower property prices, taxes, and rents.

The reputation of the marshes as an extensive area where disease and death were rampant and the associated westward movement of the city accelerated the development of what Bonnell calls "noxious" industries both around the river mouth and extending to the north beyond Gerrard Street. She describes these industries as producing what locals considered an offensive and possibly harmful stench from biological wastes and chemical processes, as well as extreme noise, filth, and general unsightliness.

Three exceptionally noxious factories, up and running by the late 1840s, were the harbingers of worse to come.

The first was William Smith's tannery on the east bank of the river, constructed in 1820 on fifty acres of property that had previously belonged to John Scadding. This enterprise provided all-important leather goods for the locals. In doing so, however, it generated odious smells and dumped toxic tanning wastes into the river.

The second major polluter in the area was the Gooderham and Worts gristmill and distillery on the lake front just west of the river mouth. By 1840, more than twenty-eight thousand gallons of whisky were being produced annually to slake the public's thirst for hard liquor. G&W may have been captains of industry, but they, and particularly William Gooderham after the suicide in 1834 of his original partner, James Worts, were not exactly model citizens. In the late 1830s, Gooderham came up with the bright idea of starting a hoggery to utilize the by-products of the distilling process. The company also opened a large dairy near the mill, with sheds on the east side of the river that eventually accommodated some four thousand cows. Ever the entrepreneurs, G&W participated in the development of the Toronto and Nipissing Railway, which not only distributed booze and other products to markets outside Toronto but also transported cattle from the agricultural hinterland in the north to their sheds on the fringes of the city. In addition to the overwhelming stench that pervaded the area, copious volumes of pig and cattle manure were simply drained into the shallow marshes at Ashbridges Bay, provoking howls of protest from the city government, other businesses in the area, and the growing number of working-class folk setting up house in the neighbourhood.

Detail from a City of Toronto map dated 1893, showing the Gooderham and Worts cattle sheds just east of the bend in the Don River. Manure from some four thousand cows was disposed of by simply tipping it into the shallow marshes to the south.

The P.R. Lamb Glue and Blacking Manufactory, established in 1848 on the west side of the river north of Gerrard, completed the unholy trinity. Lamb's boasted of paying the "highest Price in Cash ... for Tanners' Size Pieces, Damaged Hides, Cattle Tails, Horns, &c," which would then be boiled, and boiled again, in an exceptionally malodorous process to create their trademark thick, gooey adhesive. But what were they to do with all the wastes? Luckily, little Lamb's Creek, which fed into Castle Frank Brook and thence into the Don River, was situated just beside the factory. Such a convenient spot to dump all that toxic and evil-smelling sludge.

By 1856, when the city became the proud owner of a hundred-plus acres of former Scadding property, the area outside the city limits to the east of the Don still consisted mainly of dwindling forests and

An advertisement in *Hutchinson's Toronto directory*, 1862–1863, for the P.R. Lamb Glue and Blacking Manufactory. Toxic wastes from the factory contributed to the pollution of the Don River in the mid- to late 1800s.

farmlands. The scene was now set for the establishment of an industrial farm, a new jail, and, as an afterthought, a House of Refuge.

A precedent for the location of these new institutions on the fringes of the city had been established in 1855 when the Toronto General Hospital moved from the downtown area to a four-acre site just east of Parliament Street. In 1853, as noted by Bonnell, a local medical journal decried the relocation: the site was too far from the city centre; it was alarmingly close to the pestilential river with its dreaded miasma; and the poor medical students would have to trudge close to four miles to get to the hospital from the medical school at Trinity College. An editorial in the *Leader* declared that this was absolute nonsense. The old hospital was located as far west of the downtown area as the new one would be to the east; people in the west part of the city got ague, too; and there were simply no facilities for students closer to Trinity College. And, importantly, the site, with "all the advantages which are to be derived from an airy and unconfined position ... has met the general approbation of the public." Case closed. The hospital took in its first patients in 1856.

The House of Refuge, to be situated just north of the jail, was not part of the original plan. In the late 1850s, the Toronto Magdalene Asylum, a women's charitable organization whose main mandate was to protect "fallen women," obtained a lease of five acres on the industrial farm site. In 1860, the refuge opened its doors, thus providing shelter, according to city council minutes, for "the poor and indigent," as well as "idiots," and reform for "the idle, the lewd, the dissolute and the vagrant members of the community."

The site, located beyond the city limits, had two important points in its favour: it was cheap, and, as noted in an inquiry in 1858, its purchase would provide both employment "for the criminal and disorderly portion of our population" and reduce "the city expenditure in connection with the department of Police and Prisons." The assumption was that the land would lend itself to extensive agricultural use. But, as is so often the case, you get what you pay for. As the inquiry sadly discovered: "Of the entire area of about 100 acres, which it is proposed to retain for the purposes of the farm, not more than thirty acres can be brought under cultivation without the expenditure of a very large amount of labour."

However, there may have been additional but far less obvious reasons for choosing this particular semi-rural location.

Despite the increasingly polluted waterway that formed its western boundary, the site was regarded as being located in the countryside. And the countryside occupied a special position within the nineteenth-century psyche. It was viewed as a place of natural beauty, majesty, order, and tranquility, as opposed to the city, which was perceived as overcrowded and rife with disease. Prison reformers like the Englishman John Howard reflected this romantic viewpoint: prisons near a river would be the cleanest and healthiest.

In *Reclaiming the Don*, Jennifer Bonnell posits that there were complex and paradoxical factors underlying the choice of site. The three new institutions would be established in what was considered to be a "restorative landscape," outside, but fairly close to, the city and its corrupting influences. On the one hand, undesirable individuals, such as criminals, vagrants, the poor, the elderly, the "fallen," and the mentally ill would derive the double benefit of being distanced from the harmful effects of the city and placed in the reformative and healing countryside. On the other hand, isolating these damaged individuals would protect "the supposedly uncorrupted residents of the centre" from their debased influence. And so, in a strange parallel with the heavily polluted Don River, the semi-rural space would become a dumping ground for the unpleasant or ugly elements of society.

For better, or perhaps for worse, the die had been cast: the urgently required Toronto jail would be located on a fairly remote parcel of land on the far side of the Don River. The time had now come to choose someone to design and oversee the construction of the new institution.

CHAPTER 4

In with the New

Schools, churches, banks, stores, residences, town halls, court houses, jails — you name it, hotshot architect William Thomas had designed it; some eighty commissions in all since coming to Canada from his native Britain.

Toronto was booming when Thomas and his family arrived in 1843, two years after the merger of Upper and Lower Canada into the Province of Canada. With a population of more than fifteen thousand, Toronto had just three registered architects to cope with the exploding demand for new designs and buildings. For an ambitious professional forced from his native land by a brutal economic downturn, this was the equivalent of architectural heaven. Within a year of hanging out his shingle, Thomas was hard at work.

Energetic and focused, Thomas thrived as both an architect and a surveyor. Most of his work was in Toronto, with the St. Lawrence Hall topping the list of his most-admired public buildings, but a smorgasbord of Thomas-designed structures were erected throughout the Province of Canada and beyond. These included schools in London and Goderich; town halls in Peterborough and Guelph; churches in Etobicoke, London, and Niagara-on-the-Lake; residences, including his very own dwelling, Oakham House, in Toronto; and commercial and industrial buildings in Hamilton, Port Hope, and as far afield as Halifax, Nova Scotia. There were even a jail in Simcoe and a courthouse or two in the mix.

St. Lawrence Hall, designed by William Thomas in 1845, built between 1849 and 1850, and magnificently restored in 1967. It is regarded as one of Thomas's finest Canadian public buildings.

Then in 1857, as Thomas's biographers Glenn McArthur and Annie Szamosi put it, "the bubble of optimism that was generated with the advent of the railroads and sustained by the Crimean War of 1853–56 suddenly burst. In the post-war reaction, the entire world was shaken by panic and depression." Toronto was hardly immune from the economic fallout, with businesses failing and individuals plunged into ruin. Along with his architectural practice, Thomas had been speculating in real estate, and the slump hit hard. In at least one case, he threatened legal action to collect payment, and in December 1858 he noted in a letter to the treasurer of the Brock's Monument project (the towering column he had designed on Queenston Heights had been completed in 1856), that the cash still owed to him for his services would be most useful in his current dire financial situation.

With all of these challenges roiling in the background, Thomas must have been very relieved to be awarded the prestigious commission of architect for Toronto's new jail. In March 1857 he received his brief from the city council: "to prepare a plan for a jail for this city after the model of Pentonville England Reformatory Prison." With modest fanfare, the *Globe* revealed the full extent of the project: "Two wings of this gaol will only be erected at present, the estimated cost of which is about £10,000 [$40,000]. The separate system, now so much in vogue in England, has been adopted, and all the latest improved methods will be introduced, every attention being paid to the physical and moral health of the prisoners, as well as their security."

Given the primitive and hellish predecessors of the proposed institution, these orders seemed remarkably progressive. However, the winds of change had already been blowing through the correctional cosmos for around eighty years. Now, a new and immensely improved penal philosophy was set to breeze into Toronto.

The transformation had been spearheaded by British philanthropist and prison reformer John Howard, who was born in North London in 1726. Described in his bio on the John Howard Society of Canada website as an unloving father and "a strange and complex individual who could not have been everyone's 'cup of tea,'" Howard found his calling after being appointed high sheriff of Bedfordshire in 1773. The sheriff served as the sovereign's personal and military representative in the county, and Howard took his responsibilities very seriously. One of his duties was to inspect the county jail, which typically housed awaiting-trial or short-term prisoners.

What he saw revolted him; so much so that he spent the next seventeen years visiting both jails and prisons designed for long-term incarceration across the length and breadth of the United Kingdom and Europe, dying on the job in the Crimea in 1790.

"I could not enjoy my ease and leisure in the neglect of an opportunity offered me by Providence of attempting the relief of the miserable," he explained in his magnum opus, *The State of the Prisons in England and Wales*, first published in 1777.

Some of the horrors he encountered included inadequate food and water; overcrowding in "close rooms, cells, and subterraneous dungeons," with wet floors and bedding; and poisonous air. "My reader will judge of its malignity, when I assure him, that my clothes were in my first journies [*sic*] so offensive, that in a post-chaise I could not bear the windows drawn up; and was therefore obliged to travel commonly on horseback." He also complained bitterly of what he saw as morally pernicious: the mass incarceration of "all sorts of prisoners together: debtors and felons, men and women, the young beginner and the old offender," generally in one large, wretched open space.

Not content to simply document the inequities he found in the course of his travels, Howard took it one giant step further: he weighed in on the architecture of jails and prisons with a focus on security, health, and order, which he considered crucial to their effectiveness.

In addition to giving advice about the site (an airy spot outside a town or city, and if possible near a river or brook), he strongly supported the idea of separate cells for inmates: "I wish to have so many small rooms or cabins that each criminal may sleep alone.... If it be difficult to prevent their being together in the day-time: they should by all means be separated at night." Besides keeping inmates safe and preventing escapes, he believed that "solitude and silence are favourable to reflection; and may possibly lead them to repentance."

Another key point: "the women-felons [*sic*] ward should be quite distinct from that of the men; and the young criminals from old and hardened offenders." A great concern was the intermingling of debtors and felons, who, he believed, should be separated from one another. Novel recommendations were an adequate supply of fresh water, a "commodious bath with steps ... to wash prisoners that come in dirty," an oven ("nothing so effectually destroys vermin in clothes and bedding"), and an airy infirmary or sick wards. There should be a large workshop for those debtors and felons who wished to work. And, of course, a chapel was an absolute necessity. A stern warning here: those who would tear or otherwise damage Bibles and prayer-books should be punished.

Howard's revelations led to an explosion of new interest in prison construction, especially in Britain. The health of inmates became a major focus, so amenities such as clean water, toilets, baths, and ventilation started popping up in new prisons. The issue of security also received attention. Underpinning the latest designs was a pressing requirement for the surveillance of prisoners at all times and in all places. As Professor Norman Johnston puts it in *The Human Cage: A Brief History of Prison Architecture*, "constant, unseen inspection became the *sine qua non* of good jail design and administration, the mechanism whereby the prison setting could be freed of its old abuses and the prisoners protected from corruption and disruptive behavior."

Johnston adds that architects, court officials, prison directors, master builders, and stonemasons all scrambled to design structures based on three main layouts: the first, rectangular, generally modelled on existing eighteenth-century jails and older ecclesiastical buildings; the second, circular, which included polygonal, or multisided, arrays; and the third, radial, with wings fanning out from a central core. This last style became the rage, so much so that an 1826 British government publication quoted by Johnston announced that "we consider the advantages of the radiating plan to be now so completely established in preference to those of any other, that we should not feel ourselves justified in reporting favorably on a proposed plan of a new county gaol founded on any other principle."

Reformist notions spread like wildfire to other countries, finding their perfect expression across the Atlantic in the separate system developed by the powerful religious and political Quaker community in Pennsylvania. Johnston explains this system:

> The Pennsylvania Quakers gradually forged their philosophy of total isolation of each prisoner night and day. Solitude would serve several purposes: it would be punishment *par excellence*, but more importantly, it would give a man time for reflection and contrition and protect the naive from contamination by the more sophisticated, preventing also plots, escapes and attacks on keepers, which were at the time most prevalent. Religious instruction, work in the cell and visits by philanthropically inclined individuals would complete the job.

In short, the "separate" system meant absolute solitary confinement.

When it came to choosing a layout in the 1820s for the new Cherry Hill penitentiary near Philadelphia in the Eastern District of Pennsylvania (later known as the Eastern State Penitentiary or ESP), it was decided that no better model could be found than the new radial formation adopted so enthusiastically in Britain and beyond. The architect, a young Englishman named John Haviland, accordingly designed a grim and hulking Gothic "hub-and-spoke" structure with seven cell wings spreading out from an inner core. The cells measured eight feet by twelve feet with a height of ten feet, and each one was provided with heating, a tap for fresh water, and a flush toilet. But the unnerved prisoners would know that they were under constant surveillance, not only by guards posted in the central watch tower or peering through peepholes in the cell doors but by a higher presence — the sole light source for each cell was a small window or skylight, ominously called the Eye of God.

Eastern — a true penitentiary with its focus on rehabilitation through penitence and reflection — "welcomed" its first occupants in 1829. With its newfangled radial design, its massive structure, its technical innovations, including heat, running water, and ventilation, its focus on surveillance, and its hugely controversial underlying philosophy, the prison became an instant sensation. Investigators from near and far, including government representatives from Britain, France, Prussia, and other countries, streamed into Philadelphia to evaluate this trendsetter.

Strangely, this system did not gain much traction in the United States, due to a competing reform ideology and architectural design introduced at more or less the same time in Auburn, New York. The notorious and storied Sing Sing Correctional Facility on the Hudson River in New York was modelled on the Auburn system, as was Canada's own infamous Kingston Penitentiary on Lake Ontario.

Among the interested visitors to Pennsylvania was the great nineteenth-century British writer and social commentator Charles Dickens. In his *American Notes for General Circulation* of 1842, Dickens described a day trip to the ESP. Two polite and helpful officials took him round: "Every facility was afforded me, that the utmost courtesy could suggest.... The perfect order of the building cannot be praised too highly, and of the excellent motives of all who are immediately concerned in the administration of the system, there can be no kind of question."

And yet he found the whole setup totally repulsive. Why?

> The system here, is rigid, strict, and hopeless solitary confinement. I believe it, in its effects, to be cruel and wrong.... Over the head and face of every prisoner who comes into this melancholy house, a black hood is drawn; and in this dark shroud, an emblem of the curtain dropped between him and the living world, he is led to the cell from which he never again comes forth, until his whole term of imprisonment has expired. He never hears of wife and children; home or friends; the life or death of any single creature. He sees the prison-officers, but with that exception he never looks upon a human countenance, or hears a

human voice. He is a man buried alive; to be dug
out in the slow round of years; and in the mean time
dead to everything but torturing anxieties and horrible despair.

Dickens described in dreadful detail a few of the inmates he came
across. A German, incarcerated for two years, who had painted his
cell beautifully: "the taste and ingenuity he had displayed in everything were most extraordinary; and yet a more dejected, heart-broken,
wretched creature it would be difficult to imagine." A man who kept
rabbits was called out of his foul-smelling cell to talk to the writer and
"stood shading his haggard face in the unwonted sunlight ... looking as
wan and unearthly as if he had been summoned from the grave." And a
sailor who, after eleven years inside, did not, or could not, speak: "Why
does he stare at his hands, and pick the flesh upon his fingers?"

In December of 1842, the same year that Dickens delivered his
scathing report on Eastern State, a new prison opened its doors in
his own neck of the woods, North London. Cue in the "Pentonville
England Reformatory Prison," based on the "separate system, now so
much in vogue in England," which, as interested citizens of Toronto
would learn fifteen years later, was to serve as the model for the new
Toronto jail.

Pentonville had been established by Act of Parliament in 1840 for
the reform and rehabilitation of men sentenced to imprisonment or
awaiting transportation to penal colonies in Australia. Consisting of
a central hub with five radiating wings, it was designed by Captain
Joshua Jebb of the Royal Engineers, with the assistance of architect
Charles Barry, and built at a cost of £84,186 12s. 2d. (It will be interesting to compare this cost to the eventual price tag attached to the
Don Jail, which ended up being somewhat pricier than the initial estimate of about £10,000 [$40,000] as reported by the *Globe*.)

In *The English: A Social History*, British author and historian
Christopher Hibbert writes that each of the 520 prisoners incarcerated in Pentonville had his own tiny cell, measuring just thirteen feet

by seven feet. The cells were nine feet high, with a small window on the outside wall. They were admittedly well ventilated, but the in-cell toilets soon became blocked up and were replaced by foul communal "recesses." Prisoners were not allowed to communicate with one another — they "tramped along in silent rows" and wore brown cloth masks over their heads when they left their cells for exercise. At the compulsory daily chapel services, they sat in separate cubicles with their heads visible to the warder on duty but not to one another.

Although inmates were permitted to work and were fed a reasonable diet, the system had a disastrous effect on their mental health. Hibbert quotes an official report stating that "for every sixty thousand persons confined in Pentonville there were 220 cases of insanity, 210 cases of delusions, and forty suicides."

Isolation, penance, complete silence, constant surveillance: it seemed as if the future inmates of the Toronto jail were in for a very bleak time indeed.

CHAPTER 5

Cornerstones

William Thomas's plans for the splendid new jail that would incorporate progressive penal reform principles and architectural innovations were presented to the city council's Committee on Police and Prisons in July 1857, and work on fencing, grading, and levelling began early the following year.

However, the months dragged on, and it became increasingly clear that the project was in serious trouble.

In December 1858, a select committee appointed to investigate matters relating to the jail and industrial farm, and, more specifically, ongoing problems with the fencing and grading work, presented a report to the city council. The select committee was blunt: as reported in the *Globe*, aldermen overseeing the project had been derelict in their duties. "There can be no doubt that serious irregularities have taken place.... It has been customary to issue the most important instructions, relative to the gaol works, without first submitting them to a regular meeting of the [standing] Committee [on Police and Prisons]." Costly modifications, like changing the direction of the jail fence, were undertaken without any records being kept, and no tenders were received for the "work of grading and leveling the ground from the fence on the southern boundary of the Farm, which has proved to be of considerable magnitude."

Others, too, were censured. Workmen were accused of incompetence and worse. For example, a subcontractor, Peter Croly, was caught out in the "malconstruction" of the brick drain and was forced to admit "that he had committed the fraud solely for his own benefit."

The role of Thomas Young, superintendent of the works and in theory William Thomas's right-hand man, was also closely examined. British-born Young was an artist, teacher, and politician as well as an architect. He had had some experience in designing jails in the Province of Canada in the 1840s, notably the Huron County Gaol in Goderich and the Simcoe District Gaol in Barrie. Young proved difficult to work with, however, since he was both quarrelsome and litigious, defects compounded by what a newspaper described in his obituary as the "seductive but destroying influence of liquor." William Thomas was also known for his tempestuous interpersonal relationships. Thomas was furious when he learned of Young's appointment. He believed that he should have been consulted but wasn't. The two clashed from the beginning, especially since Thomas believed that Young's job performance was exceptionally poor. The superintendent was accused by one alderman of being absent from the site on occasion, and another remarked unflatteringly that he was "a person unsteady in his habits." So Thomas found himself in the invidious position of having to supervise the troublesome supervisor. The select committee tactfully noted "that without doubting Mr. Young's ability as an architect, Mr. Thomas does not hesitate to declare that if the appointment was left to him, he 'would employ a more practical mechanic.'" However, other than suffering some withering comments about his salary and transaction-recording skills, Young was generally exonerated from blame.

The highest-profile individuals criticized by the committee were the chief architect and his two sons, William Tutin and Cyrus Pole, who together made up the firm of William Thomas & Sons. "With reference to the architects of the building, and the manner in which they have conducted the business entrusted to them, it is the painful duty of this Committee to express its strong disapproval." Take the fence, for example. The design was flawed, the plans badly worded, the dimensions of the posts insufficient, and the quality of the lumber not specified at all.

And "as a natural consequence the contractors … availed themselves of this omission to work in material of a very inferior character."

In their biography of William Thomas, Glenn McArthur and Annie Szamosi marvel at the "surprising naiveté" displayed by Thomas in acceding to requests of the board and foregoing normal tendering processes. These are challenges that fledgling architects learn about in ARCH 101, and failure to adequately address them could indeed be seen as shocking in a professional man of Thomas's stature and experience. In his defence, however, he was in very poor health by that time, and it may well be that he was simply no longer able to cope with the stresses of the job.

Immediately following the release of the select committee's report, the city council had a short, sharp debate on what to do next: dismiss both of the squabbling architects? just one of them? Fortunately for Thomas, the final decision was to keep him on and let Young go.

This was hardly the end of the problems associated with the construction of the jail. In May 1859, it was the turn of Skelsey and Sinclair, the brick- and stone-work contractors, to cause mayhem. Thomas complained in a communication to the city council that "the contractors had as yet done nothing towards the work, except delivering rubble stone, while the time allowed for the completion of the basement story [*sic*] had already expired." Skelsey and Sinclair asked to withdraw from the project, which led to howls of indignation from the council. The jail was excessively expensive to build, huffed several of the aldermen, and "its unproductive character, magnitude, and distance from the courts" would be "a perpetual drain" on the resources of the city. On the contrary, countered the Committee on Police and Prisons — if the project were abandoned, the property would end up being sold at a loss. And just think what that would mean to the city's bottom line.

New contractors were finally found for the brick and stone work, and the chief architect's son, William Tutin Thomas, eventually replaced Young as superintendent of the works.

Finally, to everyone's relief, a new chapter seemed to be beginning.

Amid great pomp and Masonic ceremony, the cornerstone of the new Toronto Jail was laid on October 25, 1859. Everybody who was anybody in the corridors of power joined in the day's festivities, which started with a parade from City Hall to the northeast corner of the jail, where the ceremony was to take place. The *Globe* was on the scene, recording for its readers effusive descriptions of the august event. First, the Masons: "many ... in full dress; bearing the banners of their lodges, covered over with symbols of awful meaning. Some of them carried huge candles, others swords, squares, plumbs, and levels, while upon the breasts of all shone brightly the jewels which they were allowed to wear." Then, the firemen: "strong, useful, practical looking men, around whom no mystery gathers. They wore their handsome uniforms well ... and added much to the interest of the procession." Then, officers of the Volunteer Militia, and, finally, His Worship the Mayor, Adam Wilson, followed by the Council of the City of Toronto. Everyone fell into step behind the Toronto Union Band and marched from the assembly point to the construction site. On arrival, band after band played the Masonic Anthem with great enthusiasm.

The Free and Accepted Masons had originated in medieval times among the stoneworkers of Britain. Over the years, the Masons developed into an international fraternal organization with complex secret rituals. They came to Canada through this country's position within the British Empire and have traditionally wielded immense influence in Ontario and elsewhere. As an indication of the extent of this power, eleven of the thirty-six Fathers of Confederation, the political leaders who played a major role in stitching together the British North American colonies to form the Dominion of Canada in 1867, were Freemasons. Small wonder, then, that the honour of laying the cornerstone of the new jail was bestowed upon Lieutenant Colonel William Mercer Wilson, the organization's Grand Master. This grandee solemnly addressed the gathering and was presented with a "very handsome" trowel, which was "of silver, with a maple wood handle, and decorated with Masonic emblems."

St. Lawrence Hall's splendid great hall was a fitting setting for the sumptuous lunch that followed the ceremonial laying of the Don Jail's cornerstone in October 1859.

Although some work had been done back in the spring of 1858 on the fencing and grading of the site, there was still just a gaping hole in the ground where the building would one day rise.

No matter. The foundation stone had been ceremonially laid, and now it was time for lunch. And what a lunch it was. The splendid affair fittingly took place at the St. Lawrence Hall, arguably the most outstanding achievement in Toronto of William Thomas, the architect of the yet-to-be-built jail. Guests were no doubt overwhelmed by the magnificence of the great hall on the third floor, which was described in the 1858 *Handbook of Toronto* as "100 feet long, 38 feet 6 inches wide, and 36 feet high, with a gallery at the entrance end. The ceiling of the Hall is ornamented by flat hemispherical, enriched panelled, domed compartments, and lyres surrounding them." The space was lit by a "large and magnificent chandelier" that had a "brilliant and most imposing effect" when illuminated.

Three tables stretched the full length of the hall, but the list of invitees was so long (more than four hundred in all) that many of the dignitaries had to be seated in overflow rooms along the sides. The catering was superb, and champagne flowed freely. The company ate, sang, and caroused until the affair broke up shortly before eight in the evening.

In sharp contrast to that raucous and boozy celebration, a far more restrained ceremony had been held a month earlier just a little to the north of the jail, or rather, as one news report acerbically put it, "to the north of the hole that [had] been dug for the gaol." The purpose of this gathering, too, was to lay the cornerstone of a new building. It was attended by the mayor of Toronto, Adam Wilson, a handful of aldermen and other officials, and the architect, John Aspenwall Tully. For posterity, a number of items, including several current newspapers and a few coins, were placed in a glass case. One of these objects was a roll of parchment containing an inscription, which the mayor read out to the group before the case was carefully positioned inside a hollow in the cornerstone and cemented into the wall: "This corner stone of the House of Refuge, at the Industrial Farm, Toronto, was laid by Adam Wilson, Mayor of the city, in the presence of the members of the Corporation, this 14th day of September, Anno Domini, 1859, in the 23rd year of Her Gracious Majesty, Queen Victoria."

The House of Refuge, as you will remember, was being built on the industrial farm site to provide shelter for "vagrants, the dissolute, and for idiots." Unlike the new jail, it was up and running within a year. Its cost was a modest $30,000.

By December 1859, the extravagant Don Jail stone-setting gala was over but not really forgotten, and Toronto was nursing a sour hangover. This was not remedied when the bills started rolling in.

Some examples: $261.00 for the catering; $140.75 for the champagne; $50.00 for the silver trowel.

Beneath the headline "Wanted, Ninety-Six Thousand Dollars," was this blistering re-evaluation from the *Globe*:

> Toronto was flattered by visitors from other cities, who deigned to honour us with their company at "lunch." She was congratulated upon the happy prospect before her; for was she not to possess a gaol which should do her honour, which should eclipse all other gaols, which should become *the* building of the city? But neither they nor the institutors of the "lunch" thought of the people outside, who had no champagne, who heard the noise but could not join in the revelry — the stern blue-coated gentlemen at the doors refusing entrance to the *canaille* unfavoured with tickets! The dinner was finished, but not so with the gaol.

There was a crater in the ground waiting to be filled, but none of the eloquent after-dinner speeches or the Masonic ceremonies would succeed in filling it without the consent of the "champagneless thousands."

The follow-up was swift. As with all city expenditures, the request for additional funding had to be approved by the rate payers of Toronto. In a terse report dated December 6, 1859, the city clerk informed the city council that "the by-law for raising $96,000 had been defeated, by 587 nays to 199 yeas." The champagneless thousands, or at least their representatives, had spoken.

The lavish cornerstone celebration (or great "gaol guzzle," as the press later called it), ushered in 1860 with new controversies and onerous financial demands. By the time the saga ended in 1864, costs had ballooned. Did the citizens of Toronto eventually come to believe that they had made a grave mistake? Maybe, after all, they should have just ponied up the original and much more reasonable sum of $96,000.

CHAPTER 6

A Change of Plan

Winter 1859 rolled into spring 1860. A cornerstone had been laid, but nearly three years after William Thomas's plans for Toronto's new jail based on "Pentonville England Reformatory Prison" had been submitted to the city's Committee on Police and Prisons, building operations remained at a complete standstill.

In April 1860, for some unfathomable reason, the committee submitted Thomas's plans to the Provincial Prison Inspectors. (This should probably read "resubmitted," as at the outset the province must surely have given his designs its stamp of approval.) These gentlemen were based in Kingston, and, as it so happened, they had a prison on their very own doorstep: the Kingston Penitentiary, which had been receiving rave reviews.

To illustrate: After visiting the United States, famous author Charles Dickens had breezed through Kingston during his Great American Tour of 1842. He was not impressed with the town ("Indeed, it may be said of Kingston, that one half of it appears to be burnt down, and the other half not to be built up"), but he *loved* the prison: "There is an admirable jail here, well and wisely governed, and excellently regulated, in every respect. The men were employed as shoemakers, ropemakers, blacksmiths, tailors, carpenters, and stonecutters; and in building a new prison, which was pretty far advanced towards completion. The female prisoners were occupied in needlework."

Such a glowing testimonial could hardly have failed to capture the inspectors' attention, although, as J. Alex Edmison dryly commented in a short history of the penitentiary written in 1954: "I am sure that when the author of *Little Dorrit* visited the prison they did not put on a special flogging of Antoine, aged eight, or Elizabeth, aged twelve." (Fortunately, these inhumane practices were eventually discontinued.)

A massive limestone structure that has dominated the lakefront in Kingston for more than 180 years, this institution, which housed prisoners with long-term sentences, was British North America's first true penitentiary. For upward of a century, it served as the model for other federal prisons in Canada. Originally called the Provincial Penitentiary of the Province of Upper Canada, and now called the Kingston Pen for short, it opened its doors to its first six unwilling occupants in June 1835. The large cellblock contained 154 cells, which originally measured twenty-nine inches wide by eight feet deep by just over six-and-a-half feet high. When first built, the compound was surrounded by a tall wooden picket fence, and by the late 1840s there were industrial shops on site for various trades, such as blacksmithing, carpentry, and tailoring. Way back, there were also a large farm and stone quarries, making the institution totally self-sufficient.

Kingston Pen was modelled on Auburn Prison in New York; Pentonville on the competing Eastern State Penitentiary in Pennsylvania. Charles Dickens, you will remember, had visited Eastern earlier on in his travels and found it hateful. An 1838 essay on prison discipline by college professor Francis Lieber lays out clearly the difference between the two penological models:

> The Auburn system (so called because it is most fully, and, as some think, most successfully, carried out at the penitentiary at Auburn, New York) separates the convicts *by night*, but suffers them to work together during the day, requiring however the most rigid non-intercourse. Hence it is also called the *social* and the *silent* system. The Pennsylvania system

> ... separates each convict from the presence of his
> fellows ... secluding him night and day from all
> intercourse with the world.... Hence it is called the
> *separate* or *solitary* system.

The prison inspectors in Kingston now proposed scrapping the existing plans for the Toronto Jail, which were based on the separate system (complete and utter mind-numbing isolation of prisoners at all times) in favour of one modelled on the social system (communal work in silence during the day; confinement in tiny, solitary cells at night). The two ideologies were alike in insisting on the strictest discipline at all times.

What could have motivated the inspectors to rethink the structure, and the underlying penal philosophy, of Toronto's jail? Were they swayed by Dickens's persuasive words, or were they patriots looking for a superlative "made in the Province of Canada" prison to use as a template? Whatever their reasons, they effectively moved the goalposts halfway through the game. As noted in the Toronto city council minutes in May 1860: "The Provincial Prison Inspectors dissented from and objected to the plan of the Pentonville Prison, England, from which the plans of the Toronto gaol have, in part, been adopted."

And while they were at it, they also changed the basic configuration of the cells: "The Inspectors object to the construction of the cells along the outer walls of the building and require that the same shall be constructed in the centre, with the hall, or keeper's walk, between them and the outer walls." Although this new arrangement overturned the reformers' fundamental architectural requirement of a clear view down the centre of the cells to ensure constant surveillance, the inspectors noted that it would offer greater security against prisoner escapes. It is possible that they had been influenced by the May 1860 Quebec *Memorandum of the Board of Inspectors of Asylums and Prisons*, which stated that "there should be two rows of cells in each story placed back to back; they should open upon spacious corridors, well heated, well lighted and well ventilated."

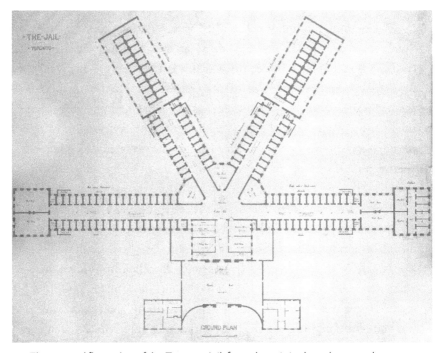

The ground floor plan of the Toronto Jail, from the original set drawn up between 1857 and 1859 and based on Pentonville Prison in London, England. These plans were rejected in 1860 after construction of the building had already begun, and William Thomas was obliged to redraw and resubmit his designs.

Puzzlingly, the inspectors also condemned the "radiating principle on which the rear wings had been originally projected." These wings had been considered but never included in the designs. Having no alternative, the Toronto city council acceded to these demands, and it was back to the drawing board for Thomas.

Once Thomas had painstakingly redrawn the plans, he made the journey to Kingston himself in July 1860 to submit them. At the same time, he requested an additional $20,000 to cover the expense of changing the plans and redoing the foundations.

By November, the din of dysfunction in the Toronto city council had become deafening, and Thomas found himself in the excruciating position of having his professional integrity and decisions challenged and ridiculed by a hostile member of the city council.

The man in question was James J. Vance, alderman for St. David's Ward, located just west of the Don River, and chairman of the city council's Board of Gaol Inspectors. Vance was a blustering bully. When on one occasion a fellow alderman proposed that the board should report on proposed changes to the plans of the jail and any costs that might ensue, Vance replied that he would ignore any motion and bring in the reports in his own good time. In fact, he declared, if his fellow alderman tried to force the issue, he would "tear the reports to atoms and strew the pieces on the Council floor before the members."

Vance was more than merely quarrelsome: he was a violent man, well known to police in Toronto. The press reported in great detail that during his term of office he was fined $10 plus costs for brutally assaulting a man "with his clenched hand, which knocked him down, and when deponent was down he kicked him, which kick broke four of his teeth." There were also credible allegations swirling about that Vance was quite comfortable accepting bribes from tradesmen and contractors.

Vance had been a constant thorn in William Thomas's side. Against Thomas's objections, he proposed that white brick should be used instead of stone for the front façade of the central block of the jail. Fellow members of the council were outraged. "If the centre was built of brick the effect might be to make the Gaol a laughing stock," protested one. While they had Thomas as the architect, they "ought to abide by his opinion," said another. "Before five years were passed the Gaol would be a disgrace to the City if the proposed alteration were made," warned a third.

Obviously realizing he could not win that particular battle, Vance shifted his attack to the heating and ventilation systems. Thomas proposed to heat the whole building with steam generated from just two boilers, scoffed Vance. And for ventilation, to erect a brick shaft at great expense. Over a twenty-year period, the cost of fuel alone would be enough to build another whole jail building. "Such were the Architect's absurdities," he concluded. "Why, the man was mad!"

As Thomas explained in a letter, "of the different methods now in use in heating buildings, I believe it will be found that steam combines all the advantages of the best, without the defects of others." Vance and the board vetoed this. "Upon mature consideration the Board ... abandoned the hot-air system on account of its inadaptibility [*sic*] to the resources of the gaol, the difficulty of obtaining a water supply for steam usage being great."

By this time Thomas's health was failing fast, and these personal and professional insults must have been the last straw.

On December 27, 1860, a bold headline in the *Globe* regretted the DEATH OF MR. THOMAS, "a well-known and highly respected architect, long resident in this city." Mr. Thomas, the paper reminded its readers, "will be remembered, not only for his kindly social qualities which endeared him to a numerous circle of friends, but for the services which he has rendered to the architecture of Toronto. To him we owe some of the most tasteful buildings of which our city can boast."

William Thomas, master architect, dead at sixty-one.

The death of Thomas, who was survived by his wife and six of ten children, could hardly have come as a shock to his family and friends. He was diabetic, described as having suffered from "long and continued illness." In late 1857, Thomas and his wife had made a last, desperate trip back to England in the vain hope of finding some relief from his debilitating disease.

With his younger son Cyrus Pole Thomas taking care of family business out east, the torch was passed to William Tutin Thomas to complete the thankless job their father had started three years earlier.

CHAPTER 7

Fire

Finally.

In January 1862, after many stops and starts, including the death of careworn architect William Thomas, construction of the new Toronto Jail was just about completed. The stern and substantial building consisted of a sixty-eight-foot-high central administration block made of stone, with two creamy-white brick wings containing cells for the prisoners. The main entrance was on the south side of the central pavilion. On the first floor was a large entrance hall flanked by rooms including the governor's office, male and female "visitors rooms," and storage closets. The second floor contained the apartments of the governor and the turnkeys, or the head guards who were entrusted with the jail keys. The chapel was located on the top floor. In the basement were a few holding cells and separate male and female washrooms for scrubbing down the newly admitted. Iron gates at the northern end of the entrance hall opened into a large, four-storey central hall or rotunda. There was some interior work still to be done, such as plastering and the installation of the heating system. But in less than two months' time, the stout wooden front doors would be thrown open for business.

Then: disaster.

On Sunday, January 19, a fire raged through the building and consumed the centre block. This was the second major conflagration in a public building in Toronto in less than a week: the previous Monday, Government House had been accidentally destroyed by the "devouring

Firemen pose with their horse-drawn engines in front of the fire hall at Berkeley Street, built in 1871. On display is the type of equipment that would have been used a few years earlier to fight the devastating fire at the jail.

element." Was the fire at the jail also an unfortunate accident? It was not. According to one sombre news report, "it is feared that … the incendiary has been at work and the gaol building wilfully fired."

It was around two in the morning when the caretaker who lived in a nearby cottage, a man named Cooney, was startled from his slumbers by a brilliant light flickering through his bedroom windows. He immediately ran to the main entrance of the jail, to find that the chapel was ablaze. To his shock, the padlock and hasp had been torn off the front doors. A violent snowstorm swept in, bringing some hope of relief, but it did nothing to dampen the flames. The smoke from the fire was so intense that Cooney could not even enter the building. Braving the storm, he sprinted westward toward the city, shouting "Fire at the new gaol!" The bell at Berkeley Street started solemnly tolling the alarm; at round 3:00 a.m. the bell at St. Lawrence Hall rang out in accompaniment, and firefighters hastily trundled out their equipment to deal with the blaze.

When it came to fighting fires in the second half of the nineteenth century, Toronto had several different kinds of equipment in its arsenal: basic and very heavy hand-drawn and hand-powered fire engines, and steam pumpers mounted on a horse-drawn carriage with steel-rimmed wooden wheels. With this type, a water-tube boiler provided steam to a pumping engine that forced water through hoses onto a fire. The hoses were hand-hauled separately on large-wheeled carts.

What unspooled over the next ten or eleven hours would not have been out of place in a Buster Keaton movie.

As the firemen scrambled into action with their horses, hand pumpers, and, it would seem, one lone steam-powered engine, the alarm bells stopped ringing. According to later reports, the watchmen at the top of the bell towers could no longer see the fiery glow — perhaps it had been obscured by the blizzard — so they simply turned off the alarms. After some head-scratching, the chief engineer ordered his men to stop their headlong rush and return to their stations. Then he set off on foot for Berkeley Street to find out for himself what the dickens was going on with those bells. Meanwhile, a police patrolman heading east along Gerrard Street in the downtown area who had spotted the blaze at the jail ran back to St. Lawrence Hall, where he raised the alarm a second time. Out came the fire engines again. However, deep drifts of snow now blanketed the city streets, and men and equipment became hopelessly bogged down. The minutes ticked agonizingly by. Another pair of horses was brought up and harnessed to the steam fire engine. Around five in the morning, the teams finally reached the jail. By this time the roof of the centre building had collapsed and the top floor was a mass of flames.

Back in 1862 you would have looked in vain for a fire hydrant at the corner of Mill Street and Danforth Road (now Broadview Avenue and Gerrard Street East); water had to be pumped up from the Don River. So the firemen swept into action and laid out their hoses. Unfortunately, even when placed end to end in a single line there were not enough of them to reach the building from the river. To their consternation, the crews now realized that some of the hose carts had not turned up. More time was wasted as messengers were dispatched for additional hoses.

At 7:00 a.m., some five hours after the fire was spotted, the first stream of water was finally trained on the flames. At this late stage the embattled firemen could only hope to prevent the fire from spreading to the side wings of the building.

About two hours later the steam fire engine burned out, and firemen scrambled frantically to bring in more equipment.

By the time the fire was finally doused around 1:00 p.m., the centre block was completely gutted; its walls charred and cracked. The heat had been so intense that the thick iron gratings on the chapel windows were bent and twisted out of shape.

In the aftermath of the conflagration, there were several suggestions as to its cause. For example, it was rumoured that someone had heard an explosion, similar to that of a powder keg being ignited, just before the fire broke out.

But the most enduring theory is the one advanced by Robertson in his *Landmarks of Toronto*. "It was supposed that a gang of bushmen had gone inside the building to get shelter from the piercing cold, and either wilfully or accidentally fired the premises." These so-called bushmen (actually, bush men *and* women) belonged to the Brook's Bush Gang, a pack of around twenty violent criminals who prowled the eastern fringes of the city in the 1850s and early 1860s. With their headquarters in a derelict barn in the woods to the east of the jail in what is now Leslieville, these "vagrants and vagabonds" had long brought misery into the lives of fearful residents. "The most vigorous proceedings should be adopted by the civil authorities to disperse and banish these bands of outlaws," fumed "Suburban" in a letter to the press in 1858.

The fact that the institution was situated in a semi-rural space outside the city boundaries warrants consideration. As historian and author Jennifer Bonnell puts it: "The lower [Don] valley had become, by the 1860s, a repository for urban discards — for sewage and industrial wastes, for prisoners, for the institutionalized poor, and for people who in other ways failed to measure up to nineteenth-century liberal values of rationality, moral rigour, and self-advancement."

Apprehensive city folk regarded that part of the valley with its inaccessible ravines and polluted marshes as a place of menace and suspicion. Beyond the valley, the largely undeveloped landscape was dotted with woodland areas, all of it suggesting a kind of "underworld" that brought with it "images of darkness, unpredictability, and other-worldliness."

From the mid-1800s, the untamed ravines of the valley and the largely uninhabited areas beyond were the haunt of marginalized people. Torontonians had become accustomed to harrowing tales of bandits preying on people crossing the Don (Queen Street) bridge or on the road to Kingston. And then there was that much-reviled Brook's Bush Gang. According to a report in the *Globe* in April 1861, "they subsist mainly by robbing hen roosts, as the farmers in the neighbourhood know to their cost; by robbing some unfortunate they may inveigle into the bush, or by the wages of sin of the women."

The wages of sin, as the Bible warns, is death.

And so it was with the Brook's Bush Gang. That same year, sixteen purported members of the gang, both men and women, were arrested after the decomposing body of John Sheridan Hogan, a local politician and former editor-in-chief of the *British Colonist*, was found floating in the Don River. Hogan had allegedly been relieved of substantial amounts of cash before he was killed. All of the gang members were subsequently released, presumably free to resume their nefarious activities in the neighbourhood. The lone exception was a "notorious character" named James Brown, who was tried and sentenced to death for his role in the murder. Despite public outcry that justice had not been done, he was hanged in front of the Court House on Adelaide Street in March 1862. This would be the last public hanging in Toronto.

However, Bonnell cautions against too simplistic an attitude toward those populations relegated to the fringes of society. She notes that although the urban elite perceived the valley as being a place of corruption and danger, marginalized individuals who took refuge there, such as the Brook's Bush Gang, regarded it as a place of safety. What was more, "despite its occasional violence, it was also a kind of social hub for those with few other meeting places to frequent."

Public fears, however, were not entirely misplaced. Policing in the area was scant: in mid-nineteenth-century Toronto, police authority ended at the west bank of the Don. Both the jail and the House of Refuge that shared its site fell under the jurisdiction of the County of York. It was not until the city annexed Riverdale in 1884 that the police started to exercise control over the east bank of the river between Queen Street and Danforth Avenue.

All that aside, it was the Keystone Cop–style ineptitude of city and fire authorities, admittedly working under extremely challenging conditions, that ultimately sealed the fate of the building. Of course, the jail's location on the wrong side of the Don River — the east side, that is — was definitely a contributing factor. It was simply too far away, separated from city and services by bad roads and rickety bridges. Today, walking briskly, you could probably cross the Gerrard Street bridge and cover the distance between the jail (A) and where the fire hall stood at Berkeley Street (B) in about thirty minutes. In 1862, travelling from point A to point B in a raging snowstorm via Bell's Bridge, the rustic Gerrard Street crossing that was washed away by a flood

Rickety Bell's Bridge spanned the Don River at what is now Gerrard Street East. It was washed away by a flood in the late 1880s.

in the late 1880s, would have taken a lot longer; and manoeuvering horse-drawn or hand-pulled fire equipment from point B to point A through deep snowdrifts longer still.

When the embers died and the smoke cleared after the disastrous and probably deliberate blaze, it was time to take stock. The building had been regarded as virtually fireproof. In hindsight, the weak link was the soaring chapel in the centre block, which had been richly fitted out with wood: wooden seats, a wooden gallery and pulpit, and a wooden division running down the centre to separate male and female inmates during church services. The situation was not helped by a profusion of carpenters' benches littering the room as construction neared completion and a thick layer of wood shavings on the floor. In contrast, the wings of the building had been saved, both because their walls were thick and because they contained little or no woodwork.

William Thomas had been aware of the fire risk, and, as a preventative measure, he had proposed the installation of a large cistern on the roof with a series of hoses connecting it to all parts of the building. The proposal had been rejected. In a supreme irony, such an arrangement might have greatly diminished the catastrophic effect of the blaze.

The damage to the jail was estimated at $30,000; the premises were insured for just $20,000. The *Globe* reported that the original building estimate had ballooned, and, as to who should shoulder the blame: "the main portion of the $34,000 over-expenditure was caused by fulfilling the requirements of the [provincial] gaol commissioners."

Now, some four years into the project, it was back to the drawing board. Once more.

In May 1862, the interfering provincial prison inspectors stepped in yet again to "suggest" further improvements. In their opinion, the recently gutted chapel was too large: they believed that it should be divided into two chapels and four rooms. The city council's Board of Gaol Inspectors meekly agreed. In July, the new architect, William Tutin Thomas, sent a letter to the city council complaining that there were still no roofs on the jail. Unless things started moving very soon, the onset of winter would cause serious damage to both the central building and the wings. In September, the city council was still squabbling over who should pay that additional $34,000 occasioned by the change to the original plans back in 1860. The provincial government had balked at the very idea of paying any part of this. According to one alderman, the government "said they had never ordered any alteration, that there were no books or papers to show they had ever promised anything, and they would never give a cent."

It would take another two years before the jail was finally completed and open for business. By that time, costs had skyrocketed. The total price for the jail buildings and farm was an astounding $256,812. The provincial government reluctantly kicked in $24,000 toward the alterations, and insurance companies paid a further $15,535 to compensate for the fire damage. And that left the city on the hook for a whopping net amount of more than $217,000.

CHAPTER 8

The End Result

What had been going through William Thomas's mind, in those heady days of early 1857, as he settled before his drawing board, with pencils, pens, watercolours, and compasses within easy reach, to create the first sketches of his prestigious commission, the new Toronto jail?

Thomas's instructions from the city council were straightforward enough: to base his designs on Pentonville Prison, London, and incorporate the principles of the separate or silent system. So his thoughts must first have turned to that imposing structure with its lofty central hall and five radiating wings.

Thomas probably spent quite some time musing about the basic functions of a prison, too. Here, he may well have come across volume 21 of the *Encyclopaedia Londinensis*, published in London in 1826. In a long entry under "Prison," this self-styled *Universal Dictionary of Arts, Sciences, and Literature* goes into great detail on the basic aim of imprisonment, which "is, of course, the prevention of vice, and, towards this end, it operates in two ways; first, by inflicting such distress on the prisoner as shall prevent him from repeating his offence; and, secondly, by exciting the terrors of the people in general, so that the anticipation of a like punishment may restrain them within the bounds of good behaviour."

In addition, the encyclopedia offers helpful hints on what a prison should look like, so as to ensure that its form would appropriately embody its function: "The style of architecture of a prison is a matter of no slight importance. It offers an effectual method of exciting the imagination to a most desirable point of abhorrence.... The exterior of a prison should, therefore, be formed in the heavy and sombre style, which most forcibly impresses the spectator with gloom and terror."

With such examples and opinions in mind, Thomas created a series of preliminary drawings of the proposed jail between November 1857 and February 1859 for submission to the Toronto city council. These plans feature a south-facing central hall with four long wings, one extending directly to the east and one directly to the west, and two diagonal wings projecting northeast and northwest. With the exception of back-to-back cells designed to accommodate felons at the ends of the diagonal wings, all the cells were to be arranged on the outer walls, allowing for easy surveillance of the corridors, à la Pentonville, from the central hall. Men and women would be accommodated in separate wings and adults and juveniles on different floors. There were administrative offices and work rooms and day rooms and a small section for debtors; there was an apartment for the governor, and, of course, a chapel on the second floor. Also proposed was a highly decorated octagonal watch-tower at the back, allowing observation of the surrounding area.

The council, however, approved a simplified plan consisting of just the central block and the two side wings, and construction began.

These initial drawings were discarded once the provincial prison inspectors rejected the Pentonville model in 1860, and the plans had to be radically revised. Fortunately, a sufficient number of those originals survive to show us how the actual building differed from what Thomas had first envisaged.

The final product was a smaller, but still hugely imposing, rectangular structure, comprised of a four-storey central pavilion flanked by three-and-a-half-storey side wings. Golden stone from Niagara and Ohio and brick from Toronto brickyards were used for the exterior of the central block, and the wings were of creamy-white brick. Stone, wood, and iron were used in both the exterior and interior trim, and the roof was made of slate.

Architects and historians agree that Thomas's overall design largely followed the Renaissance Revival style, especially with regard to the façade. Characteristic of this style, which drew heavily on sixteenth-century Italian Renaissance architecture, are large, formal buildings with symmetrical façades, prominent quoins or cornerstones, and rusticated or rough-textured stone piers and columns.

Charles (later Sir Charles) Barry, who designed the façade of Pentonville, was an ardent admirer of Renaissance Revival architecture, and, although the Pentonville model had been thrown out in Toronto, his influence on Thomas may still be seen both in the impressive bulk of the Don Jail and in the exaggerated detailing of the central pavilion, such as the rusticated piers and columns and the vermiculated or worm-like patterns carved into the stonework. These sculptural details also reflect Thomas's own love of elaborate stone-carved decoration, which you can see in his other work, such as Brock's Monument at Queenston.

The final version's tiny, iron-gated back-to-back brick cells, arranged along the centre of each wing, were designed to accommodate the general jail population at night. The windowed corridors alongside the cells were essentially day rooms where inmates would congregate during the daylight hours when they were not working, eating, or, perhaps, exercising. A few larger cells, original purpose unknown, were located on the third floor. Grimly, there were also several segregation and punishment cells that were used as an alternative to flogging the unruly. These were larger than the standard cells, but solid oak doors shut out every glimmer of light, leaving the occupant in complete darkness. As noted a century later in Bridgepoint Health documentation on the history of the Don Jail, this type of confinement was a serious matter in an institution that lauded the importance of providing fresh air and natural light to prisoners.

In addition to the cells, the jail had a suite of apartments for the governor and administrative offices for the staff. There were also a chapel, a kitchen, a sick room, classrooms and visiting rooms.

The most outstanding feature of the new building, however, was the towering four-storey semi-octagonal rotunda (later familiarly called "the dome") with its skylight and clerestory windows designed to allow in the natural light so dear to the hearts of the early prison reformers. A glass floor, subsequently covered over, allowed the light to filter down to the basement. Two balconies with cast-iron railings supported by iron brackets in the form of serpents and griffins, which had been wrought locally at the St. Lawrence Foundry, ringed the rotunda. Anecdotally, the serpents were designed to represent the lawbreakers confined in the jail and the griffins the officers tasked with confining them. The acoustics were excellent in that soaring space. Grimly, however, inmates were sometimes flogged there on purpose-built scaffolds, and the sound of their anguished cries would be carried to the cells of their fellows in the outer wings.

After all that stopping and starting and building and rebuilding, how successful from the architectural point of view was the end product?

That depends on whom you ask.

Over the years, historians, architects, and the general public have weighed in with very varied opinions on the merits of the fourth Toronto jail. Think of a bottle of red wine. One expert may describe it as "having subtle notes of raspberry and wild blueberry" and another as "tasting of berries; really oxidized," or "nail varnish and soap."

So, too, with the Don Jail.

On the one hand, you have this balanced assessment from Eric Arthur in 1964:

> It is an impressive building in the manner made famous by Piranesi the etcher and by George Dance the younger, who designed Newgate prison [in London, demolished in 1902]. Compared with the grimness of Newgate, the City Jail is a friendly building in spite of rustications, vermiculated quoins, and barred windows. Interesting elements in the design are the flanking ventilators rising out of the roof ...

which might well have come from the hand of the great eighteenth-century English architect Sir John Vanbrugh.

Then the significant flaw: "One might criticize Thomas here for the weakness of the crowning cornice and pediment and for the complete lack of connection between the central mass and the flanking wings."

George Rust-D'Eye, in his *Cabbagetown Remembered* (1984), positively raves: "Inside is a setting of spaciousness and grandeur, with a skylighted eighty-foot-high tower.... The Don Jail, with its uplifting interior and well lighted and ventilated cells, reflected the humanitarian principles of rehabilitative justice which the erection of such a magnificent building for this purpose was intended to embody."

There is one design feature that has evoked fierce controversy over the years: the menacing stone face that frowns down on you as you climb the stairs to the solid iron-studded oak entrance doors. "Be afraid; very afraid," it seems to be saying.

Rust-D'Eye's take? "Over the central doorway is a magnificent carved keystone of a man's face, with flowing beard and hair, welcoming all who enter."

Others are not so upbeat about this stony visage, also known as Father Time. McArthur and Szamosi described it in 1996 as "scowling downward as if to say, in the argot of the prisoners, 'You've done the crime, now do the Time.' This is Thomas's best expression of *architecture parlante*, denoting the spiritual function of the jail. It is massive and menacing and suitably depressing by reason of its function."

"The architectural feature was intended to instill fear in those who crossed the threshold," *The Canadian Encyclopedia* informs us bluntly. "His face could well be the disgruntled expression of the building itself, for if ever a building was cursed from its inception, it was the Don."

Over the years, many others have echoed these conflicting points of view. But when the jail first opened in 1864, its teething problems seemingly forgotten, it was reportedly described as "a palace for prisoners." Folks at that time were clearly of Rust-D'Eye's opinion.

Then, in December 1868, the *Globe* published a sensational report stretching over four columns under the banner "Toronto Gaol: Twenty-Four Hours Within Its Walls." The anonymous reporter was possibly the first, but certainly not the last, to inveigle himself (or sometimes herself) into the jail to share with readers his impressions of the conditions from an inmate's point of view. His boldness was tempered with great prudence, as he had no desire to spend a moment longer than twenty-four hours on the premises. He had thus arranged to be detained on remand and to be released on bail the following day.

The official who admitted him had no compunction in relieving him of a plug of tobacco and a few matches, and roared "Take him away!" when challenged. The turnkeys were menacing. He described some of the inmates as the scum of society, men plainly marked by vice and crime. The food was revolting, with supper consisting of oatmeal porridge. "There was no milk, nor sugar nor molasses, nor any of the little concomitants generally considered necessary to make this dish palatable, so I sat a little while looking coldly at my porridge." A table companion, after first politely asking permission, grabbed his food and hastily gobbled it up. There was the odd bright moment, though: an inmate's offer of a puff on his pipe, and the general sympathy from his fellows when the issuing of his bail bond seemed to have been ominously delayed.

Nestling amid these "day-in-the-life" details were others that pointed to what may be regarded as fundamental flaws in the makeup of the jail.

As a "casual" prisoner in temporary detention, the reporter was offered neither a cell nor a bed overnight. ("Do you imagine you can have a bed here without being bathed?" asked a turnkey in disbelief.) He spent the night "on a form eight inches in breadth" in the corridor or day room outside a row of cells, with two other inmates as uncomfortable companions.

In a paragraph headed "No Heat — No Water," our man from the *Globe* writes: "And now it began to get intensely cold. There was no heat in the cold stony pavement, I had nothing to cover me, and for hours I walked up and down that dreary corridor, with the cold shooting through every joint, my head aching, my tongue parched with thirst, for not a drop of water was to be had."

Besides the lack of adequate accommodation and heating in the Toronto Jail — then just four years old, remember — there was another serious shortcoming the reporter came across in his brief sojourn there — the general absence of sanitary facilities. This was his knee-jerk reaction immediately after being locked in: "Never shall I forget the sickening sensation that came over me, when I entered that corridor. To say that it was badly ventilated, or that it smelt badly, would not give the most remote notion of the truth, for it seemed to me to contain the quintessence of all the filthy smells that had existed from the creation of the world.... The whole place was a mass of the most disgusting horrible exhalations."

A partial explanation for the fetid atmosphere started to emerge after supper, when the prisoners were marched down a staircase to a backyard. Each one of them seized a pail. "Thinking that they were about to carry water from a well which was hard by," the reporter became "eager to show [his] industry," and grabbed two, to the "high enjoyment" of his "brothers in trouble." His efforts were greeted with a thunderous "How dare you take two pails" from a guard on duty. And later, as his long, cold, dreary night in the corridor dragged on, the ghastly truth was revealed: the stench became intolerable, and he now knew what the pails were used for.

Finally, after twenty-four exceedingly uncomfortable hours in the Toronto Jail, the reporter received his precious bail bond, and he once again "stood in the pure fresh air of heaven a free man."

In spite of protestations that he had faithfully recorded what he had seen, heard, and felt during his incarceration, his somewhat florid style suggests that a certain amount of exaggeration may have crept into his narrative.

A view from below Castle Frank in 1870, looking southeast across the Don River toward the Don Jail.

However, certain facts are incontrovertible.

In his final architectural designs, William Thomas had been obliged to embrace the fundamental precepts of the Auburn-style prison. The best an inmate could hope for was to be locked up alone at night in one of the poky little cells. In utter darkness, possibly, as there was no lighting at all in the cells, a situation that would not change throughout the lifetime of the jail. As the arrangement of the cells was back-to-back, light could filter through to them only via the corridors — which were, with the passage of time, fitted with rows of overhead electric bulbs. The plans made no provision for toilets in the cell areas, hence those foul night pails. And what were the chances of inmates being able to spend their nocturnal hours in quiet contemplation, and, perhaps, repentance? What with the free interaction between those locked up in the cells and overflow inmates in the corridors (which, it must be added, were not heated, at least in the early days), this would clearly have been impossible. And, as time went by, inmates would have companions doubling up with them in their cells, possibly even in their beds. By contrast, although those confined in Eastern-style prisons were horribly isolated and desperately lonely for their full term, at least they spent their days and nights in bigger cells with amenities such as individual windows, adequate heating, and toilet facilities.

William Thomas might have argued that, according to the Auburn principles, cells were meant only for sleeping. Prisoners would spend their daylight hours in workshops, classrooms, or planting peas and potatoes on the industrial farm. So why waste space? A poor argument, as things turned out. As time passed and theories of penology changed, inmates at the Don spent more and more time in the cells and corridors, and more and more inmates were crammed into each one.

The much-vaunted and forward-looking white and gold stone-and-brick Palace for Prisoners in Toronto, with its emphasis on the moral and physical health of inmates, was rapidly tarnishing around the edges.

CHAPTER 9

Governor of Long Standing

Perhaps with a last, lingering look at the cozy $400-per-annum rent-free house he had enjoyed for the previous eight years as governor of Toronto's third jail, George Littleton Allen moved across the Don River to become the first governor of Jail Number Four when it opened in 1864. At his new workplace, he took up residence in the administrative section of the jail itself.

Exposés of conditions within the Don Jail were fast becoming a semi-regular item in Toronto newspapers, with Governor Allen often at the centre of the criticism. In a long letter to the sheriff of the County of York, one complainant accused the governor of using the industrial farm as his own "manufactory," and brazenly pocketing the proceeds. Allen had been accused in the past of supplying liquor to inmates; this practice seemed to be flourishing still. Eventually, in 1872, the *Globe* called for "a thorough investigation into the whole management of Castle Allen."

A few days later, uninvited and unannounced, a grand jury showed up at the jail doors, and the truth tumbled out. Their visit brought to light a shocking mix of filth and sloppiness, and clear evidence of the governor's dereliction of duty: "The governor of the gaol being frequently absent, the great responsibility rests on me, and there are not enough turnkeys or men under me to properly perform the duties required, and look after the safety of the prisoners," complained one of the turnkeys bitterly.

Outrage swiftly turned to action: Allen was dismissed.

His replacement in the hot seat, John Green, was much more diligent, but he, too, often found himself facing harsh condemnation. Consider, for example, this passionate diatribe in 1887 after a reporter posing as a casual prisoner at the Don exposed the remissness and gross abuse that lurked behind its forbidding walls:

> Let us see now what is established about the internal economy of Toronto gaol — Mr. Green himself being witness. There is no classification of the prisoners that amounts to anything. The accused, the remanded and the convicted, the sober and the inebriate, the lunatic and the sane, the comparative novice in the ways of sin and the double-distilled brute and ruffian, are all tumbled higgledy-piggledy together in different corridors.... It is also confessedly common enough for four prisoners, such as Governor Green describes, to be supposedly washed in the same water, while that sometimes six pass through this terrible ordeal is admitted."

And, even more witheringly: "We are quite ready to admit that Mr. Green is a careful officer and that he tries to do the best he can with the means put at his disposal. But what a mortifying 'best' it is even on his own showing!"

John Green was an Englishman, born in Stratford-upon-Avon in 1829. At the age of twenty-one he left his native land, heading for the United States. He lived and worked in Chicago for a few years before moving to Canada. Thenceforth, his entire professional life would be spent within the belly of the Canadian beast: first as head officer of the Chatham Jail in Kent County, Ontario, then, for almost thirty years, as governor of the Toronto Jail.

There is no denying that Green's job was a difficult and sometimes highly dangerous one. In 1883, for example, he was the victim of a vicious assault — he would bear the scars for life. A female inmate, Louisa Barker, complained about another woman working alongside her in the jail. A matron escorted Barker to Green's office; the governor ruled that she had no grounds for complaint. This drove the woman into a frenzy, and, according to a newspaper report, "she darted forward and struck the Governor a blow on the head with a piece of bath-brick she had been using scrubbing the floor." She was restrained by the combined efforts of the matron and a turnkey who rushed in to investigate the source of the commotion. Green had been "felled ... to the floor insensible," and, on examination, was found to have a long gash at the back of his head. Fortunately, the doctor ascertained that there was no skull fracture. According to the authorities, Barker had lost her reason.

Green did try to do the best he could. In 1886, the markets and health committee of the Toronto city council toured the jail, and, other than remarking (as so many had done before) that the "lunatics and epileptics" they came across should be in an asylum rather than in a jail, they commended Green and his staff for keeping things in "first-class order." And, as captured in the 1891 *Report of the Commissioners Appointed to Enquire into the Prison and Reformatory System of Ontario*, some of Green's views on the Don Jail in particular and the prison system in general were quite thoughtful, even progressive.

For example, on the imprisonment of young boys in the Toronto Jail he said: "The chances are against him once he goes to gaol. I think he will learn so much in the gaol through the association with other prisoners that his experience will have an abiding effect upon him." And if boys were "sent to gaol I think they ought to be sent for the shortest term the nature of the offence will admit of." Would he recommend that children should be taken away from parents who utterly neglect them? "I would have no hesitation in doing so."

And what of other classes of inmates, "lunatics," for example? Eighty-seven of them, noted the commissioners, had been committed to the jail during the previous year. "I think it is a great mistake — a great injustice to send them to gaol" was Green's firm conviction.

He simply hated seeing groups of inmates hanging about idly in the corridors. "Any classification where a number of prisoners are associated together in corridors must be defective and undoubtedly this is the cause of many reconvictions. This applies to all classes of a gaol population." His remedy? Hard labour, and lots of it. In Green's opinion, it was a very good thing that inmates at *his* jail could be forced to work. However, it emerged that much of this highly vaunted labour was of the "make-work" variety. A visiting Toronto markets and health committee in 1889 had observed prisoners walking round and round the jail yard carrying barrows filled with sand. Green shared his dilemma with the visitors: "What is to be done? It is impossible to allow these men to loaf and lounge about the corridors, for it is then they concoct plans of villainy to be carried out when they regain their liberty." But, he added, "it was unsafe to send those men to work outside the prison walls, simply because I had not guards enough to watch them."

Contamination of prisoners was a significant problem for the entire jail population, not just minors. A remedy, said Green, would be "cellular confinement — complete isolation, the separation of each prisoner from all others." However, this system was not ideal for all types of offenders: "I have thought a great deal upon the subject. I do not think that those hardened persons [such as drunk and disorderly characters and vagrants], who are constantly sent to gaol, would be benefited.... With that great regiment of old offenders, contamination won't amount to much, but I would earnestly recommend separate confinement for all first offenders, in order that they shall not be contaminated."

But this was all just wishful thinking. Green summed it up bluntly: "This cannot be done in the Toronto gaol."

Inmates in the Don had their own litany of complaints. Limited writing materials; vermin in the bedding; being forced to "double up" in single beds; being denied admittance to religious services on Sundays; gross overcrowding: just a sample of their bitter grievances.

However, as a reminder that relations between guards and guarded were not always manifestly hostile, Governor John Green and his staff at the Toronto Jail received a letter of praise in July 1880 from an unexpected source. The missive was penned by a man named George Dickson, better known as George Bennett.

On the afternoon of March 25, 1880, employees at the offices of the *Globe* newspaper in Toronto had been startled to hear a pistol shot ring out, followed by the voice of their employer, George Brown, crying "Help! Murder!" Rushing into Brown's office, they found him confronting an attacker and nursing a bullet wound to the thigh. Brown's assailant was George Bennett, who had recently been dismissed from Brown's company for dereliction of duty. As the *Globe* explained, "his whole life lately [had] been evidently one in which the man had given way to every vicious passion, drunkenness and lust being his predominant vices." For five years, Bennett had been night engineer in the *Globe*'s boiler room. After several reprimands from his superior, James Banks, he had again come in to work drunk and, unforgivably, he then left his post unattended. The day engineer was hauled out of bed in the middle of the night to deal with a looming disaster in the boiler room.

This was the final straw. Bennett was fired the following day.

Simmering with resentment, he returned to the newspaper's offices, a loaded gun in his pocket, ostensibly to wrest a reference from his ex-employer. Brown, a Father of Confederation, owner of the *Globe*, and a powerful political figure in the Liberal Party, was having none of it. He told the man to run along and discuss the matter with his former supervisor. Bennett argued; he pulled out his revolver; and, after a brief tussle, the gun went off, injuring George Brown.

Bennett was known to police as a violent drunk and wife beater; so well known, in fact, that, as later reported in court, he had the following conversation with his arresting officer, Robert Gregory:

"Gregory, this is a big thing."

"Yes, it appears rather serious," replied the policeman.

"I won't get out of this as easily as the last."

Prophetic words. Over the next few weeks, Brown's condition worsened, and what had started out as a flesh wound morphed into "blood poisoning" — life-threatening gangrene. He lapsed into a coma, and, on May 9, he died.

The nation was in shock; messages of grief and outrage poured in.

But could Bennett be regarded as guilty of murder? Was it his fault that a seemingly minor injury had developed into a fatal condition? His trial lasted one day. The judge and jury were clearly in no mood to give him the benefit of any doubt, and he was sentenced to hang.

On July 24, the *Quebec Daily Telegraph* published an article that was typical of newspaper reports of the day. The story, stretching over more than two-thirds of the page, described in meticulous detail the last few hours Bennett spent on earth before his hanging at approximately 8:00 a.m. This was followed by a letter from Bennett to Governor Green, which he styled as "a warning to young men" not to fall, as he had done, "an easy victim of evil associates." The lengthy account ended with a second letter, with the heading "TORONTO GAOL, July 23rd, 1880."

> I here express my sincere thanks to the officials of Toronto Gaol. I have received from them the kindest attention and utmost civility in attending to my wants during my confinement here. It is remarkable the descipline [*sic*] that is exercised in the discharge of the various duties to be performed and the caution, promptitude and despatch [*sic*] which accompanies all the work done within the buildings. The persistent watchfulness with which innocent and guilty alike are regarded when once beneath the shadow of this roof makes Toronto gaol a credit to the city and the country at large. I have found Mr. Green a kind shrewd, observant man: nothing can escape his notice. The manner in which the business of the place is conducted is worthy of all praise. Farewell, Toronto jail.
>
> (Signed,) GEORGE BENNETT.

Enraged at being dismissed from his job at the *Globe* newspaper, George Bennett confronted and shot his ex-employer, George Brown. After Brown died of complications from the wound, Bennett was convicted of murder and hanged at the Don Jail in July 1880.

According to the report, Bennett was quite composed on the morning of his hanging: "At five o'clock he arose and making a careful toilet, took up his testament and commenced to read his prayers in an earnest manner.... He was dressed in a suit of black broadcloth and blue silk necktie.... Bennett had in his right hand an ebony crucifix." As unlikely as it seems, this was entirely in character: in a complete about-face, he had dedicated his last days to penitence and prayer. Just before eight, a procession set out from his room in the west wing of the jail across the main hall to the east wing, down a stairway to the basement and thence up a flight of stone steps to the northeast jail yard, where the scaffold was set up. The group included Bennett's spiritual advisers, the sheriff, the hangman, the government inspector of prisons, the jail surgeon, a handful of newsmen, and the governor of the jail, John Green. About seventy spectators were permitted to witness the execution. Then Bennett's lifeless body was lowered into a plain pine coffin, which, according to some reports, was adorned with silver ornaments. In accordance with a requirement in force at the time, executed individuals were to be buried where they had been hanged. Bennett was no exception: he was interred in the jail yard.

This was not the only time that Governor Green and his staff had been highly commended: back in November 1877, John Williams had been another doomed man who expressed gratitude just before he was hanged.

Williams, described as "a man of medium height, sparely but apparently strongly built, and about 49 years of age," was employed as a brick maker just outside Weston, Ontario. He was belligerent and abusive when drunk, which Ann, his wife of twenty years, suffered "with exemplary patience and forbearance." On the night of September 21, 1877, after consuming an inordinate amount of whisky, he battered Ann to death. At his trial, he was found guilty and sentenced to be hanged, the judge commenting that "in the course of a long professional life I have only heard of one more awful spectacle than that of your wife, dragged along the floor, and left under the bed to die." Like Bennett, Williams turned to religion during his final days in jail, studying the Bible and discussing his readings with his spiritual adviser.

Williams paused at the foot of the gallows, then pronounced the following words in a "loud, painfully firm tone": "I wish to make several remarks. I wish to thank the Governor, the Deputy-Governor, and all the officers under them for the kind way in which they have used me. I wish to thank my counsel for the way in which they defended me. I am happy that I got a fair trial, and I thank the public at large for what they have done for me. Also my clergyman. That's all."

Governor Green, who had visited him in his cell on the morning of his hanging, courteously returned the compliment, telling reporters that Williams's "deportment towards all the officials aroused in them a keen feeling of regret that the law was irrevocable, and that they had to assist on such a melancholy occasion." These are bafflingly generous words, you might think, considering the dreadful crime Williams had committed just two months previously. However, given Green's progressive opinions on the treatment of offenders, it may well be the execution of Williams that jail staff found so sad an event, even though the man did indeed deserve stern punishment for the murder of his wife.

Like Bennett three years later, Williams was buried in an unmarked grave in the jail yard.

Overcrowding at the jail was an ongoing problem.

One attempt to improve conditions and ease congestion had been the construction of the Toronto Central Prison, which opened just southwest of King Street and Strachan Avenue in 1873. Designed by Ontario's official government architect, Kivas Tully, and built by relays of prison gangs, it housed 336 men, generally serving time for minor offences such as larceny, vagrancy, or drunkenness. Hard work (making wool, bricks, and furniture, and building equipment for the railways, among other jobs), hard discipline (administered by armed ex-policemen and ex-military men), and rigorously enforced silence at all times were the basic penological principles upon which this institution was founded.

However, the Don remained ominously overstretched. In 1885, there were 177 male inmates in the jail, most of them on convictions of drunkenness or vagrancy, with only 122 cells to accommodate them. To relieve pressure on the men's side, many of the men were moved over to the women's section. As the *Globe* noted in October 1887: "Governor Green telephoned to police headquarters yesterday that he had 40 prisoners at the gaol for whom there were no cells. They were compelled to sleep in the corridors. The collection of prisoners who went over the Don Sunday morning was 54, and this is not counting a number who were allowed out on bail. The van had to make three trips."

There was more bad press in 1888. In February of that year, the city markets and health committee made a tour of inspection of the jail. Although the place earned full marks for "scrupulously clean floors and immaculate walls," the visitors found 162 men of all ages "lounging about" in corridors, "some reading, some talking together and others standing apart and staring into vacancy, as though all mind and motion had deserted them." Also of grave concern were two young girls "of chaste character and imprisoned for the first time ... compelled to associate day and night with infamous women of the lowest and vilest description."

But the same report revealed that the committee was considering changes to the Don that would directly affect the living arrangements of its governor.

CHAPTER 10

Greener Pastures

By the late 1880s, Toronto was bursting at the seams.

When the city was incorporated in 1834, it had consisted of roughly 5,400 acres, stretching from Lake Ontario in the south to a line four hundred yards to the north of Lot (Queen) Street (the approximate position of what is now Dundas Street), and from Bathurst Street in the west to Parliament Street in the east. (This excludes what were called the "liberties": areas reserved for new wards that were originally located outside the boundaries but absorbed into the city in 1859.) Within fifty years, the number of residents had climbed from 9,252 to more than 105,000, and by 1891 to more than 181,000.

The city limits had also expanded — galloping northward along Yonge Street, westward to High Park, and, vaulting across the Don River to the east, the city now also included land along Kingston Road.

Along with the exploding population, the number of criminals requiring accommodation in the city jail was seeing a sharp uptick, and there was simply nowhere to put them. "The truth is," mused the *Globe* in the late 1880s, "that the Toronto gaol was built for a city of 50,000 inhabitants and has not been enlarged with the growth of the city. It is too small, it has no regular hospital, only a couple of small rooms, which are altogether inadequate, and the heating system is faulty." Overcrowding extended to every single department. A row of narrow cells had been built in one of the corridors, with four men jam-packed

Looking north toward the Don Jail from Munro Street in 1880.

like sardines into each one. The chapel, condemned as "repulsive and hideous" and entirely unsuited for "the purposes of divine worship," had perhaps just enough room for one hundred churchgoers. This made it much too tight for the existing inmate population. The laundry room was hopelessly small; the drying room was gone, and clothes were being hung up to dry in the chapel and the corridors.

Faced with this dire situation, what was the city to do?

The only way out was to spend some money. Priority Number One was to provide a new dwelling for the governor, "which," affirmed the *Globe*, "is something no person could possibly object to." During the first two decades of the jail's life, beginning with George L. Allen, the governor had lived in the administration block of the jail itself. Now the current governor, John Green, would have his own residence in a separate building just to the southeast of his workplace. With much-needed space freed up, Priority Number Two could be addressed. This would consist of improvements to the jail, including more cells, an infirmary, and an upgraded laundry room.

It was only fair that Governor Green should have accommodation more suited to his position in the city's correctional hierarchy. His second-in-command had been treated far more generously. Back in 1865, a gatehouse had been built on jail property, punctuating the southeast side of the wooden security fence. This was initially a simple one-storey building where the gatekeeper was posted, allowing him to control access to the jail grounds. It is not clear whether this was a permanent position or filled in rotation by the turnkeys or head guards. However, within a few years, a deputy governor was hired, and the gatehouse became his home. By 1879, a second floor, with a steeply sloped roof and dormer windows, had been added, making it a modest but quite comfortable residence.

In August 1880, His Worship Mayor James Beaty formally opened Riverdale Park to the general public. This triangular-shaped parkland area was located south of Winchester Street on the west side of the Don Valley. As usual, the *Globe* was there to offer its readers a sense of the pageantry of the grand opening, which was attended by groups of ladies and gentlemen, "the former largely predominating, adding immensely to the scenic effect with their light and delicately coloured costumes." From time to time, the Garrison Artillery band entertained the crowd with a "spirited marching air." The land had originally been earmarked as a burial ground, but some five years previously it had been purchased by the city. With the help of a $1,500 grant and the labour of jail inmates (courtesy of Governor Green), it had been transformed into what one alderman called "a great resort for the people residing in the east end of the city." To loud cheers, the mayor offered some prophetic words: residents should "look forward twenty-five years, and come to a conclusion as to what the city would be like then. Every inch of available space would probably be built on, and therefore it behooved them now to make an effort to establish at various points open spaces which would serve as breathing places for the pent-up inhabitants of the Toronto of the future."

This was not just idle talk. Mayor Beaty and his council were men of action: four years later, in 1884, the park was expanded eastward across the Don River to the edge of the jail. At that time, Riverdale on the east side of the Don had just been annexed and the jail absorbed into the city.

Also, ambitious plans were underway to straighten, widen, and deepen the meandering Don River. The Don Improvement Project was a massive restructuring of the lower stretches of the river that began in the fall of 1886. The city's stated aims were to reduce pollution levels, make the waterway navigable for larger vessels, facilitate rail traffic into the city, and fill in and replace the polluted marshlands with new industrial property. Painful memories of a devastating flood in 1878 that washed away buildings and bridges gave extra impetus to the project. One of the powerful parties involved in the scheme was the Canadian Pacific Railway, which had set its sights on acquiring an additional railway entrance to the city.

"With 'the Don Improvement,'" lamented Toronto conservationist Charles Sauriol in his 1955 book *Remembering the Don*, "the last vestiges of a sylvan lower Don Valley disappeared forever."

And, as it turned out, the project was anything but an improvement. Shortage of funds, political incompetence, and unforeseen conditions when construction work began led to its failure. Also disastrous was the creation of the east-west Keating Channel along the northern edge of the Ashbridges Bay marshes in the late 1890s, with the river eventually being forced into an unnatural 90-degree turn. This increased both the risk of flooding and the buildup of wastes in the river.

However, as part of the Don project in the 1880s, new bridges were built across the lower reaches of the Don River and old ones improved; in short order, residential areas started mushrooming on the eastern side of the valley.

In 1888 (sixteen years into his tenure as governor), John Green was offered a brand new, free-standing house in this very desirable expanded part of the city. Who could possibly refuse?

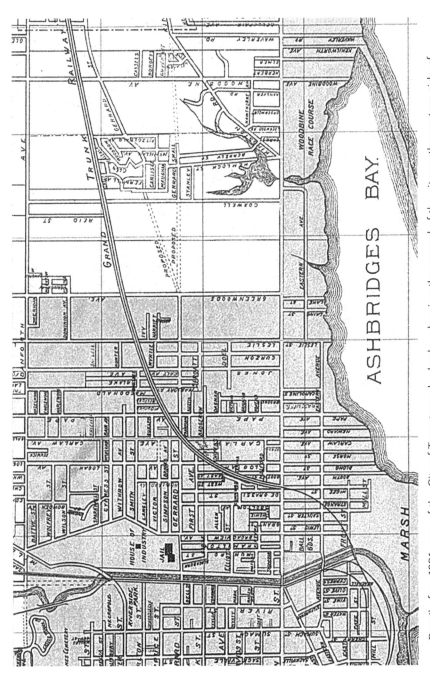

Detail of an 1891 map of the City of Toronto and suburbs, showing the spread of the city on the eastern side of the Don River. By 1884, Riverdale had been annexed and the House of Refuge [incorrectly named the House of Industry on the map] and the jail absorbed into the city.

In April of that year, architect Charles Mancel Willmot submitted plans for the new Governor's House, as well as renovations to the jail, with an estimated price tag of $28,700. This latter proposal did not meet with universal approval: Alderman G.F. Frankland, for one, strongly objected to the lavish arrangements being contemplated for the "worthless fellows" confined in the Don. The city council decided to cut out some of the improvements, among them the construction of a new laundry room, and to reduce the bill by about $8,000. As it turned out, Governor Green revealed in 1891 that the renovations ended up costing closer to $40,000 than $20,000.

According to a brief biography in Eric Arthur's *Toronto, No Mean City*, Charles Mancel Willmot was born in Yorkville village in 1855. He was apprenticed to the noted Toronto architect William George Storm. In a case of two degrees of separation, Storm had served his apprenticeship with William Thomas, the architect of the jail. Willmott spent a few years in Winnipeg in the 1880s, but other than that, he practised mainly in the Yorkville area of Toronto.

And so the Governor's House rose up on the northwest corner of what maps in the late 1800s now referred to as Broadview Avenue and Gerrard Street.

It was clear that Willmot had absolutely no desire to model his new creation on the forbidding style of its stone-and-brick neighbour, although perhaps the buff brick he chose for the residence was meant to echo the blond colours of the jail. The house, set in extensive gardens, was designed in the typically Victorian Queen Anne Revival residential style. The two-storey building stood on a raised limestone foundation and featured an L-shaped asymmetrical façade, a gable roof, a two-storey bay window, decoratively patterned brickwork, and simple woodwork.

Once the house was ready and the governor had moved in, his former quarters were reportedly fitted up with eighty-three new cells with prefabricated iron walls and bars to accommodate 113 inmates. The Willmot-designed separate Laundry Building, which was initially rejected by the city council, was tacked on to the west side of the jail in 1889. (In later years, this was used as an annex to the jail.)

Another item on Willmot's list in 1888 was an evaluation of the heating and cooling systems in the jail. According to a Bridgepoint document on the Old Don Jail, the building stayed relatively cool in warm weather, probably due more to its thick walls than to the merits of its ventilation system. Heating, however, was a different and far more serious matter. William Thomas's original plans had called for the use of steam boilers to force heated air into a complicated network of ducts and flues until it was finally expelled to the outer air through two ventilation towers on the roof. Willmot reported that the structure in the jail did not reflect Thomas's drawings — it is entirely possible that this scheme had never been implemented because of the hostility faced by Thomas in 1860 from Alderman James Vance and his allies in the city council. Following an engineer's report in 1889, the heating and ventilation systems were significantly revamped, with the installation of pipes, wooden ducts and radiators, which would have improved conditions, especially in winter.

"It is something, but not enough," was the consensus.

On December 17, 1900, beneath the sombre headline "The Harvest of Death: The Reaper Was Busy on Sunday," the *Globe* announced that Mr. John Green had died at the governor's residence at four o'clock the previous morning. His end was not unexpected, as he had been ill for some time. "He filled his responsible position with great ability, tact and efficiency," the news item concluded.

Within a week, a successor had stepped into Green's shoes: a well-known Markham, Ontario, man named Garrett Robert Vanzant (sometimes spelled Van Zant). The new governor was described in the press as being a very popular personage in York County. Now retired, he had been a hardware merchant in Stouffville, then in Markham. As a prominent Liberal, he had taken an active interest in political and municipal affairs; he was president of the Markham Township Fair, a "member of the Masonic fraternity," and a justice of the peace. In short, he was considered to be a most excellent appointee.

One of the issues that came bubbling fiercely to the surface during his governorship was a gross injustice that has plagued prison systems since time immemorial: the imprisonment of innocent people. A letter from Reverend Robert Hall in 1903 expounded on one aspect of this dilemma: "The jail is still crowded with ... aged and friendless men and women, who have not been convicted of any crime, and this condition has existed to my knowledge for the last eighteen years."

Vanzant's response drilled to the nub of the problem: "There is no doubt in the world that these people would not be taken to the asylum under any consideration. They are not insane in the proper sense of the word, but are simply old and feebleminded.... Many persons are brought here who should go to other institutions.... As soon as inmates become any trouble in any of these places they send them here." As per usual, nothing at all was done to remedy this dreadful situation.

Then there was the long-festering issue of the presence of mentally or emotionally challenged individuals in the general prison population. In 1902 a city committee paid a visit to the jail to look into a charge that "owing to the confinement of lunatics in the jail the place was a sinkhole of immorality." According to the committee,

> Seven [male] lunatics and two nurses [both men], who were also prisoners, were found in one small room, where they had been confined all winter. One of them had consumption. The women had rather better and more roomy quarters, but there were among them one or two epileptics, subject to frequent fits, and the attendant there was a prisoner also. Bertha Moor, who is awaiting trial for the murder of her child, is confined there, where she could be watched, because it was feared she would attempt suicide. Surprise was expressed at keeping her with lunatics.

The shocked committee members all agreed that it was totally reprehensible to keep lunatics in the jail. But as to who should be obliged to take responsibility for this atrocious situation — the provincial government? the jail? — they could not agree.

And so, as on many occasions before and since, nothing at all was done.

By 1906, however, it was becoming increasingly clear that, unlike his predecessor John Green — that man of "great ability, tact and efficiency" — Garrett Vanzant was not destined to die peacefully in his bed at the governor's residence after a long and respectable career in service. In December, eleven charges were laid against him by W.C. Brown, the jail's engineer. Brown claimed that Vanzant was "not a fit and proper person to be Governor of Toronto Jail" for numerous reasons, among them that he was unwilling or incapable of maintaining discipline at the jail; that he had been guilty of unbecoming and improper conduct (for example, one witness told the subsequent inquiry that he had seen the governor holding a young lady visitor in his arms); and that he had been guilty of favouritism. And the most egregious accusation: "That the open and flagrant misconduct of the said Van Zant was such as to cause the prisoners to comment thereon and ridicule the said Van Zant to the guards and other employees."

Vanzant vehemently denied all the charges. The commissioner at the head of the inquiry, who read every single one of the 977 typewritten pages of evidence, was not convinced of his innocence, and neither was the Ontario government. In June 1907, Vanzant was dismissed.

The Reverend Doctor Andrew B. Chambers, pastor of Parliament Street Methodist Church, stepped in to replace the disgraced governor. Born in Ireland, Chambers, noted the *Globe*, had "occupied many pulpits in many places in Canada." An upstanding churchman, a Mason, and "a sturdy adherent of the Conservative party" — everyone was totally convinced that, unlike Vanzant, Chambers would prove to be a most excellent appointee.

CHAPTER 11

Folk Hero

The new governor of the Don Jail, Reverend Doctor Andrew B. Chambers, was a political appointee with no prior experience; his claims to fame being that he was a Mason, a member of the Conservative Party, and the polar opposite, it seemed, of the disgraced Garrett Vanzant whom he had replaced. Chambers ran the jail between 1907 and 1917 in a caring but totally ineffectual manner.

Perhaps the most outstanding quality Chambers brought to his job was the Christian virtue of kindness. As quoted by Mark Johnson in *No Tears to the Gallows*, fellow clergyman S.D. Chown noted that Chambers "simply wanted to be a friend to everyone, especially those in trouble."

One short-term resident of the jail who certainly benefitted from Chambers's benevolence was a timid, terrified eighteen-year-old girl called Carrie Davies, on trial in February 1915 for murdering her employer, Charles Albert Massey, a scion of the powerful Canadian Massey family. She shot him, she claimed, because he had made indecent advances to her. She was desperately afraid of losing her precious virginity to the cad. Chambers granted Davies shelter in the hospital wing from exposure to the rough conditions and the tough female inmate population while her sensational case sped through the criminal justice system. The masterly efforts of her defence counsel led to an acquittal, and, weeping, she thanked the judge, the jury, and the jail.

But perhaps to underscore just how inept the new regime was, the *Globe* reported in a large, bold headline on July 18, 1908 — that is, just one year after the appointment of Reverend Chambers — that seven "desperate" prisoners had escaped from the Toronto Jail. The escape of these desperadoes, several of whom were awaiting sentence for serious crimes, was grave enough, but the circumstances of their jailbreak made it one of the most egregious (and embarrassing) getaways ever.

The offenders, among them Alexander Rose, awaiting sentence on charges of feloniously (and brutally) wounding, and Henry Churchill, awaiting trial on charges of robbing Pullman cars on the Grand Trunk Railway, had been confined in a corridor specially reserved for inmates pending sentence or trial. As Chambers explained in the records of the prisoners, they "got into the cell used as a death chamber ... and cut through the wall to the jail yard — stood on each other's shoulders to scale the twenty-foot jail wall and disappeared up a lane — were dressed in their usual clothes, so they would look like ordinary citizens." The escape was "carefully planned and executed": the men had coolly obtained a duplicate of the key to the execution chamber, and, probably over the course of several days, had cut a large opening through the three-foot-thick wall of the room, using as a tool the

"Over the Don, Toronto." This postcard, ca. 1910, depicts the jail on the east side of the Don River.

lever that triggered the trap door of the gallows. Of the seven escapees, just one was immediately recaptured, and a follow-up story in January 1909 revealed that the ringleader, Alex Rose, had been apprehended in Huntingdon, West Virginia. At that point, the remaining five offenders were still at large.

On the organizational level, Chambers's well-intentioned but completely feeble skills translated into a full decade of absolutely no leadership at the Don.

By 1917, with Canada deeply embroiled in the First World War, there was a concerted push in Toronto to introduce measures to help the war effort. So, when a call went out to cut costs and slash jobs, the city looked into what — or whom — it could cull. The consensus was that the jail was overstaffed, and both the governor and the deputy governor of the Don were let go. Although the two men were not consulted beforehand, they were compensated for their dismissal.

The governor was not replaced, and it fell upon two officials to head up the administration of the jail. The first was Frederick Mowat, sheriff for the City of Toronto, a provincial and political appointee who had his father, former premier of Ontario Sir Oliver Mowat, to thank for his cushy job and his spacious office at City Hall. Reporting to him, and often at loggerheads with him, was the man in charge of the day-to-day administration and an employee of the City of Toronto, chief turnkey Henry Addy.

Their mutual dislike and opposition came to a head in 1919 when a so-called "drifter" named Frank McCullough, who had been convicted of murdering a policeman, was locked up in the death cell at the Don Jail, awaiting execution.

The crime had taken place on November 19, 1918. The following day, the *Toronto Daily Star* gave its readers the full scoop in a story that stretched over five-and-a-bit columns. "The beginning of the tragedy occurred early in the afternoon when McCullough and another man drove up in a buggy to Madame Mayes, 372 College street [*sic*] and opened negotiations for a sale of a quantity of furs. Their actions aroused suspicion in the mind of the woman, who excused herself and telephoned No. 3 Police Station. Before Acting Detective [Frank] Williams and Constable Walter McDermott could reach the store in a police automobile the men had departed." The policemen learned that the suspicious characters had hired the buggy from Cross's Livery, and they hurried over to the stables on King and Bathurst streets in downtown Toronto. The men had not yet returned, and despite the owner's caution ("I warned him that they were big men, and would likely be hard to handle"), Williams decided to wait for them alone.

This proved to be a fatal decision.

One of the suspects, later identified as Albert Johnson, ran away, but shots were fired in a tussle between Williams and the other man, Frank McCullough. Things escalated so quickly that Williams had no opportunity to pull out his revolver. Instead, he set upon McCullough with his baton. As the two men continued to struggle, McCullough fired once more.

Williams dropped to the ground.

"I'm shot, get the doctor," he whispered.

Then he died, with a bullet through his heart. He was the first Toronto police officer since the incorporation of the city in 1834 to be killed in the line of duty.

McCullough fled onto King Street, where he was tackled and brought down by a newsboy. He was transported to police headquarters by Bartholomew Cronin, the detective assigned to the case. Cronin was to play an important role in the roiling saga that unfolded over the next eight months.

In an article published at the time, twenty-six-year-old Frank McCullough was described as "5 feet 11¼ inches in height, clean shaven, brown hair, fair complexion, protruding blue eyes, prominent forehead and cheek bones." What neither the press nor the police realized was that "Frank McCullough" was actually Leroy Ward Fay Swart, a fugitive from tiny Westville, New York. Even after these facts emerged, no one in Canada used his real name. He was so charming and disarming that most people, even the tough cops he tangled with, simply called him Frank.

McCullough had done jail time in the States before enlisting in the army and then deserting. After crossing into Canada, he carried on with his thieving ways and served a year at the Burwash Industrial Farm near Sudbury, Ontario, for burglary and assault.

This time, however, his criminal activities had landed him in the worst possible hole: the automatic punishment for murder was death by hanging. By a stroke of apparently immense good fortune, a legal colossus represented him in court in January 1919: Thomas Cowper Robinette, King's Counsel (KC), regarded as the most prominent criminal lawyer in Toronto. Relishing the challenge and tempted by the prospect of publicity, Robinette had taken on his case pro bono.

Robinette argued that McCullough was only trying to escape from Acting Detective Williams and had had no intention of killing him. If McCullough was guilty of anything, it was manslaughter. Robinette's persuasive powers came to nothing. After five hours of deliberation, the foreman of the jury pronounced McCullough guilty, the judge sentenced him to hang, and McCullough stepped into the death cell at the Don Jail to await his execution on May 2.

Conflict flared up between Sheriff Mowat and chief turnkey Addy over the "death watch," the mandatory three-man team whose duties took them right into the death cell with the condemned man. The team's task was, one at a time, to maintain round-the-clock surveillance and ensure that their charge neither escaped custody nor committed suicide.

Since all hiring and firing was handled by the province, Addy had approached Mowat for extra staffers for this demanding job. The sheriff selected two men who worked for him at city hall: Alfred Amory, a former policeman, and Sam Follis, a driver. Both seemed logical choices as they had recently manned the death watch for the previous tenant of the death cell, and they knew the drill. They promptly snagged the two daytime shifts. The problem, then, was to find a candidate for the graveyard shift.

Mowat came up with what he considered a brilliant choice: a desperate war veteran, Ernest Currell. "McCullough's Guard Served in

Trenches: Was Wounded Eleven Days After He Went into Action," explained a headline in the *Toronto Daily Star* on April 16, 1919. The returned soldier "was wounded on October 10, 1916. He had been in the trenches only 11 days when a bullet struck him on the hand. He went to the front on September 29. Prior to enlistment he was a tinsmith by trade."

Currell had a bad back and had not worked since the war. He was sick and pitifully poor; he had three children with another on the way; the family lived in a tiny house; and, on several occasions, the bailiff had come knocking. The job of night watch at the rate of three dollars a shift could not have come at a better time for him.

Mowat was emphatic. As he later told a 1919 inquiry set up under the leadership of W.W. Dunlop, provincial inspector of prisons and public charities (*In the Matter of the Prisons and Public Charities Act and inquiry pursuant to Section 9* — henceforth called the Dunlop Inquiry): "I thought there was no question but that he was a suitable man."

The rules governing prisoners awaiting execution were crystal clear: the only visitors allowed were the condemned person's doctor, lawyer, and spiritual adviser. All others would have to obtain written permission from the sheriff. Within two days of McCullough's arrival in the death cell, however, this iron rule was bent, leading to a blow-up between Sheriff Mowat and chief turnkey Addy.

The innocent cause of this hostility was sixteen-year-old Doris Mytton, the daughter of McCullough's landlady, Gladys Mytton. Doris turned up at the Don Jail, asking to see Frank. Addy refused; Doris insisted. To fob her off, Addy sent her to the sheriff, never dreaming that she would actually get permission to see the convicted murderer. But get it she did.

As author Mark Johnson succinctly puts it in his admirable book on the life and times of Frank McCullough: "The issue was who was in charge of the jail." Addy felt that if Mowat wanted to break the regulations by allowing unprecedented visits from outsiders, he certainly had the authority to do so. But what if something went wrong? As chief turnkey, Addy strongly suspected that *he* would be the one on the hook for it. And, frustratingly, there was no authority above Mowat to appeal to.

Two opposing factions were now facing off at the Don: the regular staffers, with chief turnkey Addy at their head, and the death-watch guards, who reported and were most grateful to Sheriff Mowat. This quickly exacerbated the dysfunction at the jail, a situation that the cunning and slippery McCullough took full advantage of.

It began in a small way. Death watchman Alfred Amory belonged to the Western Congregational Church, the same church that Doris Mytton attended. The Sunday after her visit to the jail, she handed Amory a letter and asked him to take it to Frank. Strictly against regulations, Amory did so. As a result of Doris's suggestions, McCullough requested the appointment of Western Congregational's pastor, Reverend R. Bertram Nelles, as his spiritual adviser.

Reverend Nelles welcomed his new role. He was genuinely concerned about the spiritual wellbeing of his charge and accepted McCullough's claims of innocence and remorse. Also, since McCullough was not a religious or church-going man, converting this notorious sinner could only lead to positive publicity for Nelles's struggling church. Before long, Nelles was conducting rousing prayer meetings for McCullough's salvation, and members of the congregation, especially the younger ones, organized letter campaigns and petitions in favour of having his death sentence commuted.

McCullough's cell was basic and sparsely furnished, containing just a bed, a rough wooden table, two chairs, a small stove, and a little cupboard. There were bars on the door and on the three windows. There were, however, some luxuries not found in a typical cell. For example, members of Mrs. Bell's Young Women's Bible Class lovingly put together care packages of fresh eggs and cookies for the prisoner, and Alfred Amory smuggled them in. But he was not the only offender. It was his co-worker, Sam Follis, who provided the cupboard to safely store McCullough's abundant supply of illicit goods. Even Reverend Nelles broke the rules, although he later 'fessed up only to bringing in candies and the occasional strawberry.

Complaints to the sheriff from Addy and his staff fell on deaf ears. Chief guard Harry Denning was especially outraged at the clownish goings-on of McCullough and his so-called guardians: "Then I saw a deck of cards in there [McCullough's cell] and that is something we don't allow in the gaol. I reported that and asked who brought them in. It turned out it was the night man who brought in the cards. Right along from one time to another things were taken in. Sometimes there would be five scuttles of coal in there. I never saw anything like the way this fellow was treated."

And, as it emerged, the biggest offender of all was the vulnerable night watchman, Ernest Currell. He had completely fallen under McCullough's spell in the course of those long nights spent together in the death cell. In addition to bringing items into the jail, he invited into his home on multiple occasions a particular friend of McCullough's, a "mysterious" young woman later identified as Vera de Lavelle. This is how Addy described to the Dunlop Inquiry an attempt by this mystery woman to visit McCullough: "She had a little parcel and I did not let her in; she wanted to know if she could see Frank and I said no, so she went away. She was well dressed, wore dark clothes, plainly made, was of dark complexion, rather French looking, I thought."

All these swirling issues were to come to a head less than three weeks before McCullough's date with the hangman. In the early morning of Wednesday, April 16, 1919, he took advantage of a violent thunderstorm and broke out of jail.

As shown by the jailbreak of Alexander Rose and his six companions back in 1908, escapes from the Don were not unheard of. This one, however, really stung.

The *Toronto Daily Star* explained in their six o'clock edition, beneath the blaring bold headline "M'CULLOUGH, MURDERER, DOPES GUARD, ESCAPES":

> Frank McCullough ... escaped from his death cell at
> the Toronto Jail sometime between eleven o'clock last
> night and five this morning. It is believed McCullough

was in possession of a quantity of veronal which, by means unknown, he was able to place in coffee drunk by his guard, who was occupying the cell with him, causing the guard to sleep until about five o'clock this morning, when he awoke and gave the alarm of McCullough's escape.

The jailers who rushed to the scene found the embarrassed Currell — shirtless, trouserless, and clutching a handwritten note from McCullough, which was clearly meant to exonerate the night watchman from blame:

Currell, old man,

I am sorry, but it had to be done. Now do not you be scared for it isn't your fault, for I doped your coffee with a sleeping powder of Veronnal [*sic*], so you see kid they cannot blame you…. Wish me luck. I am sorry but you know life is sweet, old man.
So long.
Frank

Although McCullough also informed Currell in due course that he would return Currell's "borrowed" clothing as soon as he could, he omitted to mention in this, or in any of the other chatty letters and postcards he wrote during the time he spent on the lam, how he had obtained the hacksaw he used to cut through two iron bars on his cell window before taking a perilous leap onto a retaining wall far below, inching over to the perimeter wall of the jail, and dropping to freedom.

Currell was immediately arrested and charged with aiding and abetting McCullough's escape. His alibi just didn't hold water. The "gaol surgeon" commented that veronal was not a strong enough sedative to knock a person out for hours, especially when taken in coffee, which would counter its effects. And press reports suggested that it would have required several nights' work to saw through the bars of the death-cell windows.

"Collusion!" accused Addy.

Ironically, Currell found himself locked up in the Don Jail, his own workplace. Investigations later revealed that Vera de Lavelle, who turned out to be McCullough's lady love, had hidden the saw in a box of chocolates that Currell had taken in to McCullough.

CHAPTER 12

Vera Walks Free

The *Globe* called her "Vera the Elusive."

The police were convinced that Frank McCullough's lover, Vera de Lavelle, was implicated in his dramatic jailbreak, and they were determined to track her down. The hunt ended on April 22, when Bart Cronin, the detective who had been on the case since Frank was first arrested, spotted her on Queen Street, Toronto. A simple "Hello, Vera" cut short her freedom.

Lavelle told investigators during the 1919 Dunlop Inquiry, struck to look into the circumstances of Frank McCullough's escape, that she had been born in France. She was "just a babe in arms" when her mother brought her to Toronto some twenty-one years previously. She had met McCullough at a dance. The two fell in love and were planning to marry. But, as the *Globe* put it, "the murder of P.C. Williams upset their plans." She denied helping her paramour to escape, although she admitted that they had seen each other on the night of his getaway. "I walked down from Broadview into the park. It was rather dark and spitting rain and I was afraid. I saw a figure coming across the park and he called my name and he took me in his arms and kissed me and said he was free." She had not seen him since.

Fearing political fallout from such a stark exposure of the administrative ineptitude at the Don Jail, the provincial authorities chose to shield the results of the Dunlop Inquiry from public scrutiny at the time. But the public was soon treated to a different, but eminently more dramatic, story, which prompted a brand new inquiry. Harry Drew, a reporter for the *Toronto Evening Telegram*, presented himself at the door of the jail, ostensibly to check out the women's quarters. Charles Spanton, the guard, let him in without question ("I did not think it was any of my business," he told the inquiry), and head matron and reportedly execrable cook Tanny Soady took him on a tour. ("He said 'that he did not think there were nicer quarters in Canada,'" she told the inquiry.)

And then Drew just "happened" to notice Vera de Lavelle and casually asked if he could have a few words with her. ("Well, I suppose there is no harm," replied Soady.)

Imprudently, as it turned out, because there was indeed a great deal of harm implicit in Soady's action. Rule 114 of the 1903 *Official Rules and Regulations Governing the Common Gaols of Ontario* clearly stated that "no person shall be allowed access to any prisoner for the purpose of 'Interviewing' him or her with a view to publishing a report of such interview."

The story hit the headlines in the *Telegram* on April 26. In summary: Vera was refined, honest, and innocent; Frank was a moral and newly religious man; they loved each other; and, although she had not helped him in any way, she had met him in Riverdale Park after his escape and they had said a tender goodbye.

The authorities were furious. The guard was docked one week's salary and the matron two weeks' and both of them were suspended. They were, however, immediately reinstated.

The press had a field day. As quoted by Mark Johnson, after getting the runaround from the provincial secretary, the provincial inspector of prisons and public charities, the sheriff, et al., reporters fumed that "the poor public would like to know whether the Riverdale Bastille is a jail or merely a resort where hide and seek is played at the expense of law and order."

May 2, the day that McCullough was due to be hanged, came and went.

Then, on May 8, the offer of a $1,000 reward for his recapture bore fruit. A tip led detective Cronin and his fellow officers to the second floor of a dingy boarding house on Bathurst Street in Toronto. McCullough tried to escape by leaping from an upper window, but the police were waiting below with their guns trained on him. Soon, according to a newspaper headline, the "Death Cell Door Clang[ed] Once More on Condemned Slayer."

There was huge public adulation for McCullough, but Cronin came in for his share of praise, too. As one admirer put it in a telegram: "Congratulations for having landed the coveted prize. You must be gifted with the sixth sense of locating evil-doers."

McCullough's execution was rescheduled for June 13.

The day before Frank's capture, Vera de Lavelle had been tried for aiding his escape. She faced up to seven years of prison time and was locked up in the Don to await sentence.

But she was having none of it.

To the utter confusion and embarrassment of the staff at the Don, and in spite of the fact that they had come to regard Vera de Lavelle as one of the "shrewdest, coolest and cleverest schemers with whom they had ever had to deal," she strolled away from the jail in broad daylight.

"According to the official statement," reported the *Globe* on May 31, "it would appear that Vera Lavelle and her accomplice [Ruby Masten, soon recaptured] simply took two ladders from the Laundry Building, through an open door into the jail yard, placed them against the 16-foot wall, scaled it, climbed a six-foot board fence and walked away."

This escape made it "the second jail breaking within seven weeks, and the fact that the other case was that of the man whom she is said to have been in love with, presents a dramatic coincidence."

The public was absolutely entranced: murder, a charming rogue, a beautiful woman of mystery, romance in the shadow of the gallows, star-crossed lovers yearning to be reunited, daring jail escapes (not one, but two, and both in the space of seven weeks!). It was a sensation.

The official reaction was far less dewy eyed. Sheriff Mowat skipped out of a meeting at City Hall and raced across town to the jail in a vain attempt to contain the fallout. And Provincial Inspector of Prisons

A sampling of the thousands of petitions sent to Ottawa in 1919, all pleading for the commutation of Frank McCullough's death sentence.

Dunlop was apoplectic. "It's the smallest jail in the Province, the smallest part of my work, yet it causes me more work than the whole of the rest of it. I could handle the King's business better than the Toronto Jail," he said.

With McCullough back under lock and key, efforts to have his sentence commuted resumed with redoubled force. The federal government in Ottawa, responsible for reviewing all capital cases and deciding whether or not a death sentence should be carried out, received petitions containing well over twenty thousand names, all pleading for McCullough's reprieve.

The government official who held McCullough's life in his hands was the Honourable Arthur Meighen, acting federal minister of justice. Meighen could hardly be described as a kind, compassionate, or particularly merciful man, but, to his credit, he did claim to have wrestled with the case: "The responsibility of deciding on the fate of McCullough is one of the most anxious that I have ever been compelled to undertake."

Thomas Cowper Robinette, McCullough's lawyer, fired off telegram after telegram to Ottawa in a last-ditch attempt to obtain executive clemency. Reverend R. Bertram Nelles, McCullough's spiritual adviser, travelled to Ottawa to plead with Meighen in person. The visit was ill-timed — Meighen's train steamed out of town just as Nelles's steamed in. Mere days before the scheduled hanging date, a telegram containing Meighen's final decision came through. It was not what the myriad of McCullough's supporters wanted to hear: the law must take its course, and McCullough must hang.

A wave of outrage and sympathy met this news. As the *Toronto Daily Star* reported on June 12:

> Hundreds of people stood in Riverdale Park last night outside the jail yard, and waved handkerchiefs and papers to Frank McCullough, who stood at the window of his death cell and waved his hands through the bars. The crowd became so large that a policeman was assigned to keep the spectators from going too near the jail wall. One man used field glasses to see McCullough. Shortly after nine the light was turned on in McCullough's cell and he could be seen quite plainly. A grey-haired old woman who could hardly walk, forced her way through the crowd and waved

her hand, while two little girls stayed till nearly midnight. McCullough stayed at the window for many
hours.

The next day, Friday, June 13, as was customary with a condemned
person just before execution, McCullough ate his last meal. He chose
a hearty breakfast of tea, toast, ham, and eggs. At 7:54 a.m., clad in a
striped silk shirt and belted trousers, he walked "with a steady stride"
forty paces east along the corridor to the death chamber. And, at
7:57 a.m., McCullough was hanged, paying what one report called
"the price of death" for the murder of Acting Detective Frank Williams.

The hangman on duty that day was Arthur Ellis, an expatriate
Englishman who was to become Canada's most prolific and notorious
executioner. He appeared very nervous, perhaps spooked by the hordes
of demonstrators who had kept up a continuous and noisy vigil outside
the jail walls.

In an unusual break with tradition, McCullough was not immediately buried in "murderer's row," located in the east jail yard. "A funeral
service such as is rarely given a murderer will be conducted by Rev. Mr.
Nelles, and will be a simple one just the same as if McCullough had
died a natural death."

Vera de Lavelle was still at large. This time, however, police were
in no hurry to find and arrest her, so she surrendered herself on
July 23, 1919. Evading a horde of pressmen, her lawyer, Robinette associate W.B. Horkins, and Detective Walter McConnell picked her up
on Beverley Street in downtown Toronto. She was much relieved that
she would be held in the Court Street cells at the corner of Church and
Adelaide streets instead of being returned to the Don, which held such
painful memories for her.

The following morning, she was once again in court, pleading
guilty to charges of assisting McCullough with his escape from jail,
and of escaping herself.

"I have considered the circumstances connected with this case,"
said Judge Coatsworth, "and I don't impose a very heavy sentence. Poor

McCullough is gone, the thing is all over, and I suppose you have suffered a good deal in connection with it one way or the other, so I am going to impose a sentence of two months on the Jail Farm in this case, and two months' imprisonment at the Jail Farm in the other case of assisting McCullough to escape, the sentences to run concurrently."

"After I come out I am going to start life all over again," Lavelle told the *Toronto Daily Star*, with emphasis on the last three words.

Of her sentence, she said: "I think it is very lenient."

Was she married to McCullough? "That is for you to find out. That is our secret," she replied with a laugh.

Vera quietly served out her term at the Langstaff Jail Farm just north of Toronto and quietly slipped out of sight. With her weighted words about starting life all over again, and her reference to the secret she shared with Frank, was she expecting a child, perhaps?

We shall probably never know.

It might confidently be assumed that heads would roll after this lengthy fiasco at the Don Jail, and roll they did. Two of them. The heads belonged to Miss Tanny Soady, head matron and cook, and to the jail's laundry matron. Soady's claim to shame was not the dreadful chow she supposedly dished up from her kitchen, but the fact that the two women's laxity had allowed Lavelle to break out of jail. However, Soady had also broken the rules and regulations by allowing a reporter to interview Lavelle, and this probably counted against her as well.

Another low-level, but heavily implicated, member of staff appeared in court for his part in the case. In a trial by judge and jury, Ernest Currell was found guilty on June 6, 1919, of aiding and abetting McCullough's escape, with a strong recommendation for mercy.

"This man did act contrary to his duty," a stern Judge Coatsworth told the jury. "He brought in things to the condemned man, he brought letters back and forth.... He went to sleep several times when he was at the post of duty, the very things that a soldier is shot for — and he was a soldier himself — yet he went to sleep several times."

However, as Mark Johnson points out, "time and a good lawyer proved to be in Ernest Currell's favour." Before sentence was passed, his lawyer announced that he would file an appeal. But there is no record that the case was heard again, nor any indication of a final sentence.

And what of Sheriff Mowat and Chief Turnkey Addy, the two men at the top of the chain of command, where the buck should have stopped? As the administration of the jail fell within the jurisdiction of the province, the actions and omissions of Mowat and Addy also came under the spotlight during Dunlop's inquiry into the circumstances of McCullough's escape. However, the authorities had no desire to bring attention to the chaos at the Don caused by the clash between government appointee Mowat and his provincial staff on the one hand and city employee Addy and his fellow municipal workers on the other. So, in spite of a heated exchange of accusations and some nervous moments — Dunlop singled out Mowat for particular censure for not adequately managing the death-watch guards and ignoring reports of "irregularities" in the food and other materials supplied to the prisoner — both Mowat and Addy escaped scot-free.

There was one positive outcome to the McCullough debacle. The provincial government decided that henceforth it was imperative to have a governor in control at the Toronto Jail, and that "the appointment should go to a person who has handled desperate men, and is able to conduct the jail in an efficient manner." By early July 1919, the relieved authorities had found a man who would fit the bill. On September 1, 1919, George Hedley Basher stepped in to assume command.

CHAPTER 13

A Firm Hand

Thomas Langton "Tommy" Church, the feisty mayor of Toronto from 1915 to 1921, had very strong opinions about the Don Jail. "It's not a jail at all — it's simply a stop-over place," he snapped at the time of Vera de Lavelle's escape. He laid the blame for the Don's abysmal administrative record squarely on the incompetent provincial government, because even though the city was responsible for paying guards and other officials, it was the province that actually selected them. So when it came to choosing a new governor for the jail, Church notified Provincial Secretary W.D. McPherson that he would simply refuse to certify the paycheques of any new appointees unless they were returned soldiers. He considered this a safe bet: veterans were regarded as exceptional candidates because of the comprehensive training and experience they received in the military.

George Hedley Basher. Even the name suggests a man who would not shirk from imposing order and discipline on the unruly. He certainly was a returned soldier, and, as his resumé showed, he unquestionably had the necessary qualifications for the position of governor of the Toronto Jail.

Born in Cornwall, England, George Hedley Basher worked for three years as a policeman in his native country before moving to Toronto to join the police force in 1913. During the First World War, he served as a commissioned officer in Egypt, Salonika, and France. He rose rapidly through the ranks, receiving several decorations on the way, and ended the war as a major in charge of a large military prison in Rouen, France.

Major Basher was a shoo-in for the position of governor at the Don. His first day on the job was September 1, 1919. After twelve years of remarkably sloppy management between 1907 and 1919, the jail was about to experience a very different and much sterner organizational regime.

An example of this new and tougher stance came within months. In early 1920, banking on the mystique of Frank McCullough, which lingered on in the public consciousness, a movie company had the "nerve" to apply for permission to make a film about the charismatic ruffian's life and prison escape.

"Of course the request was refused," declared Major Basher in an interview. "This year we have already had more people pass through the jail than in the entire year preceding.... The principal crimes are burglary, housebreaking, robbery with violence, hold-ups in automobiles, and there are many offenses under the Ontario Temperance Act."

And what was one of the principal factors that lured young people into a life of crime? "Moving pictures," said Basher. "The lads see these films and then go out in a spirit of bravado to emulate the villain of the screen. Some time ago I witnessed a film in which a jail escape was depicted. It was remarkable the amount of applause which the criminal received. Recently, to learn if my opinion was generally held, I asked a prison official of the United States if he attributed a large percentage of crime to the movies, and he agreed with me."

No wonder that cheeky request was turned down so firmly.

The ex-soldier soon developed a reputation as an honest, just, but very strict disciplinarian. This seemed to have been typical of the positions, both military and civilian, that he occupied during his long career in service. As a fellow soldier who served in Basher's regiment in the Second World War once put it: "His enforcement of strict discipline became a tradition in the regiment, and because he was always fair and impartial, men were proud to be associated with him. Even those who 'suffered' often in his orderly rooms were known to have boasted about having the toughest, but fairest, CO [commanding officer] in the Canadian Army."

However, there were times at the jail when Basher found himself having to temper harsh discipline with mercy. In February 1922, for example, David Harri, a prisoner awaiting execution in the death cell, went on a hunger strike, refusing anything other than cigarettes. He would wake up crying at night. He was Armenian, and there was no priest of the Armenian Church in Ontario to act as his spiritual adviser. Basher arranged with the secretary of the Armenian Relief Society in Canada to find a priest in New York or Boston willing to offer support to the anguished man.

By the end of 1922, a relative calm had descended on the jail, interrupted only by an escape attempt in late December by seven female prisoners. Had their escape not been foiled by jail staff, they would have missed church services and the traditional Christmas dinner, which included apples, nuts, pork pies, and candies.

"If anything, there is less serious crime this year than last year," Governor Basher told the press at the time. "The change in conditions is likely due to the stiff sentences given by Judges, which appears [sic] to have had the desired effect. It is altogether likely the improvement will be permanent if the ticket-of-leave people [those granting parole to prisoners] are not too generous."

But there were many challenges. In 1923, Tommy Church, formerly Toronto's scrappy mayor and now a quarrelsome member of parliament, complained that a prisoner could not secure bail over a weekend. Basher went on the defensive, explaining that although everyone who was entitled to bail should be able to get it at any hour, there was simply not enough staff on duty in the evenings or on holidays to safely bring the prisoners out. The following year, public attention was brought to the death from a drug overdose of Frank Anderson, a prisoner in the Don awaiting transfer to a federal penitentiary. Again, Basher found himself in the hot seat, explaining that although a watch was kept on all prisoners and known addicts were carefully searched, it was "impossible to defeat the ingenuity of some."

This sketch, dated 1871, is labelled "Flogging of a Prisoner at the Toronto Gaol, Friday, Jan 6." George Hedley Basher, governor of the Don Jail between 1919 and 1931, was a strong advocate of corporal punishment for "breaches of discipline" in penal institutions.

When it came to crime and punishment, Basher had very definite views. He was a stern advocate of the death penalty as a deterrent against serious crimes. He was less radical about hanging, telling a Senate-Commons committee on capital and corporal punishment in 1954 that "other methods that might be preferable should be explored," although he had no suggestions as to what these alternatives might be. He certainly believed in corporal punishment; specifically, the strap. He told the committee that such punishment was the only effective way to control violent and defiant prisoners. However, he suggested changing the name of this type of discipline to "spanking." He himself, while superintendent of the Guelph Reformatory, had ordered prisoners to be strapped, to the great gratitude, he insisted, of those on the receiving end.

"They thanked me for bringing them to their senses," he said.

In spite of Basher's strongly held opinions, however, the strap was eventually banned. But it would take until 1972 before judicial corporal punishment disappeared from the Canadian statute books.

On one notable occasion, Basher did relax the hard-and-fast rules ever so slightly.

This was in 1924, when Norman "Red" Ryan was committed for trial at the Police Court in Toronto for robbery with violence. Ryan could best be described as a career criminal. He had started small: stealing chickens and bikes as a youngster, then graduating to armed robbery, safecracking, and, in the mid-1930s, to murder.

As the *Globe* explained on January 8, 1924, Ryan was already in deep trouble at the Kingston Penitentiary for multiple unlawful acts: "A despatch [*sic*] from Kingston states: 'The trial of "Red" Ryan for escaping from the Provincial Penitentiary, September 10 last, setting fire to the stable to screen the escape, assaulting Chief Keeper Matthew Walsh with a pitchfork, and stealing an auto, will take place at the Courthouse in Kingston before Chief Justice Meredith on February 5.'"

It was therefore perfectly understandable that exceptional security measures were put in place during Ryan's stay in Toronto. Other than police and members of the press, no outsiders were allowed in the court room. Incarcerated in the Don Jail, Ryan was watched over day and night by a rotating team of three guards. He was forced to wear shackles at all times, even when he slept.

Just before his court appearance, Ryan asked to see Governor Basher. If he were given a good meal, he said, he would give the governor a surprise. On reflection, Basher agreed, whereupon Ryan handed him a seven-inch-long saw blade. How Ryan got the saw was a great puzzle to the authorities, as on being admitted to the Don he had been stripped of his clothing and given a fresh uniform.

There was no possibility that Ryan could have used the saw to make his own getaway, but escapes, and violent escape attempts, were an ever-present reality at the Don. In March 1925, Andrew Morrison and James Moss beat a guard, Thomas Richards, bloody and unconscious with a chair leg before grabbing his keys and releasing some twenty inmates incarcerated on the third floor. Several of the liberated prisoners were sleeping when the doors of their cells were flung open. They simply refused to leave their cells, believing that there was no way to escape from the building. Others, however, trashed the entire floor before a squad of policemen armed with sawed-off shotguns, hastily summoned by Basher, turned up and marched the escapees back to their cells.

Saws always seemed to be a highly sought-after commodity at the jail. In December 1926, four of these prized tools were found in one of the corridors. Two of them, both eight inches in length, had been hidden in crevices in the walls. Additionally, one of the bars in a window had been sawn nearly through. Basher was reportedly alerted to the problem by "a citizen" who knew that a big jailbreak was being planned. Basher immediately launched an investigation. The ringleader of the aspiring escapees, Norman Neal, who was awaiting transfer to the Kingston Penitentiary to serve three years for housebreaking, was placed in solitary confinement.

Two full body searches failed to reveal that Neal was in possession of a fifth saw, which he used to cut an opening measuring seven by twelve inches in the bars of his cell. He then wriggled through, earning himself the nickname "The Human Eel" from an admiring press. This was reportedly the first successful jailbreak under Basher's watch; he must have been very relieved to identify a man caught robbing a chicken coop in Oakville five months later as the elusive Eel and to get him safely back under lock and key.

And then there were the riots, also known as "disturbances," or, in Basher's words, "breaches of discipline." This was part of a statement issued by the department of the provincial secretary in January 1931:

> Major Basher, who is the governor of the local bastile [*sic*], received a message from the guard in charge that a serious disturbance was taking place at the institution. Going to the jail from his near-by residence, he found that prisoners were indulging in an organized

program of shouts, catcalls, profanity and obscenity. The prisoners at this time were all in their cells, with the exception of a few sleeping in corridors for lack of cell space.... It required the combined efforts of the Governor and staff from 6 p.m. until 10 o'clock to restore order.... The ringleaders were detected and placed in isolation cells, and quiet was gradually restored. It is established that the leaders were, in the main, lads of from 17 to 21 years of age. One of the chief complaints seemed to be regarding the deprivation of tobacco, use of which is strictly forbidden under the jail rules.

On learning of the "disturbance," the mayor, William James Stewart, "summoned his own chauffeur" and paid an unannounced visit to the jail. After an hour-long tour of inspection and a conversation with the governor, the mayor declared that the problem was not caused by conditions in the jail, even though he did find that there were inmates sleeping in the corridors for lack of cell space. "I believe Major Basher is entitled to a larger staff to maintain discipline among the prisoners, particularly the younger element," he announced. It would certainly *not* be necessary to take any more drastic measures, although the provincial secretary, Leopold Macaulay, was "said to be determined to compel the city to erect a new jail."

Tellingly, the mayor added "It should be borne in mind that the population of the jail includes prisoners, men awaiting trials, awaiting deportation and men with penitentiary records of an extensive character. It is a clearing house."

And the punishment meted out to the offenders? After receiving a report from Basher about the circumstances behind the riot, and obviously with his wholehearted support, Secretary Macaulay decreed that the seven ringleaders should be strapped. Each of the "guilty parties" was given three to five strokes with a broad strap under the observation of the jail surgeon.

By this time, Basher's days at the Don were just about numbered. In a move described by Macaulay as "not political," Basher was shunted off to the Langstaff Jail Farm or Industrial Farm, familiarly referred to as the Jail Farm. In announcing Basher's appointment as superintendent, Minister Macaulay declared that he was looking forward to a great improvement in the discipline of both staff and inmates at the farm.

Macaulay's claim that there was nothing political in his decision lends itself to suspicion. Particularly so, because he was a minister in the Conservative cabinet in Ontario. And the man slated to replace Basher at the Don was Clifford E. Blackburn, a former alderman and a prominent member of the Central Conservative Association of Toronto — or so it was emphatically stated by prominent Conservatives at an Orange Lodge banquet in May 1931. So were staff changes in the prison system still politically motivated, as they had been in the bad old days before the arrival of Basher? Was Blackburn being touted for the top job at the Don because he was a Conservative with strong Conservative backers?

If there were machinations taking place in the background, they came to naught: in the end Blackburn did not get the job. It was announced in September 1931 that the governorship of the jail had been awarded to Harry G. Denning, the former deputy governor. He was the guard who had so bitterly complained back in 1919 about Frank McCullough's privileged treatment in the death cell.

Clifford Blackburn, runner-up for the top job, was appointed deputy governor. He lasted less than four years. He was dismissed at Denning's request in May 1935, following more riots at the jail. "We have been dissatisfied for some time," was the curt comment of the now Liberal provincial secretary, Harry C. Nixon, to howls of protest from Conservatives.

As for Basher, his new job in 1931 took him a few kilometres north of Toronto to the corner of Yonge Street and Langstaff Road (now Highway 7) in Richmond Hill. The Jail Farm then belonged to the City of Toronto, and it was seen as a less-dreadful alternative to the Don. Construction had begun in 1913, and until the 1950s it served as a minimum-security institution for petty criminals and first offenders. It was a proper working farm, with barns and silos and sheds and a water tower as well as the actual jail building with cells for inmates. It is said that Basher made his daily rounds on horseback, often jumping over hedges at a gallop.

When the Second World War loomed, Basher again prepared for combat, and again, he excelled. He became commanding officer of the Royal Regiment of Canada and served in Iceland, England, and Italy. He was awarded the Order of the British Empire in 1943. At war's end, the now-Colonel Basher was appointed a special investigator in the provincial secretary's office. After a stint as superintendent of the Guelph Reformatory from 1946 to 1952 (where his charges, you will remember, reportedly thanked him for having them strapped), he was appointed deputy minister of reform institutions in Ontario.

George Hedley Basher stepped into his civilian career in 1919 to mop up the mess at the Don Jail after the jailbreaks of Frank McCullough and Vera de Lavelle. In 1952, after several even more sensational escapes, he would again grab the reins of leadership at the Don. This would turn out to be the lowest point of his professional career, and he would not emerge from it unscathed.

CHAPTER 14

War Hero

The firing of the allegedly incompetent Clifford Blackburn, deputy governor of the Don Jail, may have been met with intense hostility from prominent Conservatives in May 1935, but no one of any political stripe could have disapproved of Walter Leigh Rayfield, the man appointed to replace him.

"Because of his experience and interest in his fellow men it is expected he will be a very capable deputy governor," said Provincial Secretary Harry Nixon.

The Liberal Party had swept into provincial power in 1934 and Rayfield's appointment was in line with a new policy of selecting war heroes to fill vacancies in the civil service.

But Captain Rayfield was not just your ordinary war hero. He had earned the right to tack the rare and coveted initials *VC* (Victoria Cross) after his name.

Born in Richmond-on-Thames, England, in 1881, Rayfield came to Canada as a youth. During the First World War, he enlisted in the Canadian army and by September 1918 was a private with the British Columbia Regiment of the Seventh Battalion Canadian Infantry. In the course of two long days near Arras in northern France, he performed three separate exceptional acts of valour: he rushed a trench full of German soldiers, bayoneting two and taking ten prisoner; he neutralized an enemy sniper and captured another thirty Germans; and, he left cover under heavy machine-gun fire to rescue a gravely wounded comrade. For his service and bravery, Rayfield received the Victoria Cross, the highest honour awarded to members of the British armed forces. The last paragraph of his citation read: "His indomitable courage, cool foresight, and daring reconnaissance were invaluable to his Company Commander and an inspiration to all ranks." After the war, his good deeds continued: he was in charge of transferring "shell-shocked" and other severely disabled soldiers to military hospitals.

Prior to his appointment as deputy governor of the jail, Rayfield had served for a short period as sergeant-at-arms of the Ontario legislature, where, to the surprise and admiration of the press, he had come to work in mufti; that is, wearing a regular or civilian suit instead of his military uniform. Newspapers praised "his quiet and unassuming manner and his failure to attempt commercialization of his decoration, [which had] earned the respect of his fellow citizens in peacetime just as his valor won their admiration in war." His past professional record in agriculture, in the armed forces, as one of the officials in charge of the post-war reintegration of soldiers, and as an employee of the Toronto Harbour Commission were clear evidence of "diversified ability." In short, it was expected that the deputy governorship of the jail would be in very safe hands.

After serving as deputy for five years, Rayfield was promoted to governor in February 1940 when the incumbent, Harry Denning, retired with serious heart problems and took to his bed.

A year later, Rayfield was fielding some very bad press. A newly released prisoner accused guards of beating and torturing an inmate named Hugh Alexander "Bill" Newell, a twenty-seven-year-old airman serving with the Royal Canadian Air Force. At the time, Newell was in the Don awaiting a second trial for murdering his estranged wife, Anne, who had been strangled with her own silk stocking. Her body was found in a clump of bushes on Toronto's Centre Island. Newell was by then living with another woman.

The ex-prisoner, Michael Kelly, claimed that "six burly guards" had dragged Newell out of chapel and thrown him into the death cell — "undeservedly," according to Newell's lawyer, as he had not yet been

Capt. Walter Rayfield, VC, governor of the Don Jail from 1940 to 1949. When serving as sergeant-at-arms at the Ontario legislature in 1935, he impressed reporters by dressing in mufti; that is, in a regular suit instead of his military uniform.

convicted. Kelly alleged that Newell kept shouting, "You're breaking my arms!"

The truth was probably a lot more nuanced. Bill Newell was an angry man with a disruptive personality. Soon after his arrival at the Don, he was placed in a detention cell for hurling his food on the floor in a fit of rage. He accused the police of framing him, and at his first trial, he yelled at his own lawyer, called the crown attorney a liar, and accused the judge of "turning prosecutor." Losing patience, the judge rebuked him for being arrogant and impertinent.

"I can't make any statement," was Governor Rayfield's curt reply when asked to comment on Kelly's accusations.

Kelly, on the other hand, had no compunction about making lots of statements. "The guards are to blame for all the mistreatment that Newell or anybody else gets at the jail," he announced. "The inspector of prisons never gets to see any of these things. The governor's a good man, but he doesn't know what's going on behind his back."

The allegation that Rayfield was a good, but clueless, man must have stung.

Ongoing criticism of Rayfield's workplace included this from a former deputy provincial secretary: "The outmoded Don Jail has resumed its original status as the main reformative institution in an area containing a third of Ontario's population, and it is crowded till the walls bulge." In 1944 a *Globe and Mail* reporter and photographer were invited on a rare "frank and open" tour of the jail, with no special preparations made in advance. The pair found the jail "spotless but outmoded." It was so clean because there was no shortage of labour to keep it so. However, there was not enough work to engage the entire jail population, and most of the inmates spent their time sitting in the corridors and "gossiping." Once again, the lack of toilet facilities was highlighted. Only four cells in the whole building, the death cells, had private toilets. (And if you weren't one of those with the luxury of death-cell accommodation, you still had your trusty "portable facilities" at night time — read, "pails" — to fall back on.) The jail, according to the article, was a space waster. It had "a huge central area which towers to the roof and which is topped by an ancient skylight." Officials at the provincial secretary's office at Queen's Park who administered the institution wanted something different: a modern jail near a highway to facilitate transportation of prisoners to the courts, "which wouldn't waste space, heat, or staff labor [*sic*]." In the meantime, officials pointed out, the facilities were just about the same as those "enjoyed by a lot of pioneers and a lot of rural Canadians today."

In short: it was business as usual at the antiquated, overcrowded, malodorous institution.

However, what took place on June 10, 1944, with the news media dominated by harrowing stories of the D-Day invasion and the Allied struggle to liberate Western Europe, was anything but business as usual.

That night, there was a bloody battle in the hospital ward of the Don Jail.

For one horrible moment, Governor Rayfield must have thought he had been plunged back into a war zone. "The first thing I noticed when I walked into the ward was blood on the floor, just inside the door," he said. "It looked as if a man bled for some time. Then I saw the body of the guard lying on the floor. I put my hand on his chest, and in my opinion the guard was already dead."

The dead man was forty-seven-year-old Robert H. Canning, a veteran of the First World War who had recently been discharged from the army and had been working at the jail for just two months. Canning was found tied to heating pipes with a leather strap. His head had apparently been battered with an iron pipe found nearby. A post-mortem later revealed the cause of death as asphyxiation from pressure applied to his throat, severe enough to break his larynx.

The men accused of killing Canning were Allan Baldwin, thirty-two, who was in the Don pending appeal of his conviction for bank robbery and receiving stolen goods, and William J. O'Sullivan, twenty-one, convicted of armed robbery. After battering, choking, and tying up the bleeding Canning with bedclothes, the two men spent the next hour frenziedly sawing through the iron bars on one of the windows with a hacksaw blade. Baldwin then climbed through the fourth-floor window, letting himself down on a rope made of knotted sheets stripped from the beds. The makeshift rope broke and he plummeted down the last twenty feet or so, breaking his arm. O'Sullivan obviously thought better of following him, and when the alarm buzzer was eventually pressed, possibly by O'Sullivan himself, jail guards who rushed to the scene found him fully clad, boots and all, lying on his bed.

Baldwin's flight triggered a twenty-two-hour manhunt throughout Toronto and its surroundings, involving more than two hundred members of the city, suburban, and provincial police forces. Ten carloads of officers, led by the chief constable himself, converged on the Humber Bay area, where they eventually found the escapee hiding under the Dundas Street West bridge. Although he was armed with a fully loaded revolver, he offered no resistance.

Baldwin and O'Sullivan were tried for murder in October 1944.

"I pointed my finger at O'Sullivan who was reclining on the third bed inside the ward and told him 'you know something about this,'" Rayfield testified in court. "He just smiled."

There were two orderlies and five other inmates, reportedly mentally ill, in the ward that evening. Not one of them sounded the alarm. "I couldn't understand how this thing could have happened," said Rayfield. "I thought some effort should have been made to save this man's life."

"Did you think it was strange they didn't help?" asked O'Sullivan's lawyer.

"No," said Rayfield. "Not after I was told they were bound up and threatened."

"They were probably all scared to death," commented the judge. "They were not well to start with. They had seen the knife [in O'Sullivan's hand], and had been told to stay out of it. It was serious from the start."

After eleven hours of deliberation, the jury could not reach an agreement.

At the men's second trial, in March 1945, Rayfield told the judge and jury that hacksaw blades like the one the defendants had used to cut through the window bars were quite regularly smuggled into the jail. "We're up against that all the time," he said.

Although both men protested that Canning's death was accidental and that they had only intended to tie him up, they both received a verdict of manslaughter. The judge sentenced Baldwin to twenty-five years and O'Sullivan to ten, to be served concurrently with their existing sentences. This would, in effect, add six years to their original terms. "I think the jury has taken an extremely lenient view of your case. I have no sympathy with you at all," Mr. Justice McFarland told Baldwin curtly. He was slightly more sympathetic toward O'Sullivan — the plan had been conceived by Baldwin, he noted, "although you may have been the willing assistant."

This violent and sensational case made media waves, and legal history, for another reason as well: Baldwin's lawyer was Vera Parsons, the first woman ever to defend a person tried for murder before an assize or circuit court jury in Ontario. The press commented admiringly on her blondish hair and "peculiar" shade of green-brown eyes, and the fact, as the *Globe and Mail* put it, that she didn't fit "into the average conception of a woman lawyer who usually is pictured as of somewhat severe mein [*sic*], bespectacled, and with a penchant for tailored business suits." Also mentioned was that Parsons just happened to be an extremely talented and dedicated professional with more than twenty years' experience at the bar, who excelled as a trial lawyer.

At the time of the jailbreak, the mayor of Toronto, Frederick Conboy, announced that he intended to lodge a protest with provincial and federal authorities. "Many of these [desperate criminals] appeal their cases without any hope of winning the appeal, but with the intention of plotting their escape," he fumed. "When they are sentenced to Kingston Penitentiary they should be sent there and brought back for a new trial if necessary. When held at Don Jail they are a menace to the guards and to the citizens generally."

Prophetic words.

Just one year later, they would return to haunt provincial, city, and jail officials when another group of desperate, Kingston-type criminals would put the security of the Don Jail and the competence of its custodians to the test.

CHAPTER 15

The Polka Dot Gang

I n the spring and summer of 1945, tucked in among news stories about the end of the war in Europe, the return of soldiers, and the ongoing bloody conflict with Japan, reports started surfacing about a series of shockingly violent crimes in the peaceable province of Ontario. Beneath the headline "Crime Wave: Southern Ontario is Hard Hit," the *Globe and Mail* reported that one of the most troubling aspects of a seemingly home-grown spree was the appearance of a new weapon: "Ontario, for the first time, has to contend with the machine gun in crime. Not the noisy, cumbersome Thompson — 'tommy gun' — of the motion pictures and Chicago, Ill., but the handy Sten gun built right here in Toronto." And the "fanciest exponents" of these guns were the members of the newly formed Polka Dot Gang, who sported natty red polka-dotted handkerchiefs to conceal their faces when on a job.

The Polka Dots specialized in holding up, robbing, and brutally beating watchmen before smashing open or carrying away the safes they were guarding. Working at night, they chose their targets carefully — they hit companies such as dairies, packing plants, and flour mills, where there was sure to be a coffer stuffed with cash, or war bonds that could easily be offloaded on the black market.

In a 2015 article in the *Guelph Mercury*, journalist and author Ed Butts described a nocturnal visit paid by the gang to the Wellington meat packing company just outside Guelph in the early morning of June 25, 1945. On investigating a noise coming from the office, the unarmed night watchman, J. Forestell, was confronted by at least three intruders, who knocked him senseless and kept him unconscious with repeated blows to the head. After tying the man up, the bandits broke open the door of the safe with a sledgehammer and helped themselves to several thousand dollars in cash and bonds. These were not the only items they helped themselves to — deviating from their usual modus operandi, they took the time to grab a smoked ham, some chocolate milk, and soft drinks, and enjoyed a midnight feast on the house. By the time Forestell recovered consciousness, struggled free, and called the Guelph police, the robbers were long gone. Forestell was admitted to hospital with head injuries and a broken jaw.

The gang's robberies were always vicious in the extreme. "The man who carried the machine-gun hit me four times on the head with it," said one victim. "I crumpled to the floor." A watchman at a Hamilton plant claimed that during a raid one of the masked men hit him across the side of his face and his nose with the butt of a revolver. "I told him he didn't have to do that. He said: 'Shut up, you — or I'll put a bullet through you.'"

After several very successful heists in small southern Ontarian cities, the gang decided that it was time to hit the big time. In August, an attempt to rob a garage on Toronto's Dufferin Street was averted by a policeman. After firing at the officer, the thugs got away in a car. In September they raided a milling company on Dupont Street with greater success and made off with $1,200. The night watchman spent two weeks in hospital recovering from a severe battering. Their next job was an abortive robbery at a Dufferin Street dairy that was interrupted by what they thought was an alarm but was actually just a telephone ringing. As they fled in panic, their getaway car nearly collided with the truck of an employee coming into work early. They greeted the man with a burst of bad-tempered machine-gun fire; fortunately for him, they missed.

In spite of a few more excellent results in and outside Toronto, the luck of the Polka Dot Gang was soon to run out. On October 27, under the banner "7-CAR DRAGNET GRABS POLKA DOT SUSPECTS," the *Toronto Daily Star* described the exciting fifty-mile-an-hour three-quarter-mile chase through Toronto traffic and the arrest of five suspects, who "gave no trouble at all," according to one of the arresting officers.

The men being held in the Toronto Jail, all aged thirty or under, were Kenneth "Budger" Green, Bruce Kay, George Constantine, George Dobbie, and Hubert Hiscox. Although the membership of the gang seemed to be fairly fluid, these five were regarded as the hard core. And their leader, described by victims and witnesses as a dark-haired, six-foot-tall man with expensive tastes in clothing, was undoubtedly Kenneth Green.

Born in Toronto, Green had a tempestuous start to life. His father was an alcoholic who frequently disappeared, leaving his wife struggling to bring up their four children virtually single-handed. The children were often sent away to relatives or placed in care. Green's hot temper soon landed him in trouble, and his delinquency earned him a couple of terms in reformatories before he graduated to violent crime, and, finally, to the nefarious role of ringleader of the Polka Dots.

With the help of family and friends, George Dobbie and Bruce Kay managed to raise bail of $10,000 each (some reports put the sum at $12,000) and were released from the Don in December 1945. They promptly skipped to the United States. Within a month, they were back in court in Detroit, Michigan, on charges of possessing burglar tools. When sentencing them to four to ten years in prison, the American judge commented dryly, "We have enough customers of this type in our own country without importing any from Canada."

Green, Constantine, and Hiscox, the remaining members of the gang in Ontario, were tried in June 1946 by judge alone in the county criminal court. Hiscox was acquitted on one charge of armed robbery and discharged. Green and Constantine received terms of fourteen years apiece, to be served in the Kingston Penitentiary, for armed robbery, robbery with violence, breaking and entering, and shooting with intent. In making his decision, Judge James Parker remarked that, since the Ontario Court of Appeal frowned upon corporal punishment coupled with long penitentiary terms, he had increased the length of their sentences to compensate for the strapping he would have liked to impose.

As they had filed appeals, the two men were not immediately transferred to Kingston to serve out their time. Until the court of appeal resumed its business after the summer holidays, they would remain locked up in the Don Jail.

Clearly ungrateful at having been spared the strap, the pair lost no time in springing into action — ten days, to be precise. As the *Toronto Daily Star* explained on June 27, 1946, "Trussing two guards hand and foot with bed sheets, a number of 'dangerous criminals' led by Kenneth Green, leader of the Polka Dot gang, were foiled today in their mass attempt to break out of the exercise yard in Don jail [*sic*]." The thirty-one prisoners milling around that day were indeed a terrifying bunch; they included a man convicted of shooting and killing a merchant, a sex offender, and a trio of violent bank robbers.

The well-orchestrated escape attempt started when jail guard James Stanton was attacked by one of the prisoners walking around the small exercise oval: "[Albert] Stoutley turned and tackled me around the knees and toppled me into a window well," said Stanton. He was then tied hand and foot and gagged with "strips of sheet or towelling." His companion, Robert Johnson, was similarly bound and gagged. A third guard, Colin Barker, witnessed the scene from inside the jail and sounded the alarm.

The seven prisoners who were later tried for the offence, among them Green and Constantine, were certainly inventive, forming an "acrobats' pyramid" to scale the wall. There was some dispute among the guards as to which inmate was at the pinnacle of the pyramid. Barker told the court that it was Green, but Johnson insisted that Stoutley, who was serving eleven years for armed robbery, was at the top. Francis Sheehan, the armed guard patrolling outside the wall of the jail who foiled the jailbreak attempt, agreed with Johnson. After Stoutley's head popped up into view at the top of the wall, as one news report put it, "the inmate and Mr. Sheehan's Winchester rifle eyed each other for 'one or two seconds,' and the figure dropped back inside the yard."

The attempted "escape from lawful custody" was over.

The man responsible for the smooth operation of the jail was not at his desk while all this drama was unfolding: Governor Walter Rayfield, VC, was downtown conferring with Sheriff J.D. Conover. Rayfield rushed back on hearing the news, but his staff, under the leadership of Deputy Governor Allen Armstrong, had handled the situation with great competence. By the time Rayfield arrived, all was calm.

One of the topics on the agenda of the meeting between the governor and the sheriff could well have been the "report card" issued by newsman Ralph Allen a month earlier, which had given the eighty-two-year-old Don Jail a failing grade. Almost every spring, Allen wrote, a new grand jury would denounce its plumbing, medical facilities and policies, its "non-existent" correctional programs, and, sometimes, its dreadful cooking. On the city side, mayors had long decried it and at least one alderman had described it as a "hell hole."

But that was just the small stuff; by far the worst evil "in the long dossier against the Don" was overcrowding. The jail was always at least 50 percent over capacity, and some days nearly 100 percent. "Like canned sardines," inmates were locked into their cells (numbering 248 at the time and most of them "just over the width of a telephone booth") between 8:00 p.m. and 6:00 a.m. A few lucky individuals were allowed to work in the prison garden; the rest were locked into the long, narrow corridors beside their cells for the remaining fourteen hours, sharing a single toilet and washbowl. Inmates would kill time playing cards or dominoes, smoking and chatting, or just staring into space. They were allowed to eat their meals in a cramped mess hall and shuffle around the exercise area for an hour. There was no planned recreation, no prison library, and no other possibility of obtaining books. However, men and women inmates were allowed to buy newspapers and sensational magazines. "As a result," noted Allen scathingly, "the Don is one of the few prisons in the civilized world which not only makes no pretense of reforming its inmates, but permits them to read glamorized essays on crime and the more violent aspects of biology."

And what of the staff, numbering seventy at the time? With the jail turning over about a thousand prisoners a month, ranging from "suspected and convicted murderers and the criminally insane to casual drunks and the occasional law-abiding citizen who simply happen[ed] to get arrested by mistake," they were kept pretty busy. Their main tasks were "discouraging escapes, hounding bedbugs, keeping records, running meal and bull-ring [exercise] shifts and maintaining a decent standard of cleanliness."

The jail's top official scored a less-than-flattering mention in Allen's article. "We separate the boys from the men, and that's about all," Governor Rayfield was quoted as saying. The treatment of women and girls did not even get a mention.

In the dying days of the First World War, Rayfield had killed or captured dozens of enemy soldiers and risked his life rescuing a gravely injured comrade-in-arms. In the immediate post-war period, he had overseen the transfer of seriously disabled soldiers to military hospitals. He had served as sergeant-at-arms for the Ontario legislature and for eleven years as deputy, then governor, of the Toronto Jail. Sadly, even this brave, resourceful, and committed man was powerless to bring about any improvements to the lot of inmates in the dreaded Don.

The situation was no better in other penal institutions in Ontario in the 1940s.

Although located in Ontario, the Kingston Penitentiary was a federal institution, housing convicts sentenced to two years or more, while prisoners serving sentences of up to two years less a day were sent to provincial penitentiaries. For offenders awaiting trial, sentence, or appeal, or those serving shorter sentences, the model was still the county or provincial jail, and there were dozens of these dotted around in towns and cities throughout the province. However, like the Don, they were, for the most part, sadly inadequate relics of the nineteenth century.

The Huron County Gaol in Goderich, for example, designed by Thomas Young, William Thomas's future assistant at the Don, was regarded as being on the cutting-edge of prison design when it opened in 1842. Two wings radiated from a central hub and it contained twelve cells, nine for men and three for women. Unlike the Don, proper toilets had been installed in 1859, replacing the cesspit in the yard. However, early inmates were described as the poor, the homeless, and the insane. That jail was closed in 1972, and the following year it was designated a National Historic Site. The Waterloo County Gaol in Kitchener, dating back to 1853, proved to be inadequate from day one, with thirty-nine inmates stuffed into its fourteen single and six double cells. As noted by Ron Brown in *Behind Bars: Inside Ontario's Heritage Gaols*, their crimes included theft of bees, swearing, and disobeying a "master." This jail was shuttered in 1978, and it, too, is now a heritage building.

Perhaps the closest to the Don in size and scope was the Carleton County Gaol in Ottawa, also known as the Nicholas Street Gaol. Designed by architect H.H. Horsey, and predating the Don by two years, it was praised by the *Ottawa Citizen* as "a splendid building capable of holding 100 prisoners and ... complete in all its parts. It is the model gaol of Canada." This model jail contained cells measuring three feet by nine feet with no lights, windows, or ventilation. The cell blocks lacked heat and running water, and inmates of the Don would have recognized the toileting system — night pails. Overcrowding, brutal punishments, and the intermingling of hardened criminals, minor offenders, and the mentally ill were commonplace in what came to be described as "a medieval dungeon." It was shut down in 1972 but has taken on a new life as the Ottawa Jail Hostel. Paying guests don't seem to mind the exceptionally skinny rooms, although all the other amenities have been considerably upgraded.

Things went from bad to worse for the Polka Dot Gang after the stellar but failed acrobatic performance in the exercise yard of the Don

Jail in June 1946. Green and Constantine had extra time added on to their sentences, which they served in the Kingston Pen. The man reputed to be the gang's machine-gunner, Hubert Hiscox, who had initially escaped penalty, was trapped by police in early 1948 while carrying out a solo late-night robbery. Rather than be captured and face a term in the Pen, he detonated a bottle of nitroglycerine and blew himself up. Kay and Dobbie served out their time in the United States. Kay subsequently disappeared, and Dobbie was deported to his native Scotland. Constantine returned to his unlawful ways after his release from Kingston and spent many more years in and out of prison. After a failed escape attempt from the Pen in 1948, Green seemed to have resigned himself to captivity. He was not, however, destined to walk out a free man. A short announcement in July 1954 revealed that he had died of viral meningitis after a brief illness. He was just twenty-nine years old.

Time had also run out for Governor Rayfield. In January 1949, he had to cope with a "disturbance" (long-term inmates showering short-term inmates with pea soup in protest against being forced to eat in the corridors because of a lack of space in the dining room), followed by a hunger strike by around forty prisoners. "We're doing the best we can," a harried Rayfield told the press. Less than six weeks later, he was dead, stricken with a coronary thrombosis at his home on a Saturday evening after a hard day's work. He was sixty-seven years old.

In October 1950, Rayfield's successor, former deputy governor Allen Armstrong, died suddenly and unexpectedly after just eighteen months on the job.

In 1952, a self-described long-serving "die-hard trained in the old school" guard, who said he had resigned from the jail because he was disgusted with the lax discipline, told a Royal Commission exactly what he thought about Rayfield and Armstrong. The former, he insisted, "should never have been governor of Don Jail"; the latter "was getting old and wasn't too well. He was just waiting for his pension." Rayfield's predecessor, Harry Denning, was elsewhere described as "a kindly man of wide sympathy and easy approach." In spite of some criticism, however, these three successive governors had at least tried to move away from George Hedley Basher's harsh disciplinary routines of the past and usher in a softer, more respectful regime.

The attempted jailbreak of seven inmates, including two members of the notorious Polka Dot Gang, had the makings of a huge embarrassment for city and provincial authorities. They must have breathed a sigh of relief at dodging that particular bullet. But the situation at the jail had not improved and there seemed to be little likelihood that it ever would. In 1948, on receiving *another* grand jury report about the awful conditions, County Judge James Parker remarked: "So far as improving conditions in the jail is concerned, it's like making a silk purse out of a sow's ear."

CHAPTER 16

The Great Escape

You could tell from the tone of her letter, sent to Mayor Allan Lamport of Toronto in September 1952, that the lady was interested and engaged.

My dear Lamprey [*sic*],
The "Over Sixty Club" desires to express its sincere sympathy in the dilemma in which you find yourself today.

We realize that the full blame for the jailbreak should not be resting on your shoulders even if you did appoint a controller's brother to a post for which he was quite unfitted.

Here is a smart tip for the raising of funds to pay for a new prison.... When the wretches are rounded up why not have a public hanging of all four on a Sunday afternoon in front of the grand stand at Exhibition Park? People would come from far and wide to participate in such a gala festival and seats would sell for as much as choice vantage points along the coronation route.

Think it over Lamprey. The idea will make you famous.

Sincerely yours,
Margt S. Rogers,
Secy.

The four wretches referred to by the secretary of the Over Sixty Club were Edwin Alonzo Boyd, Leonard Jackson, Willie Jackson, and Steve Suchan, collectively known as the Boyd Gang. The mayor's dilemma was that on September 8, 1952, the foursome had collectively escaped from death row in the Don Jail, three of them (incredibly) for the second time. The unkindest cut for Mayor Lamport was that he was being accused of something completely beyond his control.

The fiery and outspoken mayor had already made his feelings crystal clear, calling the administration of the jail "the operation of a bunch of morons," so it was perhaps a wise idea to delegate his response to this letter and the dozens of others he received after the jailbreak to his more diplomatic executive assistant: "As you assume, the blame for this occurrence does not rest with the City as the operation of the jail comes within the jurisdiction of the Provincial authorities, who appoint the Jail Governor and the guards. The City had nothing whatever to do with the appointment of the Controller's brother to the post of Jail Governor."

Moreover, added the executive assistant, "I am afraid that your suggestion regarding a public hanging of the four escapees, when recaptured, would not meet with the approval of the public, whom [*sic*], I am sure, would consider this an indecent and inhuman method of carrying out any death sentence that might be imposed. In any event, of course, the City has not any jurisdiction over such matters."

The headlines on page 1 of the September 8 edition of the *Toronto Daily Star* blazed out the news in three lines of bold print that filled a third of the page:

REWARD $4,000 FOR EACH
BOYD, SUCHAN, 2 JACKSONS
SAW WAY OUT OF DON JAIL

The next day, "Wanted, Dead or Alive" the *Globe and Mail* trumpeted on its front page. This was followed by a banner in big, bold letters: "$26,000 IN REWARDS," and, on the same page, another article with the headline: "What Fool Put Them in Same Block With Club Car Privileges? Mayor Asks."

A grim-faced Mayor Allan Lamport visits the Don Jail on September 8, 1952, following the second escape of the Boyd Gang — this time from death row, supposedly the most secure area in the jail.

The Toronto City Police report dated September 8 was a bit more muted:

> At 6:58 A.M. this date an Alarm was received re a disturbance at the Don Jail. All Cars available in the City and Provincial Police were despatched [*sic*]. It was found that four prisoners had escaped. Alonzo Boyd, Leonard Jackson, William Jackson, Steve Suchan. These prisoners had been confined in four seperate [*sic*] cells in one block. Cell doors were opened by a key and three iron bars sawed out of a window which gives access to a retaining wall which divides the Graveyard from the Excercise [*sic*] Yard. By walking along this wall they could walk either east or west to the end of the Jail then a drop of 18 ft. to the ground.

The public was enthralled by this latest chapter in the unfolding saga of the Boyd Gang. For the past three years, people had been regaled with episode after lurid episode, both factual and embroidered, of the gang's exploits. And what a plethora of details: Flamboyant bandits! Daring bank robberies! Fast cars! Beautiful women! Bungling police, frustrated politicians, gun-happy bank officials! But also, grimly, a police officer, murdered in the line of duty.

Meanwhile, mortified police in Toronto and beyond launched the biggest manhunt in Canadian history. They were determined to get their men, and, this time, to hold them.

It had all started in rather a small way.

On September 9, 1949, thirty-five-year-old Edwin Alonzo Boyd dabbed rouge onto his face, donned a brown fedora, gulped down half a bottle of Irish whiskey, and, clutching the Luger pistol he had taken from a dead German soldier during the Second World War, set out to rob a bank. He was inspired to do so, he told the *Toronto Star*'s Dale Brazao in a 1996 interview, after reading a newspaper report about a mentally challenged teenager who had made off with $64,000 in a bank robbery.

"After that, I said, 'What am I doing working?'"

What, indeed.

Boyd, born on April 2, 1914, had an early induction into the seedy side of life. His father, Glover, was a constable with the Toronto Police force. His beloved mother, Eleanor, died of scarlet fever in 1930. Edwin ("Ed" to family and friends) had bitter childhood memories of his troubled relationship with his father. As quoted by Brian Vallée in *Edwin Alonzo Boyd: The Story of the Notorious Boyd Gang*, Ed said, "He had a temper, and whenever he got mad he would take me down [to] the basement and pick up a hockey stick or a broom handle, whatever was handy, and give me a few good swats."

Ed cut himself loose from his father's influence, and in 1932, as the Great Depression tightened its hold on the country, he hopped a freight car and spent the next few years in and out of trains, casual jobs, and jails for a series of petty offences, including theft and bumming money from suscep-tible householders. In 1936, a break-in at a service station in Saskatchewan led to more serious charges of break, enter, and theft, and earned him a three-and-a-half-year sentence in the Saskatchewan Penitentiary at Prince Albert. Meanwhile, Glover Boyd worked tirelessly to have his son released on parole. The efforts of Ed's highly respected policeman father finally paid off, and in March 1939 Ed was on his way back to Toronto.

Speaking of his father to Vallée, Boyd said, "He thought my going through the penitentiary system would make a big difference in my life, but all it did was teach me how to handle myself under authority."

That skill was soon to be tested, with so-so results: with the Second World War looming, Boyd enlisted. He had multiple absent without leave (AWOL) charges levelled against him during his military service, and was both promoted and demoted several times. After serving in England, France, and Germany, he returned to Toronto in 1945 with an English wife and three children in tow. He found a well-paid posi-tion with the Toronto Transit Commission (TTC) but quit after just eight months. Was it a case of the job being too mundane after the thrills of wartime, or was he pushing back against his nagging wife?

"One thing I couldn't stand was people telling me what to do," Boyd told Vallée. "I'd had enough of that in the penitentiary and in the army. I enjoyed working at the TTC and I could have had a good career there, but I got tired of listening to [his wife] Dorreen. She wanted to run my life — so I quit."

Boyd drifted from one dead-end job to the next. Then came 1949 and his first foray into robbing banks. In spite of having to scamper away from the scene of the crime in a hail of bullets, Boyd netted $2,256. He was hooked. Over the next two years he carried out at least six more heists. Finally, he'd found something he was really good at. In later life, Boyd complained that he would have been so much more successful in his chosen occupation if he'd not been hobbled by inept accomplices. And, in fact, after a bungled robbery in late 1951, his partner in crime, Howard Gault, snitched on him, and Boyd found himself in the Don Jail on six counts of bank robbery and one of attempted robbery.

It was there that he met fellow prisoners Leonard "Tough Lennie" Jackson and Willie "The Clown" Jackson (no relation). His collaboration with these hoodlums, and later with Valent Lesso, alias Steve Suchan, ushered in a new and much more dangerous phase of his criminal career.

Boyd was the titular head of the Boyd Gang (a name given by veteran crime reporter Gwyn "Jocko" Thomas of the *Toronto Star* to a loosely associated group of hoods who sometimes worked together, and sometimes as individuals). With his "matinee idol" good looks, his bravado, and his swashbuckling antics, such as brandishing a gun and leaping over the counter of a bank during a robbery, Boyd was a natural for the role. However, he was not really a violent man, and probably not the true leader of the gang. As Toronto Police sergeant of detectives Adolphus Payne, who investigated the series of robberies committed by the gang over a period of three years, explained to the judge in October 1952 during Boyd's trial for multiple bank holdups, Boyd was "a very safe man with a gun." He added that Boyd "has less respect for his own life than for the lives of the people he robs or the police; he has been fired on many times, but only once did he ever return the fire, and then over the heads of police."

When it came to violence, "Tough Lennie" Jackson was your man. Like Boyd, Jackson left home and rode the rails at an early age, and, again like Boyd, was in and out of trouble with the law. In 1939, he enlisted and collected a litany of wartime offences, often for being AWOL. Bored and footloose after his discharge, he tried a stint in the merchant marine, then drifted back to Niagara Falls, Ontario, his hometown, then to Toronto, then back to train hopping.

Riding the rails was always fraught with danger: railroad police or "bulls" would arrest, beat up, or even kill non-paying customers, known as hoboes. Hoboes would have to run alongside a train as it was gathering speed after leaving a railroad yard and hop into a freight car. Sometimes they missed their footing and fell to their deaths, or lost a leg. And so it was with Jackson: in 1946, he slipped when trying to jump aboard a freight train. His left foot was severed, and doctors had to amputate just above the ankle. He left hospital six months later, depressed and fitted with a wooden prosthesis.

By 1950, Jackson was again in Toronto, working as a waiter at the Horseshoe Tavern on Queen Street West. He envied the clientele for their fancy cars and probably ill-gotten wads of cash. No epiphany sparked his decision to change careers. He simply came to the same conclusion as Boyd: working at a dead-end job would not get him the rewards he craved. He had to rob a bank or two. Between February and July of 1951, in fact, he carried out at least five armed and violent robberies in association with a gang called the Numbers Mob. By that time, *he* was one of the elite, driving a shiny metallic-blue Oldsmobile and flashing bundles of banknotes.

Then, on July 30, 1951, Jackson came face to face with the man who would prove to be his nemesis: Toronto Police sergeant of detectives Edmund "Eddie" Tong, who had been out looking for him. Following a tip-off, Tong and three other officers raided Jackson's lodgings in Toronto. His room was empty. But when Tong left the building through the back entrance, he came across Jackson climbing the fire escape. Both Jackson and his accomplice, Frank Watson, were taken into custody and charged with five bank robberies.

Eddie Tong was a loving family man, generous and funny, but a very tough cop when he needed to be. He was well known to the criminal community in Toronto, and he was exceptionally successful at getting its members off the streets and into jail. He was also skillful when it came to getting information. According to reporter Jocko Thomas, who knew Tong well, "He had a certain way about him. Stool pigeons and informants liked to give him information." Tong had been on the trail of the Numbers Mob for about six months. He had made several arrests and recovered money and weapons.

On October 25, 1951, twenty-five-year-old William Russell Jackson joined Boyd and Lennie Jackson in number 3 corridor at the Don. Willie was awaiting an appeal of his sentence for robbery with violence: seven years in the Kingston Penitentiary and twenty lashes. He earned the nickname "the Clown" for his propensity for firing off one-liners, but his criminal behaviour was nothing to joke about. Police records described him as "seldom out of jail." His rap sheet included vagrancy, car theft, and robbery with violence. Typically, his robberies netted him between five and seven dollars. His last crime had been a brutal mugging: he stole a few dollars from an elderly man after beating him senseless with a beer bottle.

Shortly after Willie's arrival, Lennie Jackson approached Boyd with a proposition: he was considering a jailbreak. Did Boyd want to join him? Jackson had everything planned out. Hacksaw blades? Check. He had a few hidden in his prosthetic leg. The bars in the window? No problem. They were made of soft iron. It would be like cutting through butter. The steel mesh over the window? That could be bent back to allow a man to wriggle through to work on the bars. And the forty-foot drop to the ground? Again, no problem. They could tie sheets together to make a rope. And use another rope to help them scale the eighteen-foot-high prison wall and drop to the other side. Then: freedom.

Boyd was facing a long prison term. It did not take him very long to consent. Willie Jackson became the third party to the agreement. Boyd would do most of the sawing; Willie would take over when necessary. The other fifteen prisoners in their section would help by distracting the guards.

The stage was now set for The Boyd Gang: Escape from the Don, Take #1.

CHAPTER 17

Cop Killers

I t all went like clockwork. On Sunday, November 4, 1951, while fellow inmates answered evening roll call on their behalf, Boyd and the two Jacksons wriggled through the window, rappelled to the ground below, scaled the outer wall of the prison and dropped down to freedom. Boyd thought that Lennie would be seriously hindered by his prosthetic leg, but, surprisingly, he turned out to be the most nimble of the three.

The last member of the unholy quartet should have made his appearance at this point, but he didn't. Lennie had arranged with fellow bank robber Steve Suchan to pick them up in his car on the Don Roadway (which, in those days, extended north past the jail). But Suchan was nowhere to be seen.

Suchan later told Lennie that he had simply forgotten. Boyd, however, was reportedly furious that Suchan's carelessness had so nearly derailed their plans.

Suchan, originally Valent Lesso, was born in Czechoslovakia and immigrated to Canada with his parents in 1936. He attended school in Cochrane, Ontario, and then moved to Toronto in 1946. He was a talented violinist, but in 1950 he swapped his instrument for cash and a .455 Smith & Wesson revolver. In March of that year, Suchan became an inmate at the Guelph Reformatory for attempting to pass forged cheques. After his release, he worked as an elevator operator at the King Edward Hotel in Toronto, and it was there that he met and became friendly with Lennie. Within a year, the two pals were robbing banks together.

Much later in the evening of November 4, Suchan finally collected the three Don Jail escapees from the apartment where they had taken refuge. Now there were four, all of them armed and dangerous.

The next fifteen weeks were totally miserable for the police. By November 20, the gangsters were back doing what they did best: robbing banks. In short order, they hit a downtown branch of the Bank of Toronto for $4,300 and the Leaside branch of the Royal Bank of Canada for a whopping $46,270, reportedly one of the largest cash grabs in Toronto's history.

Jail personnel were not having a pleasant time of it, either. Two long-serving guards were dismissed for what a subsequent inquiry called "inattention" and the press called "negligence." They were eventually rehired and transferred to a different institution. The governor of the Don, Charles Sanderson, was reprimanded for failing to ensure that his guards were doing their duties properly. Ontario Reform Institutions Minister John Weir Foote called the reprimand a "regrettable incident," but it marked an abrupt tumble from grace for the governor.

Sanderson had stepped into the post following the death of Allen Armstrong some seventeen months previously. *Globe and Mail* reporter David MacDonald described the forty-two-year-old Sanderson as "a short, chunky man … whose quiet voice and cherubic face wouldn't qualify him in Hollywood as a jail warden."

He had immediately started making waves — in a good way.

Inmates were set to work sprucing up the exterior of the forbidding pile (often referred to by visiting grand juries as "a Black Hole of Calcutta" or "a stinking dungeon," notes MacDonald helpfully), and pretty pastel shades replaced the battleship grey of the walls within. Colourful murals adorned the main corridor, rotunda, and dining room. Even the air was sweeter, with the usual pungent scents replaced with fragrant aromas of disinfectant and deodorizer.

"If I thought my only job was to keep men behind bars, I wouldn't be here," Sanderson said simply.

He felt that the correctional system was a scandal, much of it caused by enforced idleness. "We aren't pampering prisoners," he said. "We still have discipline. But by keeping them busy and keeping their minds occupied we're preventing them from just sitting around and talking crime."

Prisoners could now enjoy "recreational diversions" like cribbage, rummy, and bowling tournaments, and there was even an essay-writing contest. Instead of walking round and round the circular sidewalk in the high-walled exercise yard, inmates could play quoits.

An appreciative young worker with the John Howard Society, an advocacy group for correctional and criminal justice that provided support services at the Don, summed up the transformation: "I just can't believe that this is the Don. The change seems impossible. And yet it's true. Everybody is talking about it — and the governor."

But nothing lasts forever, it seems. By January 1952, on the heels of the Boyd Gang's well-publicized escape, Sanderson had been shunted out — promoted to superintendent of the Burwash Industrial Farm near Sudbury. His replacement at the Don was Thomas Woodward Brand, an appointment that probably had everything to do with another January promotion: that of George Hedley Basher, both former governor of the Don Jail and superintendent of the Guelph Reformatory, to deputy minister of reform institutions.

Brand, like Basher and indeed Sanderson, was an ex-soldier. Basher had first come across him during a prison riot in 1947. Impressed with Brand's cool handling of the situation, Basher had brought him in as assistant superintendent at Guelph. Now, with the Don Jail dissolving into chaos, Basher wanted his own strong-armed man in charge.

Initially, this seemed to work well. Although Brand retained many of Sanderson's progressive programs, he introduced various measures to tighten up security: for example, he restricted traffic behind the jail, he had an armed rifleman positioned at the Isolation Hospital overlooking the exercise yard while it was in use, and he organized a search of the yard with a mine detector — which turned up a tin cup, a shoehorn, and a pair of pliers. His recommendations included the installation of more floodlights, a steel cabinet for the proper storage of arms and tear gas, and the fingerprinting and photographing of all jail employees.

By March 1952, just one of the Boyd Gang was again under lock and key. Days before Christmas, Willie Jackson had made the error of getting drunk in a Montreal pub and flashing his .45 revolver and a roll of cash. With two years tacked on to his existing sentence, he was sent straight to the Kingston Penitentiary.

Then Eddie Tong, the same detective who had nailed Lennie Jackson in July 1951, received word from an informant — who, bewilderingly, turned out to be Jackson's half-sister, Mary — that unnamed bandits were using a black Monarch sedan to ferry hot goods to Montreal. Those mystery men were actually Jackson and Suchan. Mary's motive? Possibly that she was in a souring relationship with Suchan, and she craved revenge on him and the "other woman," who owned the car. Tong and his partner, Detective Sergeant Roy Perry, kept the suspect vehicle under surveillance for several days, and on March 6 pulled it over on College Street in Toronto. Tong got out of the police cruiser to question the two men in the Monarch. Suchan was in the driver's seat, with Jackson beside him. Grabbing his gun, Suchan shot at Tong; the bullet tore through the policeman's chest, mortally wounding him. In all, Suchan and Jackson fired six shots. Perry, still in the police car, was hit, too, but he threw up his arm and miraculously stopped a bullet aimed at his head.

Suchan gunned the engine of the Monarch, the gangsters sped away — and all hell broke loose.

Tong was no stranger to the villainy of vicious criminal gangs. In addition to arresting Lennie Jackson and fellow Numbers Mobsters in 1951, Tong had been a member of the squad that took down the notorious Polka Dot Gang in the mid-1940s. Now, for Tong, the perils of tangling with violent criminals were chillingly clear.

"Tong Fights for Life; Failing, Says Hospital," was the solemn headline in the *Globe and Mail* on March 8. The bullet was wedged near his shoulder blade, and the prognosis was not good. Even if he survived, he would probably not be able to walk again.

On March 6, 1952, Toronto Police officers Eddie Tong and Roy Perry pulled over a suspect vehicle on College Street in Toronto. The occupants, the Boyd Gang's Steve Suchan and Lennie Jackson, opened fire, leaving the police cruiser riddled with bullets and Tong with life-threatening injuries.

The story had suddenly taken a sinister turn: it was no longer a case of dashing folk heroes versus bumbling Keystone Cops.

Police reaction was swift and intense. According to the *Toronto Daily Star* on March 7, "squads of detectives working around the clock swept across Toronto today hunting two known gunmen whom they accuse of trying to kill Sergt.-of-Dets. Edmund Tong and Det.-Sergt. Roy Perry at College St. and Lansdowne Ave. yesterday.... Detectives carried high-powered rifles in raids which they thought might produce the suspects. They said they were prepared to shoot it out."

And shoot it out they did.

Police investigations led them to Montreal, where they staked out Suchan's glitzy Côte-des-Neiges apartment. Thirty hours after the incident in Toronto, Suchan walked straight into a police ambush. Taking no chances, the detectives shot him three times. He was admitted to hospital in serious condition and under heavy police guard.

Jackson's takedown was even more violent. On March 11, Toronto detectives, together with local police, trapped Jackson and his wife in a basement apartment in Montreal. More than two hundred shots were exchanged before the fugitive surrendered. He would probably have continued firing furiously to the bitter end if his pregnant wife, Ann, hadn't begged him to think of the baby. Jackson had been shot four times in the arms and abdomen, and he, too, needed emergency medical treatment.

After all that, Boyd's arrest was an anti-climax. Sergeant of detectives Adolphus Payne had a hunch that he might find Boyd's whereabouts by keeping tabs on the gangster's brother Norman. The payoff came on March 15, when Payne surprised Boyd and his wife in bed in a second-floor apartment on Heath Street in Toronto. Police found revolvers and $23,329 in cash in a briefcase beside his bed.

Toronto's relentlessly self-promoting mayor, Allan Lamport, rushed to the scene so he could be seen emerging with the police and the captive.

"I'm pleased to meet you. Should I smile?" Boyd asked the mayor.

"If I were in your place," Lamport shot back, "I wouldn't smile."

Toronto policeman Jack Gillespie, who was on first-name terms with Lennie Jackson, was a member of the team that brought him down in Montreal. Although Gillespie fired the shots that wounded the gangster, he had a certain sympathy for the man and visited him in hospital. According to author Brian Vallée, Jackson told Gillespie that he would get out again.

"Don't tell me I have to go through all of this again," said Gillespie.

"No. Don't worry; you won't have to go through this again."

As for Tong, by March 10 a relieved public, which even included several criminals who phoned police to offer good wishes and their blood when a call went out for donors, believed that Tong was out of the woods: "Sgt. Tong Much Better," reported the *Globe and Mail*. But their hopes were short-lived. On March 24, the paper sombrely informed its readers of the sudden death of Edmund Tong. "It is a pity that just when he had seemed to have got past the danger point in his recovery, he was struck down by an embolism."

Murder of a police officer. This was a capital offence. And Tong's alleged killers, Steve Suchan and Lennie Jackson, now faced the ultimate penalty: death by hanging.

CHAPTER 18

The End of the Line

According to the old saying, "It's not what you know, but who you know that counts." Or, sometimes, "It's who your mother knows." In the spring of 1952, lawyer John Josiah Robinette was burning the midnight oil in his office when one of the cleaners, a woman named Elizabeth Lesso, approached him with a request. Her son, she explained by way of an introduction, was a good boy. However, he was in trouble and he needed a lawyer. Would Mr. Robinette please help him? She then revealed that her son's name was Steve Suchan, and that he had been charged with the slaying of Toronto policeman Edmund Tong.

As George D. Finlayson reports in *John J. Robinette, Peerless Mentor: An Appreciation*, Lesso broke down in tears, saying, "He is charged with another man, and the other man is a very bad man."

Robinette felt sorry for her. He agreed to take on the case.

Remember the eminent lawyer who struggled in vain to save Frank McCullough from the hangman's noose in 1919, after McCullough shot Detective Frank Williams? That was Thomas Cowper Robinette. John Josiah was his son. Now, in a strange parallel thirty-three years later, Robinette the younger was also engaged in defending a cop-killer.

As it turned out, J.J. had a little longer to prepare his brief than he had anticipated. On September 8, one day before the grand jury was due to convene to consider the indictment of Suchan and Lennie Jackson for murder, something unexpected happened.

Following the gang's first escape, Boyd had again found himself locked up in the Don Jail. This time, the authorities were taking no chances. Boyd occupied one of four cells in No. 9 Hospital, a former infirmary on the second level. It was also known as "death row" because of its location just a few steps away from the gallows chamber (previously a latrine), and because prisoners convicted of murder generally ended up spending time there before they were executed. The walls and ceilings of the cells were made of metal, with steel doors and grilles. High up on the east wall of a narrow corridor in front of the cells was a small window. It had been fitted with double bars, a necessary measure because it was just a short drop to the top of a wall that intersected with the outer wall of the jail. For extra security, a microphone connected to the governor's office was installed in a screened air vent in the corridor so guards could listen to whatever might be going on. A heavy oak door separated this area from the landing accessible to the general inmate population. There was a new alarm system in place. At night, an armed guard was stationed in the grounds outside the walls of the jail, and two policemen kept watch at the rear of the building.

On May 14, Willie Jackson was back in the Don, transferred from the Kingston Penitentiary to face charges for two robberies in late 1951. Boyd was amazed and delighted to find his pal occupying one of the vacant cells in No. 9 Hospital. In June and August respectively, the two other members of the gang, Suchan and Lennie Jackson, their injuries healed, were also assigned cells on death row. Prison officials breathed sighs of relief. All four desperadoes were now housed in the most secure and heavily monitored section of the jail.

Lennie arrived without his prosthesis but with a burning desire to get out. It was the amiable Willie who came up with the tools to make this happen. Boyd claimed that Willie was given a small piece of flat steel, a file, and a hacksaw blade by his lawyer — something that the lawyer vehemently denied. Boyd gave two different accounts of how they had acquired the master key to their cells. According to one version, Willie playfully snatched the key that opened all four cell doors from one of the guards and imprinted the shape on his hand. After some trial and error, Boyd managed to use this impression as a template to replicate the key on the piece of flat steel. However, he gave the police a different version: he had made the key by "observing the key which was brought in by the guards." Improbable as both these stories seem to be, the fact was that the men were finally able to let themselves in and out of their cells whenever they wanted.

They now had the means — and, as it turned out, the opportunity — to prepare for a getaway. For two hours each morning, while the guards were busy arranging transportation to court and breakfast for the other inmates, the oak door that separated death row from the rest of the floor was locked. So the gang was free to work without human surveillance. While Boyd and Willie took turns at sawing on the bars of the window in the corridor, Suchan and Lennie took turns at holding a pillow over the screened air vent to muffle the microphone. They started with one of the outer bars and, when that was just about cut through, proceeded to hack away at the matching inner bar. After each session, Boyd would conceal the cuts with a mixture of dirt and soap, the same ploy that had worked so successfully during their first escape. The process was agonizingly slow, and they lived in fear that a zealous and sharp-eyed guard would spot their handiwork and sound the alarm.

On a late August morning, they were ready to go. Once the oak door was shut and locked at 4:45 a.m., Boyd removed the two bars and started to wriggle through the opening. To his horror, he got stuck halfway. The aperture was too narrow.

"So I got hold of Willie and I said, 'You try it, Willie,'" Boyd said in an interview with authors Marjorie Lamb and Barry Pearson. "Just to make sure, I thought, I'll put lots of butter on his hips. So there's Willie, bare naked, and he's got — we're rubbing butter on his hips. We tried to shove him through and he wouldn't go through.'"

Boyd may not have known it at the time, but the window he was trying to squeeze his buttered friend through just happened to be the same one that Frank McCullough had used for his jailbreak thirty-three years earlier. When Major Basher was appointed governor, he had ordered it to be bricked up. However, when the large room was converted into four separate death cells in 1934, jail authorities had unbricked the escape window to allow in more light and air. Because of that dangerously close wall outside, they added another set of bars, making it the only window in the whole building with a double layer of bars.

Back to the drawing board: the gang would have to put back the severed bars and hope they wouldn't fall out and that the cuts wouldn't show. Then they needed to saw through another two bars. It took two more nail-biting weeks for them to finish the job. In the early morning of September 8, they were finally on the move. Not much preparation was needed. Lennie put a couple of pairs of thick socks, some strips of newspaper, and his enamel drinking cup over his stump. Boyd removed the bars and scrambled out the window and onto the wall. The rest of them followed.

According to Boyd, he was merely acting in an advisory role; he had no intention of actually decamping with the others. "Each of them went through quite easily," he told Lamb and Pearson, "although Suchan was fairly snug. I'm sitting (outside) waiting for them to come out, and then I was going to go back in again, and lock myself up and lock their cells too, so that it's a real mystery [to the authorities]."

His fellow escapees were not entirely convinced that this was a sensible plan. "Gee, are you sure you want to do that?... You know what's gonna happen when they find us missing? What're they going to do to you?"

Boyd said that he was just about to squeeze his way back into the building when Suchan noticed a policeman down below, outside the prison wall, whistling and talking to himself. "We laid there — and it's getting daylight," said Boyd. "Boy, the dawn is rising and it's getting so light that we can see each other's faces clearly. We could see people walking … the odd car's passing…. Then I realized I was stuck. I had to go too. And I thought, 'What the hell. That's the way the cookie crumbles.'"

The foursome hesitated for several more heart-stopping minutes — should they go back inside? If they did, they were toast. Then the policeman went over to a door in the wall, tapped to be let in, and was gone. The gangsters dropped as quietly as possible off the eighteen-foot-high outer wall and scuttled into the dense bush of the nearby Don Valley.

By 7:00 a.m., the day guards sounded the alarm. Within minutes jail officials and police were swarming all over the scene, searching the grounds and the roof. Ace crime reporter Jocko Thomas, who was sent by his newspaper to cover the story, remembered an inmate yelling out a window, "Hey, you flatfeet, they're not here, they're gone!" A despondent police inspector beside Thomas said to him: "I think he's right."

For two days the gang moved north through the Don Valley, which was wild and undeveloped in the early 1950s — no paved pathways through the ravines to make for an easy passage, and the Don Valley Parkway, the expressway that now bisects the valley, was still years away from completion.

"Even without his foot Lennie moved pretty good up the Don Valley," Boyd told Vallée. "He never let anything slow him down. But he was suffering terribly from hay fever and asthma and he seemed like a beaten man. He was never the same after he was shot up in Montreal."

On Wednesday morning they stumbled across an abandoned barn on Leslie Street in northern Toronto, where they took refuge. They subsisted on food stolen from neighbouring farms until Friday, when Willie made a sortie and returned with groceries and cigarettes.

But time was running out. The escapees had been spotted in the area, and the sightings reported to the police. These civic acts were no doubt fuelled by the generous reward ($26,000!) being offered for information leading to the gang's arrest. Police efforts, which had dropped to a simmer, came fiercely back to the boil.

The newly minted CBC English television network ran a report on the Boyd Gang's September 16 takedown. Enthralled viewers were treated to a (completely fictitious) police chase, a car being forced off the road, and motorcycle police riding in tandem, searching for the suspects.

In a hard-hitting article beneath the headline "Not So Tough," which ran in the *Globe and Mail* on September 18, Frank Tumpane revealed that the truth was far more prosaic:

> Everybody — police officers included — had given us
> to understand this quartet would act, when cornered,

like Hollywood's notion of last-ditch gunmen. You would have thought they were Billy the Kid, Jesse James and Jack Dalton with Boyd, of course, completing the program as Robin Hood.

But instead of that it turns out they weren't so tough after all when confronted by a couple of determined policemen who had guns in their hands and knew how to use them.... The glamour boys were unkempt, unshorn, unshaved and hungry when the police finally found them. Their days of freedom they spent in an abandoned barn, eating canned beans and stolen apples to keep alive. How's that for the glamorous, plush life of Canada's so-called master criminals?

The Boyd Gang's Leonard "Tough Lennie" Jackson escaped twice from the Don Jail. He faced trial in September 1952 for the murder of Toronto police officer Eddie Tong.

The saga of the Boyd Gang had now reached its final chapter — which was short but not sweet.

The day after they were recaptured, Lennie Jackson and Steve Suchan were arraigned on murder charges. At that point, Suchan, or Suchan's mother, rather, had already retained lawyer John Robinette. Jackson had no counsel. This was before free legal aid was available in Ontario, and he apparently could not afford a lawyer.

The judge assigned to their case, Chief Justice James Chalmers McRuer, also known as "Hanging Jim" and "Vinegar Jim," was a man in a hurry. He waved away all requests for adjournment, and the trial date was set for September 22. The judge was not without scruples, however. As J. Patrick Boyer describes in his book *A Passion for Justice*, McRuer

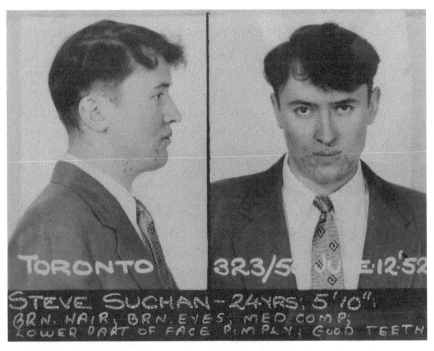

In March 1952, Boyd Gang member Valent Lesso, alias Steve Suchan, shot and grievously wounded Eddie Tong, who later died of his wounds. Along with Lennie Jackson, Suchan was tried for murder in September 1952.

spent one of his lunch hours wandering through the corridors of Osgoode Hall in downtown Toronto until he managed to snag a young barrister, Arthur Maloney, whom he persuaded to take on Jackson's case without a fee. A daunting challenge, as Maloney was given mere days to prepare for this high-profile and high-stakes murder case. As always, a guilty verdict would mean an automatic death sentence.

In court, Justice McRuer lived up to both of his nicknames: as the case proceeded, it became clear that he was unsympathetic towards the accused, if not downright hostile. It didn't help that Jackson incriminated himself under cross-examination. But, ultimately, none of this made any difference. The Crown's case was so strong that the defence lawyers, brilliant as they were, were powerless to save their clients from the gallows. The pair was found guilty of murder, and their appeals were dismissed.

Boyd and Willie Jackson were both tried for a potpourri of bank robbery offences. Boyd ended up with eight life sentences and Jackson got thirty years. Both men were paroled in 1966.

Suchan and Lennie Jackson were hanged back-to-back at the Don Jail in the early morning of December 16, 1952. "As a sidelight on the state of civilization in the City of Toronto, capital of Ontario, Canada, in the year of Our Lord 1952," fumed J.V. McAree in a blistering article three days later, "a future historian is likely to note that on a winter night a crowd of 1,000 people, including children and babes in arms, assembled before the Toronto jail where two murderers were to be hanged. These people could see nothing of the execution; if they could their numbers might have been swollen by another 50,000."

Even before the foursome met their respective fates, the fallout from their exploits had been enormous. Suspensions and dismissals were the order of the day among jail and other officials suspected or accused of negligence or corruption. And the report of a Royal Commission into conditions at the Don had just been published. Perhaps that would go some way to uncovering what one reporter in the age of Boyd referred to as "the inadequacy of the present old pile of stones," whose "usefulness was outlived long ago."

CHAPTER 19

A New Beginning

In the aftermath of the Great Boyd Debacle, Deputy Minister of Reform Institutions Colonel George Hedley Basher made it perfectly clear whom he held responsible for the chaos at the jail. Simply stated, he believed that if his orders regarding the treatment and security of the gang had been followed, they would never even have reached the window in the corridor outside their cells, let alone hack their way through it. In October 1952, he apprised the *Royal Commission Appointed to Enquire into Conditions at the Don Jail, Toronto*, that "it was felt the governor (Mr. Brand) had failed to insure [*sic*] that the special instructions were followed, the deputy governor (Mr. Noble) had failed to give a satisfactory account of his activities during the night, and the six guards had been supposed to be watching the prisoners." Having promoted Thomas Brand, his own man, to a leadership position in the jail, Basher was now more than ready to sacrifice the new governor to save his own reputation.

His Honour Judge Ian M. Macdonell had his own (conflicting) views on the matter. "It is greatly to be regretted that Colonel Basher did not issue [his] instructions in the form of written orders, which could also have been given to his Inspectors to ensure that the orders were carried out," he wrote in rebuke. And the choice of Brand as governor was a poor one. He had had only about six years of experience in correctional institutions, most of them in subordinate positions. He had been governor at the Don for just a month when Boyd landed back there in March. Granted, Brand had made efforts to tighten up security and had introduced other improvements, but, noted Macdonell: "I feel that the responsibility of not keeping the four prisoners who escaped under constant supervision fell upon his shoulders. I have reached the conclusion that Mr. Brand did not have the executive ability nor experience to cope with the difficult situation with which he was faced."

Following the publication of the report in early December, *Globe and Mail* readers learned that the Ontario premier and the reform institutions minister "made a clean sweep of the Don Jail executive ... at the same time saying they were not demoting anyone." Brand was shunted off to the Burwash Industrial Farm, where he would, ironically, be serving as assistant superintendent under Charles Sanderson, the man he had displaced as governor of the Don less than a year previously. Completing the dizzying round of musical chairs, the new governor of the Don would be H.R. Paterson, the current assistant superintendent at Burwash. All the guards suspended during the inquiry were reinstated.

Basher and Macdonell may have clashed on who should be held accountable for the mess at the jail, but on one point they were in perfect agreement. "The time has come to think of putting up an addition to the Don jail, on vacant land on the jail property," said Basher. "The addition should be completely modern, and should have separate cells to give the greatest security for handing the 'more dangerous' type of prisoners."

"Unfortunately," wrote Macdonell, "the jail has become in effect a miniature penitentiary ... [It] has to serve as a clearing house for all prisoners of the County ... [and] there is always a considerable population of dangerous criminals, of what is termed the 'Kingston type.'" And among the twelve recommendations of his inquiry was this one: "A new security wing, capable of accommodating 250 of the more dangerous type of prisoners, should be built without delay, on land adjacent to the jail owned by the City. It could be connected with the existing building by tunnel or otherwise. The new building should be provided with safety cell blocks and other modern security measures."

Over the next few years, nothing at all was built, and the clamour grew louder.

In early 1954, a grand jury stressed the urgent need for a larger jail and proper housing and treatment for mentally ill inmates. Mayor Lamport dismissed their views as "just a grand jury report. We've had that before." But Chief Justice McRuer, the judge who had sent Boyd Gang members Suchan and Jackson to the gallows two years previously, was incensed that the complaints were taken so lightly. "If those who … [were so dismissive] saw the calibre of men who act on grand juries, I'm sure they wouldn't continually disregard the recommendations of such bodies," he told the press.

A year later, Sheriff J.D. Conover warned that the danger point had been reached, with sometimes as many as 525 male inmates being crammed into a space that could comfortably accommodate only 318. "The time will arrive, if it is not already here, when, for security reasons, the jail must refuse to accept any more prisoners." According to the *Globe and Mail*, Sheriff Conover said that the "antiquated Don" could simply no longer cope with an increase in the city's population. He had a good point: the year 1954 had seen the formation of the Municipality of Metropolitan Toronto or "Metro," which was a fusion of the city and twelve surrounding towns, villages, and townships. In 1955, its estimated population hovered around the 1,365,000 mark.

The Elizabeth Fry Society, dedicated to helping and advocating for women and girls within the criminal justice system, strongly condemned the fact that all the women inmates had now been transferred to the Mercer Reformatory for Women on King Street West, Toronto. That seventy-five-year-old provincial institution could barely cope with the female offenders already serving their sentences there, let alone with this new influx from Toronto's impossibly overstuffed jail. The Mercer was the first prison built solely for women in Canada. It had as its aim the rehabilitation of inmates aged sixteen and older found guilty of offences regarded as socially undesirable; for example, prostitution or having a child out of wedlock. It must be noted, however, that overcrowding, while serious, was possibly the least of the Mercer's multiple shortcomings; over time, it developed a chilling reputation for the abuses inflicted on its inmates, such as beatings and experimental drug and medical treatment.

Finally, in March 1955, there came some good news: authorities from the recently formed Metro Toronto and the Ontario Department of Reform Institutions, which shared the jurisdiction of the Don Jail with York County at the time, were talking. Beneath the headline "$1,500,000 Jail Plan Includes Cells for 300," Alden Baker itemized for *Globe and Mail* readers the few pros and many cons of the Don's existing setup. The pros: short-term inmates kept the jail clean, and meals were "substantial, with roast beef yesterday." Then, an overwhelming litany of criticisms. In a nutshell, not much had changed since the building first opened some ninety years previously. The place was regularly full to bursting and beyond, with up to 579 inmates "of all categories" being shoehorned into tiny cells — these inmates included "mental patients" who should not have been there at all; the toilet facilities in the cells ("a bowl") were atrocious; other essentials such as the kitchen ("in a damp basement"), the hospital ("barren"), and the admissions area for new inmates ("a dingy dungeon-like corridor") were appalling; and, as noted by Sheriff Conover, boys were still being intermingled with men and first offenders with hardened criminals. One difference was that there were no longer any women inmates, as they had all been shunted off to the basement of the Mercer Reformatory. And there was now a twenty-by-eight-foot corridor furnished with two wooden benches and a payphone to serve as the reception centre for inmates' relatives and friends.

Particularly disturbing was the lack of proper facilities for the sick. "We badly need a fifty-bed hospital," said the jail physician, Harry Hills. "Many men in the cells are entitled to a hospital bed." Chronically ill inmates and those found to be sick on arrival were sent to a specific corridor in the jail.

The dangers lurking in this situation were underscored by a 1955 report from the National Sanitarium Association. A recently introduced program to X-ray all prisoners on admission had revealed thirty-four cases of tuberculosis over the previous six months. This translated into one individual with active TB for every 187 inmates.

The arrival at the jail of Lloyd Nashkawa brought simmering anxieties to the boil. A twenty-two-year-old transient fruit picker accused of stabbing a fellow worker to death in Jordan, Ontario, Nashkawa was in an advanced stage of the disease. "He's quite ill and should be in a sanitarium," complained one of the jail staff. "I think it's a disgrace." Basher, as deputy minister of reform institutions, refused a request from Toronto mayor Nathan Phillips to have Nashkawa moved to a hospital for proper care and treatment. According to Basher, the head of the TB division of the health department had assured him that the man was being properly isolated and adequately treated in one of the death cells at the Don. The mayor shared the staff's concerns: his reports had indicated that the accused was a danger to the 120 personnel and 400 inmates in the jail.

Site plans were ordered by the Metropolitan Executive Committee for the proposed addition to the jail, with costs to be shared by the province. In August 1955, Metro Toronto Council approved the construction of a new wing along the eastern wall of the existing building, to consist of cells, a modern kitchen and a hospital, and administrative offices. Barnett and Rieder of Kitchener, Ontario, were named as architects.

By October, costs had risen by an estimated $326,000, but there was no turning back. When the new wing was officially opened in November 1958, the outlay had jumped from the original $1,500,000 to $2,000,000. In purchasing power, this would be roughly equivalent to $17,830,000 today. At that stage, according to a *Globe and Mail* report, the five-storey addition provided accommodation for 236 men and 60 women (the *Toronto Daily Star* put the latter number at 65) awaiting trial or transfer to other institutions. This would increase the joint capacity of the two Don jails to around 620.

At the opening, Ontario Minister of Reform Institutions Thomas Ray Connell announced that hard work and military-type discipline were the very best therapy for prisoners. He also deplored the amount of tax money required for the administration of justice. Back in the 1860s, it cost seven cents a day for each inmate. Almost a hundred years later, this amount had risen to *forty-five cents*. The good news,

By March 1956, the construction of the new Metro Toronto Don Jail, just east of the old one, was well underway. The jail was officially opened in November 1958.

though, was that the Christmas dinner menu that guests were shown at the spanking new building included chicken soup, roast pork, vegetables, and an English-style pudding, in contrast to the stale bread, oatmeal, and weak tea served to prisoners when the Old Don was first opened.

Colonel Basher did not have much opportunity to weigh in on the pros and cons of the long-awaited extension. Within a year of its grand opening, he was himself in the firing line, although he indignantly denied it. "Eyewash," he said of rumours that he was resigning as deputy minister of reform institutions because the department had been severely criticized for its lack of progressive methods. He was actually retiring. "I will have had forty years' service with the department by the end of the month," he told reporters. "You can't go on working until you drop." His departure was followed by a major departmental reshuffle — in line, according to George Calvin Wardrope, who had just succeeded Connell as reform institutions minister, with a policy of working toward a more humane and less punitive penal system in Ontario.

A few days later, the *Globe and Mail* published a glowing "Tribute from Basher's Army." The writer, G.M. MacLachlan, described himself as a former comrade-in-arms and wished Basher health and happiness in his "well-earned retirement from many years of arduous detail for the people of Ontario in reform work." He added: "Colonel Basher is probably the only CO [commanding officer] in the army of the late war about whom his men composed a song. No one ever dared sing it in his presence during the war." But now, when veterans got together, they invariably belted out a rousing rendition of "We had to join up. We had to join old Basher's army."

In October 1960, newspapers were publishing a different kind of tribute: sombre obituaries of Colonel Basher, who died at his home in Whitby, Ontario, at the age of sixty-nine. In praising Basher as always fair and just, his ex-executive assistant and successor in office, J.A. Graham, delivered this homage: "The Province of Ontario, and especially this department, has lost a devoted servant and experienced adviser. Speaking more personally, I feel acutely the loss of a very dear friend."

George Hedley Basher had come through the fire of two world wars: he had been formed in and by the military. He was a committed proponent of both capital and corporal punishment. As governor of the Don Jail, his command had been based on rigid discipline and strict adherence to the rules. Soon after moving into the Ontario government as deputy minister of reform institutions, he had attempted to regain direct control over the facility by putting an end to the more relaxed governorship of Charles Sanderson and replacing him with his own protege, Thomas Brand. These machinations had backfired. And by the late 1950s, the penological pendulum had swung, as pendulums always do. The old, harsh, military-style regime had moved into a more benevolent phase, where there was no place for a hardliner like Basher.

CHAPTER 20

Crowded Corner

July 1958. The City of Toronto was abuzz with excitement and anticipation. A royal visitor — Princess Margaret, sister to Elizabeth II, Queen of the United Kingdom and sovereign of Canada — was due to arrive at the end of the month, and the city was planning to roll out the red carpet in her honour. Even though the princess would be in public view for the grand total of one hour and thirty-five minutes, Mayor Nathan Phillips was at pains to stress that there had been "no harsh words" over just how insultingly brief the Toronto leg of her tour was going to be. He assured the press that during that time there would be ample opportunity for every one of the approximately 1,400,000 residents who now made up the population of Metropolitan Toronto to catch a glimpse of her.

The plan was for Princess Margaret and her entourage to spend the night of July 30 on board a special train, probably somewhere in the vicinity of the Rosedale and Don stations. At noon the following day the train was to pull up alongside the "ancient" footbridge, painted a gleaming white for the occasion, below the zoo in Riverdale Park. The party would cross the bridge over the Don River on foot — waving as they went to members of the public and a mass of schoolchildren in the park — be spirited away in a waiting motorcade to meet city and provincial dignitaries, have lunch, drive through the Canadian National Exhibition grounds, wave to more crowds, then leave by train soon after 3:00 p.m. to attend a special theatrical performance at Stratford, Ontario.

The princess's visit would be short, that was clear, but whether it would be sweet was another matter entirely. The *Toronto Daily Star* put things in a nutshell in an editorial on July 30, 1958: "What Princess Margaret will make of Toronto we dare not conjecture. A railway siding near an airport and another on the banks of the Don are not exactly enchanting."

But the *real* problem was the Don River itself. Beneath the witheringly satirical headline "Our Perfumed Don," a second editorial lambasted the mayor and other Toronto officials, who "have good cause to be ashamed of the filthy condition of that section of the Don river along which Princess Margaret will be driven to Riverdale park. With belated zeal they have rushed a crew of laborers [*sic*] armed with rakes and pikes and disinfectants to tidy the ground and sweeten the atmosphere that Her Highness may not learn how Toronto has befouled one of its beauty spots."

What a black eye for the bustling metropolis of Toronto, which now stretched from Etobicoke in the west to Scarborough in the east and had swallowed up North York to the north. It even boasted its own subway (granted, just a seven-odd kilometre stretch along Yonge Street between Union Station and Eglinton Avenue) and was planning a new expressway to run through the Don River Valley: the now infamous Don Valley Parkway.

The article went much further, however, comparing the situation to "stories told of courtiers waving handkerchiefs dipped in perfume before the nostrils of the king of France as he drove through the tenements of Paris" to protect his delicate sensibilities from the stench emanating from open drains. This was not the Middle Ages, though: "here in Toronto we have turned a river into an open sewer that was complacently accepted until the prospect of a royal visit called attention to its offensiveness."

As a matter of urgency, demanded the *Star*, the river should be safeguarded from pollution caused by indiscriminate dumping, with no wrangling over which department should be responsible for keeping things clean. (The newspaper's call to arms predictably fell on deaf ears, and the banks and waters of the river soon relapsed into their customary "fetid morass.")

However, with the clock ticking furiously on that afternoon in July 1958, the princess crossed the river and waved and was then speedily shepherded northward from Riverdale Park. Her hosts would hardly have wanted to draw her attention to the smallish rectangular site just to the southeast, at the corner of Broadview Avenue and Gerrard Street East, where a building was in the final stages of completion: the new Toronto jail.

Architectural flourishes that graced the Old Don (a façade richly embellished with carved golden stonework, a distinctive keystone face scowling down from above the iron-studded oak front doors, a towering rotunda decorated with fantastical cast-iron griffins and serpents, to name but a few) were not a feature of what was once described as the nondescript structure now directly abutting its eastern flank. Made of red brick with a flat roof, the five-storey Modernist jail was in the shape of a square *U*, with a high wall blocking off the open end facing Broadview Avenue. The main entrance was on Gerrard Street. The cell blocks were located along the north and south arms of the *U*. Arranged back-to-back, each consisted of a row of eighteen cells with their doors leading out to a common walkabout area.

One of the most outstanding characteristics of the old building — the natural light that poured into the airy rotunda and cell corridors — was clearly not a priority in the new one, which had narrow slits for windows. As one former guard puts it: "The inmates couldn't really see out at all."

No doubt the decision-makers felt that there was no need to worry about the niceties of architectural design when the east wing was stuffed to the gunwales with shiny modern features.

In a November 1958 news story entitled "Addition to Don Jail Filled with Gadgets Open for 'Business,'" reporter Gwyn Jocko Thomas introduced some of the highlights of this "gleaming new building, a veritable 'prison paradise.'" Because of the acute lack of "prison-space" in Toronto, both jails would be more or less filled to capacity. However, if prisoners had a choice, being incarcerated in the new building would be a much better option. Male and female inmates (yes, unlike its over-stuffed neighbour, there were women in this one) would enjoy "luxuries unheard of in Ontario prisons," such as air-conditioning, beds with mattresses — and bed linen! — with plenty of space to move around. Each cell was also fitted with its very own cast aluminum toilet.

The stainless steel kitchen with all its state-of-the-art equipment would do any hotel proud. Dishwashing would be handled by a giant machine, thus giving more "leisure time" to the inmates who were previously obliged to do this job. And, added Governor David Dougall proudly, the "chronic drunks" who used to be tasked with peeling potatoes would be out of a job. A machine would take care of the potatoes, thus saving close to two bags a day. No rotting food smells in this kitchen — there were walk-in coolers to store waste until garbage day rolled round.

There was now a proper hospital and an X-ray laboratory. At the time of opening, a full-time technician examined every inmate admitted — around one thousand per month — often coming across cases of tuberculosis. There were also dedicated rooms and improved facilities for meetings with lawyers and visits from family and friends.

The Big Keys that had opened the doors in the Old Don had no place here. Locks on the main door and cell blocks were to be electrically controlled. Hopefully, the new place would succeed in achieving one of the primary functions it had been designed for — that is, to keep inmates in. But the governor didn't sound overly confident on that score. "You have to depend on your staff and if they let you down, someone might get away," he explained.

If there were escapes, however, they would absolutely not be launched from the exercise yards, which had happened from time to time in the old building (think Polka Dot Gang). Prisoners would take their exercise on the flat roofs surrounded by eighteen-foot-high wire fences, with another two feet of barbed wire coiled on top for good measure. An armed guard would be posted behind bulletproof glass in the lookout tower atop the central section of the *U* with a clear view of both the men and women's exercise areas. Dangerous criminals would be allowed out in the paved ground-level courtyard between the two arms of the *U*, which had a thirty-five-foot-high cement wall, again easily monitored by the guard in the tower.

With this new building squeezed between the old jail and Broadview Avenue, the quadrant at the northwest corner of Broadview and Gerrard Street had become exceedingly cluttered by the early 1960s. It featured a veritable hodgepodge of buildings, their variety underscoring the fact that the passage of time had changed the Don Jail from a lonely outpost on the wrong side of the river to an institution anchored in the vibrant community of Riverdale, now very much a part of Metro Toronto.

The south side, facing Gerrard, was bookended by the St. Matthew's Lawn Bowling Club to the west and the Riverdale Library to the east.

Lawn bowling, also known as bowls, features often white-clad men and women genteelly rolling biased balls along a flat lawn toward a small white ball called a jack or kitty. The sport was huge in Canada around the turn of the twentieth century. The St. Matthew's Club was founded in 1899 and moved from its original site to Riverdale Park in 1905. The clubhouse, designed by Robert McCallum, city architect of Toronto, was built the following year. Its more outstanding architectural details were a gable roof, horizontal wood siding, and a distinctive wraparound veranda. It was located at the western edge of the site, with twin bowling greens just to its east.

The Riverdale branch of the Toronto Public Library (TPL) on the northwest corner of Broadview and Gerrard dates back to 1910. The Georgian Revival style building was also designed by McCallum. It has the distinction of being one of Toronto's Carnegie libraries, founded through a grant made to the TPL in 1903 by American industrialist and philanthropist Andrew Carnegie. The library has an elegant curved front and is made of red brick with white Ohio sandstone trim. It sits on a piece of land that was once part of the Don Jail governor's garden.

The area between the bowling club and the library on Gerrard Street was filled in, from west to east, by the Gatekeeper's House and

The northwest corner of Gerrard Street East and Broadview Avenue, show-
ing the existing buildings prior to redevelopment of the site around 2007:
(1) Hannah Building; (2) Riverdale Hospital; (3) 430 Broadview Avenue; (4)
Hastings Building; (5) Laundry Building/Annex; (6) Old Don Jail; (7) New Don
Jail; (8) St. Matthew's Lawn Bowling Clubhouse; (9) Gatekeeper's House; (10)
Governor's House; and (11) Riverdale Library.

the Governor's House, dating back to 1865 and 1888 respectively. The former initially served as the gatekeeper's post, but after a few years it was gussied up to accommodate the deputy governor of the jail. In the 1960s, the latter building was still being used as the governor's residence. Behind them, and separated from them by the curving Don Jail Roadway, sat the looming bulk of the Old Don Jail.

In the early 1960s, another building had risen up just north of the historic jail. This was the new and vastly improved Riverdale Hospital.

Since the very beginning, there had been a hospital or similar establishment on this site. The first such building was the House of Refuge, completed, but not yet furnished, by the spring of 1860. In addition to beds, tables, and chairs, other must-haves included a keeper and matron to head up the staff. The chairman of the Board of Gaol Inspectors, Alderman Vance, the man who had been so intent on making jail architect William Thomas's life miserable at the time, weighed in with his own unique slant on the job requirements for these individuals:

> While having to deal with and govern the lewd, the dissolute and profligate, the indigent, the idle and refractory, the strong, the stubborn and vicious, the maimed, the blind, the Heaven-stricken, the aged, the orphaned and the wretched, the impostor, the innocent and the idiotic; and when considering the while that the grand object of the various treatment is the reformation and protection of each separate individual, it cannot be objected that the Board exaggerates the ability required in one to whom such trust may be assigned.

However, by 1872, the needs of those afflicted and desperate individuals were no longer a priority. From inconspicuous beginnings in the late 1860s, a smallpox epidemic was sweeping across the globe, leaving millions of deaths in its wake. Toronto was not immune to this scourge, and the House of Refuge was converted into a temporary smallpox hospital to cope with local cases. By 1891, the risk of smallpox seemed to have receded, but with a huge influx of immigrants bringing the population of the city to 181,000, other diseases, such as scarlet fever and diphtheria, became prevalent. The smallpox hospital, now appropriately renamed the Isolation Hospital, took care of patients suffering from these contagious diseases.

In September 1894, under the headline "Civic Incendiaries," the *Globe* noted that the city council had ordered the woodwork of the smallpox hospital to be torched in preparation to tearing down the walls. And so, in an eerie replay of the fire deliberately set in the Toronto Jail while it was under construction some thirty-four years previously, flames lit the night sky, and the former House of Refuge was reduced to ruins. "The citizens will pay for the bonfire for several years to come, as the forty-year debentures issued for the cost of the [original] hospital have still some ten years to run," ended the report dryly.

In 1893, as noted in *The Riverdale Hospital: 140 Years of Breaking New Ground*, the grand and brand new Centre Building of the Isolation Hospital had opened. As demand for beds grew, three other structures were added. The first of these was the South Building in 1904, which was renamed the Hannah Building after being renovated in the early 1940s. In 1911, the North Building was built specifically for patients with scarlet fever; and in 1927, another facility, the Hastings Building, was constructed for the treatment of infectious diseases. The institution was finally taken over by the municipality of Metropolitan Toronto in 1957 and renamed the Riverdale Hospital to reflect its fresh focus on convalescence, rehabilitation, and long-term care.

In 1959 it was announced with great fanfare that a $4,685,000 Riverdale Hospital was being planned for elderly patients. The original thought had been to convert the existing facilities, but it was subsequently decided that a completely new structure would be much more economical. The Modernist semi-circular hospital designed by architects Howard Chapman and Len Hurst ended up costing around

$6,000,000. Called the "Taj Mahal of bed-care centres" when it first opened in 1963, its playfully curved lines were meant both to squeeze as much hospital as possible onto the limited space available on the site and to give patients wonderful views over the parkland to the north. Its admirers lauded its additional architectural and decorative features, such as the eighty-foot-long curved mosaic tile mural, the Japanese terrace garden, the steel mushroom-shaped canopies, and the coloured glass exterior walls.

Two of the older buildings — the Centre and the North — had been demolished to make room for the "half-round" hospital, which left four Riverdale-related properties on the site: the half-round; the Hannah and Hastings buildings to its west; and a large parking lot, one of several on the site.

Finally, clinging limpet-like to the eastern flank of the old jail on the Broadview side was the last piece of the jigsaw: the new Toronto Jail, designed as a more humane and spacious alternative to its toxic neighbour.

Building this additional facility was but the latest in a series of attempts over the years to improve conditions and reduce overcrowding in the Don Jail. One early example had been the notorious Toronto Central Prison for men convicted of minor offences, which opened in 1873 just southwest of King Street and Strachan Avenue. In their 1891 report on prisons and reformatories in Ontario, the commissioners noted that "it is by no means unusual to hear that prisoners when about to be sentenced, implore the judge or magistrate to send them to the penitentiary rather than to the Central Prison. They even ask sometimes to be sent for three years to the penitentiary rather than for two years to the Central Prison." Basing their opinions on the "evidence of a number of gaolers, police officers, and others," the commissioners put this dislike down to the strict system imposed at the prison.

The facts were far more sinister. The place had developed a reputation for brutality and deprivation. Under the leadership of the first warden, both an alcoholic and a rigid disciplinarian, rumours abounded of prisoners being beaten to death, and even being buried in secrecy. There was no running water for the first five years, and no electricity for a further five. The food was foul, allegedly due to a series of sweet deals between suppliers and corrupt prison officials. Although successive wardens tried to bring in improvements over the years, the place was irreversibly tainted. By 1915, all inmates had been transferred to the newly opened Guelph Reformatory, and the failed prison was shut down.

But that was then. This was now: the second half of the twentieth century. Correctional authorities were confident that this latest up-to-the-minute effort at jail building was not doomed to end in failure, as had all its predecessors.

For the moment, however, there were two Don jails housing men and women on the crowded corner of Gerrard and Broadview, the old and the new, working in tandem. In spite of all the grand juries and the denunciations from the public and the press, the Old Don Jail was still very much in business.

CHAPTER 21

At Death's Door

The man with the dubious distinction of being the last, lone murderer to await execution on death row at the Don Jail was Quebecker René Vaillancourt.

Not content with sowing mayhem in his native Montreal, Vaillancourt, out on bail at the time, made his way to Toronto on January 31, 1973, to rob a bank. The *Toronto Star* later reported that the twenty-four-year-old had already racked up thirty-six charges for relatively minor crimes such as breaking and entering, car theft, public mischief, possession of stolen goods, and skipping bail. He had a significant piece of stolen property in his possession when he cruised into town in his black Oldsmobile: a .38-calibre Smith & Wesson Special that he had taken from the house of a policeman.

He later told police that after spending the night at the Gladstone Hotel, he got up early and drove around, finally settling on a promising target: a Canadian Imperial Bank of Commerce branch at Danforth and Coxwell avenues in east Toronto. Parking his own car, he "borrowed" a 1965 Pontiac Parisienne to use as a getaway vehicle. His normal haul for breaking and entering in Montreal was only around $200, but he was hopeful — Toronto banks had *way* more money. He was correct in this assumption, as the robbery netted him the tidy sum of $1,800. He fled in the Pontiac, which he dumped on nearby Drayton Avenue. Then, he headed toward his own car on foot.

Constable Leslie Maitland, accompanied by trainee Constable Brian McCullum, was in the neighbourhood responding to a call about a bank robbery, probably the one Vaillancourt had just committed. Spotting Vaillancourt in the street, Maitland pulled over his police cruiser and stepped out to speak to him.

As reported in the *Star*, this was how Vaillancourt described what ensued: "When I seen that he was coming for me I took out my gun. He was about seven feet from me and I told him to give me his gun. I waved my gun at him. He didn't do it and he told me to give my gun to him. He kept coming towards me. He wanted to catch me. I just shot and he fell down on the side walk."

The first bullet struck Maitland in the chest, and he was probably dead before he hit the ground.

"I chased the other policeman trying to shoot him. He didn't have a gun out. I got in the car and shot at him from inside the car."

McCullum did not take out a weapon because he didn't have one. As a trainee, he was unarmed. It was his lucky day. Vaillancourt fired at least four bullets in his direction but all of them missed.

Maitland, a six-year veteran of the Metro Toronto Police, was a married man with two young boys. His wife, Pauline, was pregnant with their third son. Maitland's funeral was a solemn affair, attended by police officers from across Canada and the United States. His coffin was ceremonially carried between two rows of saluting policemen.

Vaillancourt knew that he was in real trouble. "I killed the policeman," he admitted to investigating officers. "I'll plead guilty and draw my sentence. They will hang me for this but better that than being in jail all my life." By the time his trial rolled round in September 1973, he had changed his mind. He pleaded not guilty, but the result was the same: he was sentenced to hang, and ended up on death row to await his execution.

On October 23, 1975, the *Toronto Star* published a feature piece beneath the headline "Rene Vaillancourt: 692 days on Death Row." The article described in great detail his life as a convicted murderer awaiting execution. Other than prison officials, a Roman Catholic priest, and the jail pastor, Vaillancourt saw no one. After two-and-a-half years in solitary confinement, always under the watchful eye of a guard, he was pasty faced and had put on between thirty and forty pounds. He read French-language magazines and sometimes played Scrabble, chess, and cribbage with his guard. He occasionally read the Bible and wrote letters. However, he had stopped taking his daily ration of exercise — thirty minutes walking up and down an adjacent corridor. Reportedly, he never asked questions about a certain metal door, painted red in vintage photos, that he passed en route. Behind that door lay the execution chamber.

In the same report, the *Star* noted that Vaillancourt had just learned that he would not be hanged as scheduled on October 31. He had been granted a nine-month stay of execution by the federal solicitor general, Warren Allmand.

Although the question of whether to retain or abolish the death penalty was still being hotly debated in 1975, the fact was that no executions had taken place in Canada since December 1962, when Ronald Turpin, twenty-nine, and Arthur Lucas, fifty-four, were hanged back-to-back at the Don Jail.

Ronald Turpin was a small-time Toronto hood who had spent his formative years in and out of foster homes, and later in reformatories for crimes such as shoplifting, burglary, and escaping from custody. Repeated brushes with the law had left him with a pathological fear of policemen, who, he was convinced, were out to get him. So on a frigid February night in 1962 when Toronto police officer Frederick John Nash pulled him over for driving with bald tires and a broken front headlight, his instincts impelled him to fight rather than flight. He was hardly guiltless at the time: he was making a hasty getaway after stealing $632.84 from the Red Rooster Restaurant in Scarborough. Constable Nash found a loaded Beretta semi-automatic pistol that Turpin had hidden under the car seat. After a brief scuffle, shots were fired. Turpin was wounded in the arms and face, but Nash, a thirty-one-year-old married man with four children, lay dying on the roadway.

Arthur Lucas was a different and far more menacing kind of hood. A Black American based in Detroit, his previous offences were serious in nature, including forgery, drug trafficking, armed robbery, and pimping. He had links with organized gangs in the States and had allegedly driven to Toronto in November 1961 to take down Therland Crater, the prime witness in an upcoming drug trial in Detroit. Both Crater and his girlfriend, Carolyn Ann Newman, were found with their throats slashed in what looked like a highly professional gangland-style execution. Crater had also been shot four times. The evidence at Lucas's trial for the murder of Crater was for the most part circumstantial and relied heavily on the testimony of an unreliable witness: Morris "Red" Thomas, a drug addict and Lucas's so-called friend. It was also difficult to square the extreme efficiency of the execution with a slow-moving man who was described in psychiatric reports as having the mental capacity of a "moron."

If you were found guilty of killing someone, you would be sentenced to death. That, quite simply, had been the law since the British legal system was imposed on Britain's territorial possessions in North America by Royal Proclamation in 1763. In 1961, however, legislation was passed in Canada to reclassify murder into two categories, capital and non-capital. This meant that offenders would face the death penalty if they committed a planned or deliberate murder, murdered someone in the course of committing another violent crime, or killed an on-duty police officer or correctional officer. All other types of murder were classified as non-capital and would carry a sentence of life imprisonment.

Lucas stood accused of premeditated murder and Turpin had killed a policeman. They were both tried for capital murder and sentenced to death on May 10 and June 13, 1962, respectively. A barrage of protests was launched on their behalf, and as their legal appeals wound their way through the courts, right up to the Supreme Court of Canada, they spent their days on death row in the Don Jail talking, playing chess, and reading the Bible with their spiritual adviser and true friend, Salvation Army Brigadier Cyril Everitt, chaplain of the jail.

All these efforts failed: their sentences were upheld.

Lucas and Turpin ate their last meal at 6:00 p.m. on the evening before they died, December 10, 1962 — steak, potatoes, vegetables, and pie, all so soft they could be eaten with a spoon. Knives and forks were strictly forbidden. Shortly afterward, Walter Williston, Lucas's appeal lawyer, arrived to confirm the sombre news. The federal cabinet, which had the final say on who would live and who would die, had refused to commute their sentences. They would both be hanged just after midnight.

In a 1965 article in *Maclean's* magazine entitled "The Final Hours of the Last Two Men Executed in Canada," Alexander Ross reported that Williston told the men, "If it's any consolation to you, you may be the last men to hang in Canada."

"Some consolation," snorted Turpin.

A small but angry crowd had gathered at the corner of Don Jail Roadway and Gerrard Street East on that bone-chilling December night, carrying posters declaring that "CAPITAL PUNISHMENT IS NO DETERRENT" and "HANGING IS ALSO MURDER."

Their protests were in vain.

At midnight, Canada's last executioner, a man who called himself John Ellis, escorted the two condemned men, their hands handcuffed behind their backs, forty paces east along the corridor to a steel door that had no handle on the outside. This was the door to the two-level execution chamber. They were accompanied by a group composed of the sheriff, the governor of the jail, four guards, and the chaplain. There were perforated metal plates on the inside edge of the door that lined up with similar plates on the wall just inside the chamber when the door was closed. According to a former guard who served at the east wing of the jail, and who had received anecdotal information from "old timers long past," once the group stepped into the room, the governor would "drop the bolt"; that is, he would slide a metal bar through the matching holes in the wall and door plates. The door would now be securely fastened from the inside, and, with no handle on the outside, the execution could not be stayed.

After positioning the prisoners back-to-back on the gallows trap door on the upper level of the room, Ellis placed black hoods over their heads and nooses around their necks. At just two minutes after

The Don Jail's gallows were ultimately removed, but their ghostly outlines remained etched into the walls of the execution chamber.

midnight, he pulled the lever and Arthur Lucas and Ronald Turpin plunged into history as the last two men ever to be hanged in Canada.

John George Diefenbaker had led the federal Conservative Party into office in 1957, and, even though Lucas and Turpin were not saved, fifty-two of sixty-six death sentences were commuted under his watch. In 1963, the Liberals swept into power. They were vehemently opposed to capital punishment, and they made their point of view clear in December 1967, when Parliament voted to suspend the death penalty for civilian crimes for a period of five years. In 1973, this suspension was extended by another five years. Two years before the moratorium was to end, and mere days before Vaillancourt's stay of execution was due to expire, a formal vote was taken in the House of Commons to answer this burning question: Should Canada retain or abolish the death penalty?

It was impossible to predict which way the vote would go.

The public was firmly in favour of capital punishment, and this was backed by powerful organizations such as the Canadian Association of Chiefs of Police. But personalities on both sides of the political divide came out in strong opposition. Former (Conservative) prime minister Diefenbaker said of the death penalty: "It's too dangerous, and innocent men can be executed and have been executed." Prior to the vote, the current (Liberal) prime minister, Pierre Elliott Trudeau, voiced his thoughts in a passionate speech in the House of Commons: "Are we, as a society, so lacking in respect for ourselves, so lacking in hope for human betterment, so socially bankrupt that we are ready to accept state violence as our penal philosophy?"

The individual leading the efforts to force Bill C-84 through Parliament was solicitor general and human-rights activist Warren Allmand. Like Trudeau, he was a committed abolitionist. "I don't think Canadians are bloodthirsty people," Allmand told the CBC in 1975. "I know a lot of them don't agree with me now. But I think I could convince [them] that capital punishment is a bad thing."

Allmand had an unexpected ally in his quest. Through the clamour and controversy swirling around the retain-or-abolish question rang the clear and courageous voice of Pauline Maitland, the widow of Constable Leslie Maitland. Interviewed by telephone from her home in Glasgow, Scotland, where she had moved after her husband's death, she said of René Vaillancourt, her husband's killer: "I hope, as I have always hoped, that the decision will be not to hang him. That is not the answer."

During the parliamentary debate on July 14, 1976, Allmand read part of a letter from Pauline Maitland pleading for the killer's life to be spared. Bill C-84 scraped through the House of Commons with 131 votes for and 124 votes against abolishing the death sentence for all civilian crimes in Canada. It was replaced by a sentence of life imprisonment with no chance of parole for twenty-five years.

By the mid-1980s, the tide of public opinion was turning. "Why kill people who kill people to show killing people is wrong?" asked a button worn by members of the John Howard Society. A motion to restore the death penalty was convincingly defeated in June 1987. And in 1998 Canada achieved full abolitionist status when all references to the death sentence, even for offences under military law, were eliminated from the *National Defence Act*.

So, René Vaillancourt was not ultimately obliged to walk the forty paces from his cell to the gallows chamber when his nine-month stay of execution expired. In mid-1976, the Don Jail relinquished its solitary death-row occupant. Vaillancourt was transferred to Millhaven Penitentiary, a federal prison, to serve out his life sentence.

Death row, that grim space where, among others, much-loved Frank McCullough had made himself so thoroughly at home back in 1919, where the Boyd Gang had spent long hours in the early 1950s feverishly hacking away at the window bars to make their escape, and where Arthur Lucas and Ronald Turpin had whiled away their time playing games, reading the Bible, and chatting to their friend and spiritual adviser, Cyril Everitt, was now officially closed for business.

This did not mean, however, that the cells remained empty. In November 1976, twenty-year-old Eddie Hertrich and his brother were moved into the four-cell corridor, or "range," now renamed 9 Holding.

It was a "pigsty in there," says Hertrich, with "dried blood and feces everywhere." Spiderwebs, too. The brothers complained bitterly, and guards brought them buckets and disinfectants to clean up the area. Hertrich remembers that there were rats in the cells. They nicknamed one large rodent "King of the Road"; other rats would scurry when the King came calling. In April 1977, after twenty-three months in the Don, seven of them in the former death row, Eddie was acquitted of major drug charges and released. His brother was convicted.

The repurposed death cells remained in use until the end of 1977. By then, the existence of the jail itself was hanging in the balance.

CHAPTER 22

Down with the Don

Folks in the Western world like to usher in the New Year by cracking open a bottle of champagne and raising a toast. Frank Drea was dead set on celebrating the arrival of 1978 by doing some "razing" of his own: he had plans to demolish the Don Jail.

James Francis "Frank" Drea was the minister of correctional services in the Ontario provincial cabinet at the time. He had not held the job for very long. He started out in his professional life as a reporter and columnist for the *Toronto Telegram* before working as public relations director for the United Steelworkers of America. After a stint in radio and television, he turned to politics. A fierce Conservative, he was voted into the Legislative Assembly of Ontario in 1971. However, it was only in September 1977 that Progressive Conservative Premier William Davis, as the *Toronto Star*'s Queen's Park columnist Jonathan Manthorpe put it, "ushered the rumpled form of Drea into the cabinet ... and the world [had] not been quite the same since." Drea, described as a "hard drinker with the demeanor of a fighting Irishman," started small. He immediately announced that inmates of provincial institutions would be served only tea with their breakfast in the future, because coffee prices were a rip-off. He also felt that it was a waste of money to give inmates imported orange juice when there was excellent Canadian apple, tomato, and grape juices to be had. He pooh-poohed the idea that female guards should not be supervising male inmates; on the contrary, having women around in institutions had considerably "cleaned up the act" of the male jail population.

On a more serious note, he had made the point within minutes of being sworn in that there were too many people in prisons who should not be there. Dangerous criminals should be treated firmly but fairly, and the rest, through work, should put right the damage they had done instead of necessarily being imprisoned. His plan for the old Toronto Jail was his biggest and most ambitious yet. Here's how he explained his intentions to the legislature on November 10, 1977:

I will close the old Don Jail on December 31, 1977 ... forever. I have asked my colleague, the Minister of Government Services, to have tenders prepared for demolition contracts.

I see no value in preserving the old Don Jail. To do so would require the taxpayers to pay many hundreds of thousands of dollars to meet acceptable public fire safety standards. Heat and maintenance alone cost nearly $500,000 a year. Without additional expenditures there would be a persistent pest-control problem.

It is repugnant to me that preservation would mean that the curious would line up to see four steel-enclosed death cells, a gallows where 70 persons [the actual number was 34] have been executed, and jail corridors and cells which, for more than a century, have witnessed the worst in the human condition.

Upon completion of demolition, inmates will develop and maintain a massive flower garden for the benefit of patients of Riverdale Hospital. I regard this as a far better land use....

I am sure that all Honourable Members will share my satisfaction that 1978 will see the disappearance of this notorious 112 [sic]-year-old institution.

During the jail's controversial existence, stated the minister, more than one million persons had stepped over its forbidding threshold. The physical limitations of the building had affected inmates and staff alike, imposing unacceptable hardships on both. No jobs would be lost, he hastened to add, as staff employed there would be transferred to other facilities. Similarly, inmates would be moved to detention centres in Etobicoke and Scarborough, and, of course, to the adjacent New Don Jail at Gerrard and Broadview.

So: the Old Don would be replaced by a flower garden.

The decision to close the Old Don had been a long time coming. To recap: numerous grand juries had weighed in over the years about the actual structure and what went on within its walls. They condemned, among other things, the cheerless cells and corridors, the wretched sanitation, the poor medical facilities, the mind-numbing idleness of the inmates, the hopelessly inadequate psychiatric care, and the deficient training and support afforded to correctional officers. One such panel had famously reported that "this ancient building is an overcrowded dungeon, somewhat like the Black Hole of Calcutta." In 1933, the Toronto Jail was referred to as "the Bastille of Toronto the Good." Conditions in the jail were described as "filthy [and] the odour from night pails [was] pathetically putrid."

The deficiencies of the Don had also been documented in numerous reports. The *Royal Commission Appointed to Enquire into Conditions at the Don Jail, Toronto* was launched in 1952 to investigate the Great Boyd Gang Escapes. It had a broad mandate to report on management, security, and staffing at the jail; the adequacy of accommodation and security in the building; and the treatment of inmates. The commission found that staff morale was low, due to such factors as poor working conditions, inferior salaries, and low status. The building was deemed inadequate and hugely overcrowded. A select committee of the Ontario government report in 1954 (the awkwardly titled *Report to Study and Report upon Problems of Delinquent Individuals and Custodial Questions, and the Place of Reform Institutions Therein*) stated dryly that the Don was a good example of just how outdated a jail could become. Bottom line: it provided neither proper custody nor segregation for prisoners, and it lacked the means to facilitate reform. The *Royal Commission on the Toronto Jail and Custodial Services*, also known as the Shapiro Commission, was just wrapping up at the end of 1977, and the report, stretching to a whopping four volumes and around 1,600 pages, would be published a few months later. This commission had been struck in 1974 to look into allegations of mistreatment of inmates, the role and function of correctional officers, service demands on the staff, and their recruitment and training.

Not to be outdone, individuals, too — city officials, correctional officers, inmates, the media, and members of the public — had repeatedly castigated the building from the very beginning of its existence.

According to the media, Drea's words to the legislature in November 1977 declaring his plan to have the antiquated building demolished were met with applause from all political parties. But not everyone was onside. The question of what to do with the Don had reignited a long-simmering and passionate debate, the topic being whether it is better to preserve historical artifacts, no matter how dreadful, or to tear them down.

Still fresh in the public mind, as noted by Jamie Bradburn in an article entitled "Historicist: What to Do with the Don Jail," was the fate of the old Provincial Lunatic Asylum at 999 Queen Street West, Toronto. Designed by John Howard, the architect responsible for the third Toronto jail, the building opened its doors to its first 211 patients in 1850. In 1976, the facility, by then named the Queen Street Mental Health Centre, was torn down amid huge public controversy over its social and architectural legacy. Like the more-or-less contemporaneous jail, the asylum had had a checkered existence. Initially lauded by authoritative *Globe* editor George Brown as "exceeding handsome, commodious, healthful and safe ... a monument to the Christian liberality of the people," it had come to be regarded as a brutal and brutalizing structure, serving simply to warehouse people with mental health or addiction problems. In this case, those who decried the pain and stigma associated with the building prevailed over the advocates of heritage conservation who regarded it as a "superbly designed and humanely planned edifice," and the wreckers moved in. The street address was changed in 1979 from 999 to 1001 Queen Street West to symbolize a break with the horrors of the past. What remains of the old facility today is part of the old wall that once enclosed it, a former carpenter's shop, and a storage shed, which have all been designated as heritage properties.

The Mental Health Centre was "an extraordinary building," says John Sewell, who had joined the battle to preserve it. He was an alderman at that time, later mayor of Toronto. It was "very discouraging" when the structure was torn down.

As an indication of just how divisive things could become, an editorial in the *Toronto Star* of November 12, 1977, beneath the headline "Don Jail building too awful to preserve," completely agreed with the corrections minister. The jail, a "monument to human misery," had to come down. The paper scoffed at the various suggestions that had been mooted to utilize the about-to-be-retired building — converting it into a community centre, using it as to accommodate youth groups or Golden Age clubs, or converting it into a museum, factory, or recording studio.

> Many old buildings are worth preserving. But the stench of misery will never disappear from the Don. Over 70 [*sic*] people have died on its gallows. Hundreds have died on its narrow cots in cramped, rat-infested cells as a result of beatings, illness, alcohol and despair.... It has been the scene of numerous murders, suicides, homosexual rapes, riots, blackmail and perversion.
>
> Enough. To let the old pest hole escape the wrecker's hammer would only serve to sentimentalize cruelty and barbarism. Tear it down.

On page A8 of the same November 12 issue of the *Star*, historian Donald Jones weighed in with a passionate call to save the Don.

Granted, the building was a disgrace to the city, and over the years more than a million people had been confined in its cells under sometimes unspeakable conditions. But "history cannot be blotted out by the destruction of buildings. If the evil association of a building is a reason for its destruction there is a greater cause for the Tower of London to be destroyed than the Toronto Jail. In London, they placed the crown jewels in one of its rooms.... The building must be allowed to stand so that no one will forget how we once treated one another. The world needs visible proof that mankind has progressed."

Determined to save the jail from the same fate as the recently demolished "lunatic asylum," Sewell and fellow preservationists came up with a stratagem that proved to be wildly successful: a poster with a coloured photo of the façade of the jail that urged people to "Take a closer look!" at the Old Don Jail. Sewell maintains that this powerful message made a difference.

On December 18, 1977, the *Sunday Star* solicited suggestions from local celebrities as to what to do with the old jail. Here are some of their tongue-in-cheek offerings. This one came from lawyer Jerry Grafstein: "It's a natural for a day-care centre, Canada's most progressive day-care centre for children under 5 years old where we'd teach them English, French and one other language." This was architect Jack Diamond's recommendation: "We could turn it into the headquarters for the Humane Society and give the kittens more room. Of course, we'd have to upgrade the physical conditions. Laws protecting animals are more strict than laws protecting people." The suggestion of John Reeves, photographer and author, was to "turn the old part of the jail into a number of rather small condominiums." Jack McClelland, publisher, had a different proposal: "Give it to us. We'd turn it into a publishing house. We'd put all our authors and most of our editors in those cells to work. They feel it's the same conditions they work under now anyway."

The noisy and furious public debate intensified. Typical of the views expressed is this selection from the letters to the editor in the December 22 edition of the *Toronto Star*. "By destroying the Don Jail, we are not being practical, realistic or honest — just hypocritical, tunnel

Take a closer look! THE OLD DON JAIL

A landmark since 1859, this outstanding historic building represents the work of the prominent architect, William Thomas, and the skills of the finest craftsmen of the day. Preservation of such an important and vital link with our past is essential. We must prevent the destruction of one of the oldest public buildings in the City of Toronto. Information may be obtained by telephoning: Mrs. Clark, 367-7492; Mr. Clement, 367-7570.

"Take a closer look!" A hugely successful poster campaign in 1977, spearheaded by the Toronto Historical Board and city activists like John Sewell, tipped the balance in favour of saving the Old Don Jail.

visioned and short-sighted," vented one reader. Just retain the façade of the building, suggested another. "Let's hear some sane and rational discussion relating to history, architecture and esthetics as to whether the Don should be demolished instead of the sentimental claptrap being thrown about at present," wrote a third. Give us "more, not fewer, places of execution," was the suggestion of a clergyman from Belleville, forgetting, perhaps, that the death penalty had been abolished in Canada the year before. He urged "the rapid construction of one or two additional places of execution with all due haste." And, most poignant of all, this from a man who called the place "a disease of Toronto": "It doesn't matter now whether it stands, as the hurt has been done. You can tear it down, Toronto, but you still have a self-made curse — because there will always be the words: 'Remember the Don!'"

This roiling conflict led the city council to request a six-month reprieve to study possible uses for the site.

On December 31, Drea arrived at the jail with a wrecking crew in tow. Retiring Assistant Deputy Minister of Correctional Services Harry Hughes was among them, as was journalist and social activist June Callwood, referred to by the *Globe and Mail* as "one of the most insistent Don Jail haters." They carried silver-painted sledgehammers and took turns at taking ceremonial whacks at the cornerstone. Understandably parched from all this activity, the group celebrated by partaking of a glass or two of tea or apple juice.

Among the invitees was Ontario's ombudsman Arthur Maloney. He wandered around the death cells with members of the media, reminiscing about the time he'd spent at the Don during his former career as a criminal lawyer. Maloney's failed defence of the Boyd Gang's Leonard Jackson back in 1952 turned him into an ardent opponent of the death penalty. Jackson, you will remember, was hanged with Steve Suchan in December of that year for the murder of police officer Edmund Tong.

Drea's resolve seems to have buckled under the weight of public opinion, and he sardonically conceded that the "magnificent monument to human misery" would live on, at least in the short term. But on one point he remained adamant: the gallows had to go. Like Maloney, he was fiercely opposed to capital punishment, so there was no way that he would allow the structure to become part of a restoration project, or the bounty of souvenir hunters. Not on his watch. Ever the showman, however, he had initially said that the gallows would be destroyed publicly inside the jail on December 31. He backtracked. "There would be a danger of fire because acetylene torches would have to be used," he told the media on December 22, the day after the gallows were spirited away. Also removed were locks and cell doors. As for the noose: "It has been gone for at least three years. You should see how many requests I've had for a piece of hemp." John McGinnis, director of the Toronto Historical Board and clearly not someone on the hunt for souvenirs, was incensed: "We are just concerned about what amounts to vandalism on the part of a Government ministry. Nothing should have been taken out of there until we had an opportunity to look at it."

Following the closure of the Don at the end of December 1977 and the influx of male inmates at the jail next door, the female inmates who had been housed on the fourth and fifth floors of the "new" building were transferred to the Metropolitan Toronto West Detention Centre in Etobicoke.

Mayor David Crombie, Alderman Sewell, and representatives from the province and the Toronto Historical Board banded together to form a committee to study alternative uses and users for the decommissioned jail. A slew of architects, developers, and preservationists was called in to serve as advisers. An earlier proposal from the Irwin Toy Company to turn the building into a wax museum had gone nowhere. Other suggestions fell by the wayside, too. This state of affairs continued into the 1980s: no decision had been made, and, it seemed, none was being contemplated.

"Don Jail may yet outlast Frank Drea," mused the *Globe and Mail* on January 4, 1978 — prophetically, as it turned out. Drea died in January 2003, with the fate of the jail still in limbo. Just a few months later a proposal was put forward that would definitively answer the burning question, "What should be done with the Old Don?" But it would take another ten years for those plans to come to fruition.

CHAPTER 23

From Bad to Worse

Like the poisonous miasma once perceived to rise from the swamplands at the mouth of the Don River, spreading disease and death in its wake, the stigma associated with the Old Don Jail soon, and irreversibly, attached itself to its neighbour.

But it was not merely a question of perception.

The physical setup in the 1958 addition was certainly an improvement, with toilet facilities available in all the cells, for example. However, conditions became so deplorable that a public institutions inspection panel recommended in 1979, less than two years after the Old Don had been cleared of its inmates, that the whole shebang (old and new sides both) should be torn down and replaced with a modern building. The seven-person jury lambasted the disgusting kitchen storage room in the east wing and noted the pervasiveness of mice and fruit flies throughout the building. And those much-vaunted toilets? They should all be ripped out and replaced with stainless steel units.

In 1982, the Ontario Ministry of Correctional Services was "discussing" the chronic overcrowding at the jail and "vigorously pursuing" short-term solutions. The wing had originally accommodated some 300 inmates. Now, according to a ministry spokesperson, the number sometimes swelled to around 570.

In 1984, an inmate was rushed to hospital after being slashed in the throat in a vicious fight with another prisoner — the weapon was a metal file, smuggled in who knows how.

Jail staff came in for their share of criticism. In one case, a "young and impressionable" Crown witness was placed on several occasions in the same cell as the hardened drug dealer he was due to testify against. However, Frances Lankin, now a Canadian senator but at the time a correctional officer (CO) at the jail, pushed back in an indignant letter to the *Toronto Star* in 1979: "When will the media publish some of the news events supportive of correctional staff that occur?"

Because there were those who tried to make a difference.

Take Kari Niemi, a CO who retired in 2011, for example: "How do you behave against other human beings even if they've done things against the criminal code?" he asks. "Service them with the basics — send them to court for the rest. Don't make life miserable because of what they've done."

Niemi says that working as a guard was "not comfortable," and you had to be "careful to do things in a safe way." He certainly faced physical confrontations, typically when inmates started a fight and he had to step in to break it up, but he never felt at personal risk. Niemi is a big man with cool blue Nordic eyes — hard to imagine that anyone would want to tangle with him.

However, a long-time female CO who worked at the Toronto Jail — I'll call her Ms. X, as she prefers to remain anonymous — says that she had no bad experiences during her time in service. On one occasion, inmates in the corridor or range where she was working learned that it was her birthday. "They sang me happy birthday," she says. And once, when the lights went out, leaving her in the dark and without support among the inmates on the range, one of the "regulars" took her by the hand. "Don't worry," he assured her, "I'll take you to the front."

Ms. X complained about the unfairness of work assignments and the sometimes awful scheduling. "The best part was the inmates ... their attitude. If you treat them well, they will treat you well." That did not mean you became a "doormat."

In 1987, Lee Steven Chapelle spent two weeks in the Don Jail. Just nineteen years old at the time, he had been released to a halfway house from Millhaven Penitentiary, but after a parole violation he was sent to the Don, the provincial centre nearest to where he was living at the time. More recently, Chapelle's twenty-one years of extensive experience behind bars in Canadian provincial and federal correctional institutions have enabled him to carve out a career as prison consultant, lecturer, author, and motivational speaker. He describes his very brief stint in Toronto's infamous jail as giving him a "tourist perspective" of conditions there. A sample of his memories: a "penitentiary-like" jail, tougher than most; lots of bars, as opposed to concrete walls; a punching bag right on the range to allow inmates to get rid of their frustrations; the population "a tight-knit group of city people"; the "familiarity" between inmates and correctional officers, who generally "left the inmate population to police itself." As a young federal prisoner with "no history or bad beef with anyone," his short stay, he says, was problem free.

In 1989, it became evident that the New Don was not exempt from another serious problem once encountered in its obsolete neighbour.

At its grand opening back in 1958, then-governor David Dougall conceded that there might be escapes from time to time ("You have to depend on your staff and if they let you down, someone might get away"), but no jailbreak, he said, would ever, ever, successfully be launched from the exercise areas perched five storeys high on the rooftops and enclosed by tall wire fences with barbed wire on top.

He was wrong.

"DANGEROUS SEX OFFENDER SCALES WALL OF DON JAIL" shrieked a headline on June 1, 1989. The previous day, according to several graphic reports, Frederick Rodney Merrill, a convicted lawbreaker "who had honed [the] art of escape," clawed his way up and over the now razor-wire-topped fence, ran along air-conditioning ducts to the west edge of the roof — trailing blood as he went — dropped onto the roof of the old jail, crossed to the other side, and slid around sixty feet down a drainpipe to the ground. He was last seen hobbling over the Don River and Don Valley Parkway via the pedestrian bridge in Riverdale Park.

Merrill was a United States citizen awaiting sentence after pleading guilty to the sexual assault of a fifteen-year-old girl and the beating of a woman in separate attacks in Metro Toronto in March 1988. The forty-two-year-old Merrill, described as six-foot tall with greying brown hair, a thick moustache, and a heart-shaped tattoo inscribed with the word *Mom* on his upper right arm, was being supervised by a lone, unarmed, "elderly" guard when he made his escape. This was in spite of a requirement that two guards should be in the exercise area with inmates at all times, and it led to angry protests from the Ontario Public Service Employees Union about chronic understaffing at this "maximum security institution." According to the union, there were now 111 correctional officers, down from 137 a few years prior, to service an average population of around 600.

Merrill had a history of jailbreaks and attempted jailbreaks in the States. He became known as the "Peanut Butter Bandit" after his escape from a maximum-security prison in Connecticut using a hand gun his mom had lovingly delivered to him, secreted in a jar of peanut butter.

"I guess he's going to be known as Canada's most wanted man," said a spokesman for the Connecticut Department of Correction. They wanted him back to face sentence for rape, kidnapping, and robbery. "All I can say is good luck finding him," added the spokesman, unhelpfully.

A Canada-wide alert was issued for Merrill, with the media reporting that eventually more than one hundred police officers joined the manhunt, backed up by divers, tracker dogs, and a helicopter. Merrill was on the lam for sixteen days before being nabbed by three young constables, who found him ransacking cupboards in a home in Brampton, Ontario, at 3:00 a.m. Embarrassingly for the Toronto Jail, authorities chose to send him on remand to the Toronto East Detention Centre, and not back to the jail. He served a twelve-year sentence in Canada before being returned to Connecticut to face charges there.

The rooftop exercise yard from which Merrill made his daredevil escape would fall into disuse, and the watchtower that overlooked it was turned into offices. Eventually, the only exercise area for inmates was the bleak ground-floor yard between the north and south arms of the jail. It was covered with netting to discourage reprehensible folk from standing outside the wall on Broadview Avenue and tossing objects like packages of drugs or weapons to family or friends within.

Not that those imprisoned in the Don seemed to experience much difficulty in obtaining illicit substances.

As former inmate Eddie Hertrich explains, the netting covering the exercise yard was not totally effective; for example, hash-filled sockets or long tubes tossed over the wall could still drop through the mesh to those waiting below. There were other drug-delivery channels as well: men would come in from court or from the streets with substances in vials or sheaths swallowed or hidden in their body cavities. And some of the guards and other staff were willing to bring in contraband for a price. They would sometimes "fight for the privilege," says Hertrich dryly.

The jail continued on its downward spiral.

Hertrich, once considered a threat to public safety, retired in disgust from his life of crime in 2014 and subsequently published a book called *Wasted Time* about his experiences inside the Canadian correctional system. In all, he spent thirty-five years in various Canadian institutions. Around four of those years were in the Don Jail, where he was incarcerated on nine separate occasions between the mid-1970s and the early 1990s. This puts him in a unique position to evaluate the deteriorating conditions over time.

Early on, each cell contained a single bunk, making a total of eighteen inmates on each range. Later, the cells were double bunked, which translated into thirty-six men on each range. This led to "more altercations, more problems." Eventually, a third man was accommodated on a mattress on the cell floor, and that, says Hertrich, "got crazy." Rival gangs or rival dealers, he adds, would end up on the same range, and their bad feelings would erupt. The situation wasn't quite as serious on the streets, where they didn't constantly see one another. But once arrested and placed in the same overcrowded space they would "have to address their rivalries."

In 1990, a coroner's jury delivered a strongly worded verdict recommending that the jail should undertake "a fundamental change in its attitude and approach" toward mentally ill prisoners. This followed the death from gangrene in November 1989 of Mark Buhagar, a Mississauga man with a history of mental illness who had been in jail for eight days pending trial for attempted car theft. Following a heated argument with correctional staff, he was placed in "lockup," or confined to his cell. After causing a flood by plugging the sink and toilet, the troubled and troublesome man was moved to a segregation cell. A pathologist told the inquest that the cell was found to be teeming with the bacteria that had caused Buhagar's gangrene.

In January 1994, an interim report sounded the alarm on yet another ugly manifestation within Ontario's correctional facilities. The report, called *Racism Behind Bars*, was put together by the Commission on Systemic Racism in the Ontario Criminal Justice System. Its mandate was to investigate systemic racism, which was defined as "the values, practices, and procedures that result in black and other racial minority people receiving worse treatment than white people." After extensive formal and informal interviews, observation, and analysis of documentation, the commission found both overt and systemic racism in the provincial system, as revealed by racial hostility and intolerance in jails and prisons, racial segregation of prisoners, and racial inequality in the delivery of prison services. The commissioners noted that racial segregation was particularly prevalent at the Toronto Jail. One of their conclusions was that "the culture of corrections ... must change."

Thanksgiving 1994 was a gloomy affair. No common celebratory dinner, or anything remotely like it. After an attempted jailbreak, the entire inmate population was confined to their cells. Visits and even phone calls were banned.

In 1998, the lawyer of John Paul Roby, accused of sexually abusing dozens of young boys over a period of more than twenty years, claimed that his client had been threatened by other inmates, verbally abused by jail staff, and refused breakfast and a shower before his court appearance. The trial judge called this alleged abuse possibly "criminal."

That same year, forty-one-year-old Rodolfo Pacificador was granted bail after spending six-and-a-half years in pretrial custody in the Toronto Jail — believed to be an immoral and iniquitous record. He had been held pending extradition for allegedly assassinating a politician in his native Philippines before fleeing and claiming refugee status in Canada. Pacificador described his very first sleepless night as the third man in a two-person cell, which he spent on the floor with his head close to a reeky toilet, watching mice darting in and out of the cell.

What had long been smouldering just beneath the surface exploded into public consciousness in May 2003 with a news story that became a sensation, not just for what it contained but for how it had been obtained. After a judge had cut seven years off the fourteen-year sentence of a man convicted of attempted murder, robbery, and confinement because he had already served time in the "medieval, brutal" Don Jail, Liberal Member of Provincial Parliament (MPP) Dave Levac of Brant, the opposition party's public safety and security critic, obtained permission to tour the jail. In tow were two "assistants," one of whom just happened to be (conveniently unidentified) *Toronto Star* reporter Linda Diebel. As the *Star's* former Latin America correspondent, Diebel had visited her share of "Third World hellholes" in more southerly climes and was eminently qualified to comment on this one, handily located in her own backyard.

What she saw, heard, and smelled shocked her.

The jail, she wrote in a blistering exposé, "smells like vomit, urine and years of caked-in, grimy mould. Every prisoner in his bright orange jumpsuit, every overworked and harried guard, breathes this toxic stench in with every breath. And, then, there's the din, the mind-numbing din of hundreds of prisoners — 647 yesterday in a facility with a capacity of 504 — yelling, banging and driving themselves crazy."

A guard expressed his extreme concern about the safety of what he called "human pyramids," who Diebel described as standing "on each other's shoulders to hoist themselves up against the bars, just to get a glimpse of the sky in little windows across concrete corridors."

"We're packed in here three to a cell. There's no room. Sometimes the toilets are overflowing. It's really bad," said an inmate who was in jail for cocaine possession.

Jail employees told Levac that morale was low among staff, especially following the Ontario Conservative government's budget cuts in 1996. Understaffed and overstretched — "the strain is there, that's for sure," said one official.

The tour wound through the kitchen, where something that looked like pea soup was liberally splattered across large areas of the floor, prompting a staff member to warn the group to watch their step.

"Well, I won't pull any punches," was Levac's parting shot to jail officials. "You've got a tough place here."

Levac faced censure for smuggling in a reporter, and by so doing breaching the *Members' Integrity Act*, 1994. The integrity commissioner's report was published on July 23, 2003. What made the MPP's offence more reprehensible was that the jail was in lockdown at the time with public visitation completely suspended (a situation bitterly resented by inmates) as part of efforts to contain the spread of Severe Acute Respiratory Syndrome (SARS) in the Greater Toronto Area. Levac clearly knew, wrote the commissioner, that he was misleading correctional authorities by not identifying Diebel as a journalist, although he accepted the MPP's claim that he had not been aware of any special measures regarding SARS. "Mr. Levac," concluded the commissioner, "did not meet the standards imposed by parliamentary convention. The ends, — exposing the conditions at the Toronto Jail to the public through the media did not justify the means — participating in a plan designed to assist in providing a member of the media access to a correctional facility." However, since he saw this as merely "an error in judgment," he recommended "that no penalty be imposed."

Levac, and Diebel, were off the hook.

In early 2008, the "festering problem" of racism was again in the news. Selwyn Pieters, a Black Toronto human-rights lawyer who had once worked as a guard at the Don Jail, noted that racism had existed among COs in the jail for at least twenty years, but provincial officials had done little to rectify the problem. Since 2005, around fifteen COs, most of them Black, had received hate mail, seemingly written by co-workers. A particularly disturbing case was that of Charlene Tardiel, who had just taken special leave after receiving death threats over the Christmas period. "We have to go in and be looking over our (shoulders), not knowing if one of our colleagues is actually doing these hate crimes," she told the media. "It's a matter of fear. Am I going home to see my family today [or] be the next black peace officer that's dead on duty?"

Around thirty COs, both Black and white, walked off the job in protest.

Union steward Hayton Morrison said that the letters had been turned over to the police. "It's the most vile, hateful, racist kind of thing you could ever imagine, riddled with profanity," he fumed.

The status quo dragged on, seemingly interminably.

And a sad fact was that not only those behind bars but their families and friends were sucked willy-nilly into the machine. A typical visit to an inmate, seated at one of a bank of telephones in the visitation room and communicating across bulletproof glass, lasted just twenty minutes. Getting to that point would swallow up most of the day.

Richard Poplak, an author and journalist who interviewed Toronto's notorious bicycle thief Igor Kenk on multiple occasions in the Don while doing research for a graphic novel in 2009, speaks of the visitor experience. After making an appointment, visitors would show up and stand in line outside in all weathers — no cellphones allowed. Most of them were women, "old hands" waiting to see their husbands, sons, or boyfriends. After going through security and signing in, they waited some more, this time on a wooden bench in a small room. Once a visitor's name was called, they were buzzed into the visitation room for their twenty-minute session. These places are "time thieves," says Poplak. "And there is no compensation for time stolen."

By then, the writing was already on the wall for the nondescript Toronto Jail. Its looming demise wasn't due only to dreadful conditions — extensive changes had swept over Toronto since the jail's grand opening in the late 1950s. In 1998, the provincial Conservative government tossed out the city's existing Metro structure, and the former municipalities of Toronto, York, East York, North York, Scarborough, and Etobicoke were fused into one enormous "megacity" under a single administration. As a city, it is now the largest in Canada and among the top ten in North America. How big is it? Back in 2009, when the jail started winding down, the population of Toronto stood at more than two-and-a-half million. Toronto Police Service statistics for that year gave the number of reported Criminal Code offences as 180,283. To give just a sample of crimes committed: 5,444 were robberies, 22,964 were non-sexual assaults, 2,667 were sexual assaults, and sixty-two were homicides.

Existing facilities were beyond overstretched, and, to rectify the situation, the Ministry of Community Safety and Correctional Services announced in May 2008 that an institution capable of housing close to two thousand offenders would be built to replace the existing Mimico Correctional Centre, the Toronto Jail, and the Toronto West Detention Centre. It would take six years, however, for the Toronto South Detention Centre, the second-largest jail in Canada, to be officially opened.

Gail Desabrais, as deputy superintendent administration, was a senior member of the team tasked with closing down the Toronto Jail and diverting inmates to other facilities while simultaneously trying to maintain its smooth operation, a process she described as having "one foot on the gas and one on the brake." She, too, complained of the state of affairs in the jail. Around 2012, she noted, there was a problem with black mould in one of the ranges, and it had to be shut down.

And what of the accusations of inmates being beaten up by staff? "You will always have the bad apples," like the manager who provoked then assaulted an inmate, was taken to court, and got off on "a technicality." "Too bad it overshadows the really good officers that are out there," said Desabrais: those with "a sense of pride" in what they did. Screening, she said, needed to be improved to prevent the hiring of people with serious anger issues.

In a thoughtful article in *Toronto Life* in 2010, following the death in the Toronto Jail of Jeff Munro, a diagnosed schizophrenic, over a bag of chips, Nicholas Hune-Brown drilled down to the heart of the problem. What was actually being achieved with inmates at the Don? Rehabilitation? Reintegration into society? Punishment, even? The answer: none of the above. The jail was simply a warehouse, but one where prisoners were "treated worse than the most dangerous convicted criminals serving time in federal penitentiaries."

Overcrowded, understaffed, sunless, stinking, simmering with violence that could explode over something as trivial as a bag of chips or someone spitting on the floor — many fervently wished that the Toronto Jail would simply vanish off the face of the earth.

CHAPTER 24

Adaptive Reuse

n mid-2004, a glossy brochure, put together by the architectural firm Urban Strategies Inc. for Bridgepoint Health (the new name for Riverdale Hospital), landed on the desks of the movers and shakers at City Hall. According to the title, it was *A Master Plan for the Bridgepoint Health — Don Jail Site*. The plan for the redevelopment of the quadrant on the northwest corner of Broadview Avenue and Gerrard Street East had been several years in the making, with discussions and input from some two hundred people who lived or worked in the neighbourhood, including hospital staff and patients, members of local business associations, and other stakeholder groups, as well as city and provincial politicians.

The driving force behind this master plan was Marian T. Walsh, who had become the president and CEO of Riverdale Hospital in the late 1990s. Back then, the fate of the venerable hospital was in the balance. The Conservative government of Ontario under Premier Mike Harris, citing the need for cutbacks, wanted to shut Riverdale down, but the community rallied fiercely to save it. Walsh was against taking the hospital off site — "people here needed care," she explains — although she did come to the conclusion that the existing facilities were functionally obsolete. She was convinced that the residents of Riverdale and far beyond required a modern, state-of-the-art health care centre to handle their complex needs.

The acquisition of the Old Don Jail happened "by accident," says Walsh. Closed to the public, it was quietly mouldering away into total disrepair.

This is not to say that the Old Don had stood completely empty since very early 1978, when its last residents were escorted out of the building and the iron-studded oak doors securely locked. Some six weeks later, the building again echoed with the sounds of cell doors swinging open and clanging shut. These February 1978 inmates, however, were very different from their predecessors. They went home at night, possibly stopping for a nightcap on the way, and their sentence was a brief three days — the time it took to shoot the first five minutes of a Canadian feature film about a couple of small-time hoods striving to make it to the big time. Originally called *Fast Company*, later *Bad Company*, the movie was directed by Canadian author, filmmaker, and investigative historian Peter Vronsky.

Vronsky says that as a public relations stunt the filmmakers issued invitations to the press (they looked like "court summons or arrest warrants") for a catered lunch on site.

"Of course, we served wine with the lunch," he adds.

Reaction was glacially slow. Two months later, says Vronsky, the *Toronto Sun* reported that Ontario Corrections Minister Frank Drea had hit the roof when he heard that drinks had been served in the jail. To a reformed alcoholic and the man who wanted to tear down what he called the "dirty, grimy, stinking" building, this was clearly anathema.

Then: nothing.

It was "a mini-scandal for a day," says Vronsky.

Tom Cruise flipped bottles in the Old Don Jail as a bartender in the 1988 blockbuster *Cocktail*; the bar scenes were filmed in the rotunda. If you don't blink, you can see gargoyles and walkways behind him in some of the shots. Along with other movies and TV shows, scenes from the 1998 teen drama *Cruel Intentions* were also shot there.

Frank Drea's reaction to these latest outrages would no longer have been newsworthy. By 1985, he was yesterday's man in Ontario politics. He served as chairman of the Ontario Racing Commission until bumped from the post in 1994 by the provincial New Democratic Party (NDP) government under Bob Rae.

It would be interesting to know how he might have reacted to a report in the *Toronto Star* in January 1993 that, by the following Friday, "the correctional services staff and chaplains who have been using part of the old building for office space will have been moved into other quarters, and people will be prevented from entering the Don. Only the newer Toronto Jail, a nondescript, brick structure attached to the Don, will be used. Officials with the government services ministry, which owns the Don, say the building is unsafe."

Fast forward to the very early 2000s, when Marian Walsh found intriguing the idea of taking on this decaying relic of a crueller time and "changing a place of incarceration into a place of healing."

The jail became a key element in the transformation and restructuring of the site, which had been regarded historically as that unsavoury place across the Don River where dangerous lawbreakers were warehoused and dangerous patients were treated for contagious diseases.

According to the Bridgepoint master plan, the three on-site care facilities then collectively known as Bridgepoint Health — the 1963 Modernist semi-circular or half-round hospital and the much older Hannah and Hastings buildings — no longer met "the needs of today's complex care and rehabilitation patients or standards for modern health care delivery."

According to Frank Lewinberg, the principal architect at Urban Strategies who worked closely with Walsh on the project, even the half-round building didn't work as a hospital. "You couldn't move wheelchairs around," he says.

And that was a serious problem. As noted in the master plan, the patient population had changed over the years, with many more medically complicated and functionally impaired individuals in the system than there had been in the past. Seventy percent of patients now used wheelchairs, and there was no possibility of installing ceiling-mounted lifting systems to ease them from bed to chair. Air ducts were antiquated and low ceiling heights dictated that medical gasses could be supplied only via portable canisters. There were no dedicated wash-rooms or showers in the wards. Each floor had approximately sixteen toilets and just one shower to serve around one hundred beds.

At the time the master plan was presented, ownership of the site was extremely complicated, with part of the land belonging to Bridgepoint (the two jails, the Gatekeeper's and Governor's houses, a building on Broadview to the east of the half-round, and a couple of parking lots); part belonging to the City of Toronto and leased to Bridgepoint (the three hospital buildings and a couple more parking lots); and a section owned and operated by the city (the St. Matthew's Lawn Bowling Club, the Riverdale Library, and the Don Jail Roadway, which curved in front of the old jail to connect Gerrard Street and Broadview Avenue).

The plan put two options on the table. The first was the "Comprehensive Community Master Plan," which would see Bridgepoint taking on the redevelopment of the entire site. A new health care centre would be built to the far west and the Old Don Jail would be incorporated, adapted, and reused. Four additional blocks of land would be reserved for future development. The provisos were that the New Don Jail would be "relocated" from the site (read, "torn down"), that Bridgepoint would secure "fee simple" (absolute ownership) of the lands it currently leased from the city, that the city-owned bowling club would be exchanged for a new public park in front of the Don Jail, and the Don Jail Roadway would be realigned.

The second option was a scaled-down "Hospital Redevelopment Plan." Bridgepoint would build its new health care facility on the lands it currently leased from the city, with the addition of land occupied by the Don Jail annex/former laundry and the building on Broadview to the east of the half-round.

Nothing is ever simple.

If the Grand Bridgepoint Master Plan went ahead, a casualty of the extensive restructuring project would be the existing Bridgepoint Health facilities. And that distinctive half-round building had its devotees. To quote just one: "It is handsome, it has art, it has style. Regardless of how fine the replacement is, if this building goes I'll be sad. And a bit mad." And Christopher Hume of the *Toronto Star* wrote in January 2006: "Completed in 1963, the half-round is one of those rare structures whose every gesture and detail speaks of the age that produced it. Exuberant and wildly optimistic, this is an architectural relic from a time, the last in our history, when the future loomed brighter than the past.... Certainly, the semi-circular monument designed by Chapman & Hurst should be saved. It is unlike anything else in Toronto, a genuine landmark and part of our history."

Fierce public debate had citizens coming out on both sides of the issue, but ultimately the comprehensive master plan was approved by the city on January 31, 2006. Heritage groups promptly appealed the decision to the Ontario Municipal Board (OMB), which, in its turn, approved the redevelopment of the site in 2007.

Paula Fletcher, councillor for Ward 30 (Toronto-Danforth) acknowledged how strongly people felt about the fate of the building and noted that the OMB had been faced with a difficult decision. As she put it, the sad truth was that "the Don Jail and the half round both can't remain in the Bridgepoint master plan."

Frank Lewinberg agrees: "We couldn't save it and build the new hospital in the same location. There was no question in the minds of the decision-makers that we should go ahead."

By mid-2014, anyone wandering past the once-crowded northwest corner of Broadview Avenue and Gerrard Street East for the first time since the early 2000s would have rubbed their eyes in disbelief.

The St. Matthew's Lawn Bowling Club was gone, its historic clubhouse shunted in 2009 a few hundred metres northeast to a new spot on Broadview at the edge of Riverdale Park — predictably, to complaints from locals who claimed to have been totally unaware of the proposed changes or who protested the loss of the level land it would take up and the trees that were cut down to accommodate it.

Gone, too, was the historic Don Jail Roadway, where crowds had stormed police barricades and shouted "Murderers!" and "Killers!" just after the midnight double hanging of Ronald Turpin and Arthur

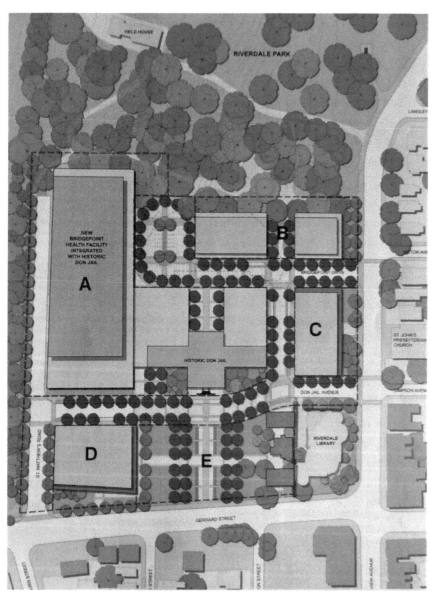

The Comprehensive Community Master Plan for the Bridgepoint Health —
Don Jail site was approved by the city in 2006. Bridgepoint took on the redevelopment of the site, which included a new health facility and the reuse of
the Old Don Jail as its administrative centre. The areas labelled B, C, D, and E
were zoned for possible future use.

Lucas on December 11, 1962. In early 2013, a much more sedate group attended the unveiling of the new Jack Layton Way, its name chosen in honour of the former Federal NDP leader who died from cancer in 2011.

The heritage Governor's House, now rehabilitated and extended, had been leased to the Philip Aziz Centre for adaptive use as a non-profit children's hospice called Emily's House, with the Gatekeeper's House as its administrative centre.

Reassuringly, the Riverdale Library remained in its customary spot, still serving the neighbourhood as it had done since 1910.

The site was dominated by the new hospital, now called Bridgepoint Active Healthcare, which had imposed its full ten-storey, 464-bed footprint on a prime location overlooking the Don Valley. Christopher Hume, who in 2006 had passionately opposed the demolition of the old half-round building, now conceded with admiration that the new Bridgepoint was "all about light, space, and patient comfort." It was also about public access, with Riverdale Park to the north and east and gardens and terraces extending to meet it from Gerrard Street.

As for the grand scheme of things: "The site is still waiting for its future," says Lewinberg. Bridgepoint received four properties that were zoned for buildings nine residential storeys high. They could potentially build whatever they like, even housing units, as long as they stick within the height restriction of nine storeys. Ideally, though, the sites "should all be health related."

However, he adds with a smile, "The next [development] may not occur in our lifetime."

A competition in 2014 to rename the green space between Gerrard Street and Jack Layton Way elicited enthusiastic suggestions such as "Gallows Park," "Hangman's Haunt," "Penance Park," and even the "Lucas-Turpin Memorial Park." The name eventually chosen was Hubbard Park, to honour William Peyton Hubbard, who had become Toronto's first Black alderman in 1894.

The much-reviled Toronto Jail — the "new" Don Jail — that clients of Toronto's Out of the Cold program, with heavy irony, sometimes called "The Don Hilton" was cleared of its residents in December 2013 and formally decommissioned in January 2014.

John Minarik, a correctional officer who retired in 1991, served in both buildings. He says that the new wing was a terrible place, and terribly built. "There was no ventilation," he says. "You would sweat in your tie and hat." From the 1960s onward there were big steel plates "holding in the walls" on the east side of the building. In his opinion, "if they ever ripped down the old jail, the new one would have fallen over."

As it turned out, it was the new one that faced the wrecking crews. And there was not a single squawk from the public when that featureless brick building came down — no angry protesters waving placards on the streets, no poster campaigns going viral, no pleading letters to the newspapers, no online petitions.

The Old Don Jail, a jail no longer, is still there, renamed the Bridgepoint Administration Building and containing office space for administrators, educators, and clinical specialists.

Father Time still frowns stonily down as you mount the stairs to the heavy oak front doors, although he is quite a few shades lighter these days, following a years-long heritage scrape and polish. The restoration was finally completed in 2013, accompanied by challenges, surprises — and macabre revelations from beyond the grave.

CHAPTER 25

Digging Up the Past

Around noon on Saturday, August 7, 1920, eight-year-old Philip Goldberg left his home at 112 McCaul Street, Toronto. With eleven cents jingling in his pocket, he was headed for the moving-picture show near the corner of Queen and McCaul streets. His family was disturbed when he hadn't returned by four o'clock; by midnight they were frantic. Less than two hours later, two of Philip's older siblings were at the morgue, where a hideous task confronted them: positively identifying the body of a young boy as that of their brother.

At 4:35 that Saturday afternoon, a passer-by, Robert McMurtrie (also spelled in reports as McMurty or McMurtry), had found Philip lying between two billboards on a vacant lot adjacent to High Park in Toronto's west end. The boy was still breathing but he was bleeding heavily. Initially thinking that the child had tumbled from one of the billboards, McMurtrie hailed a man he described as hurrying away from the scene, asking him to watch the boy while he went to get help.

As McMurtrie later told police, the man's reply was, strangely, "I had nothing to do with it. I know nothing about it."

When McMurtrie returned with a policeman, the man was gone, and the boy was dead.

But Philip Goldberg had not had a traumatic fall: he had been brutally murdered. In addition to several head and throat wounds, each one severe enough to have been fatal, the boy had suffered what the *Globe* called "bestial offences."

Police surmised that the unknown man was the perpetrator of the savage murder and rape. Investigations revealed that he was Frederick L. Davis, a neighbour of the Goldberg family and a man known to Toronto police. Described as being in his midforties, he had one gold tooth and wore a wig. He also had open sores, possibly from advanced syphilis, and walked with a pronounced limp. But Davis was not waiting around for the police to nab him; he fled to the United States. It took nearly a year, but he was eventually tracked down to Auburn Prison in New York, where he was serving time for burglary and the theft of machinists' tools in Rochester. Detective Bart Cronin — you will remember him as the man who played a significant role in the Frank McCullough case just two years previously — was sent down to Auburn to confront the suspect.

Yes, said Davis, he knew Philip Goldberg. He had taken him to the movies on that August day. Afterwards, he bought ice cream cones in Grange Park for himself, the boy, and two or three little girls.

"Where did you go next?" asked Cronin.

"To High Park."

For Cronin, that was the clincher. He charged Davis with Philip Goldberg's murder. After a few moments of silence, the man said: "I'm not a bad fellow at heart. Liquor was at the bottom of this thing."

On his release from Auburn, Davis was extradited and sent back to Toronto for trial in January 1922. Robert McMurtrie positively identified him in court as the man he had seen scurrying away from the crime scene. It didn't help Davis's case that the police read a confession, admittedly unsigned, into the records. But what really sank the accused was what the press called "the keen wit" of an eight-year-old girl. Sarah Friendly swore that she had seen Davis in Grange Park on the day of the murder. He was accompanied by a little boy, dressed in "brown running shoes and black stockings and pants fastened and buttoned and blue little hat." The man offered her and her friend Rachel Weindrow ice cream cones. "Absolutely not," said Sarah, "we don't take anything from strangers." She categorically denied the defence lawyer's suggestion that her memory had been jogged by photos the police had

shown her or by Bart Cronin's prompts at the identification parade at
police headquarters, rather than by her actual recollection of the event.

Just before Sarah stepped down from the witness box, the judge,
Justice William Renwick Riddell, asked her if she would take a message
to her school teacher: "Tell her the Judge says you are the best witness
he has seen for many a long day."

The jury may have set some kind of Canadian record in coming to
their decision. As tersely documented in the trial report:

> Jury retires at 3 p.m.
> Jury reports with verdict at 3.02 p.m.
> REGISTRAR: Gentlemen of the Jury have you
> agreed upon a verdict?
> FOREMAN: Yes, guilty.

Riddell sentenced Davis to death. In his mandatory special report
to the federal minister of justice after the trial, Riddell noted that Davis
had informed the jail surgeon in Toronto that "when a boy in England
under 10 years of age he was initiated in homo-sexual practices by a
grown man." In a chilling case of abused turning abuser, Davis also
"gave a history ... of obscene but not criminal practices with young
boys and men in Toronto."

In spite of the defence's attempts to have Davis committed to
"some public institution" on the basis of his mental and physical condition, he was led by executioner Arthur Ellis to the gallows at the Don
Jail just before 8:00 a.m. on May 9, 1922. According to the *Globe*, he
"walk[ed] to his doom with steady mien." According to the jail physician, Davis's health had deteriorated to such an extent that he could
not have lived more than another two years. An hour later, Davis's
body was buried in the northeast corner of the jail yard, where a short
burial service was held.

The harrowing details of this crime resurfaced, both literally and
figuratively, during excavations at the Toronto Jail in late 2007 and
early 2008. At that time, a site investigation led by Dr. Ron Williamson

DIES ON SCAFFOLD.
Fred L. Davis, who paid the penalty with his life at the jail this morning for the brutal murder of young Philip Goldberg.

Photograph of Frederick Davis from the *Toronto Star* of May 9, 1922, the day he was executed for the savage murder of eight-year-old Philip Goldberg.

of Archaeological Services Inc. was launched as a core requirement for the approval of the Bridgepoint Health master plan.

During the ninety long years between 1872 and 1962, thirty-four men had been hanged at the Old Don Jail. Sources such as old site plans and archival newspapers had indicated that burials had sometimes taken place in the northeast exercise yard, formerly called "Murderers' Row" or "Murderers' Graveyard." The jail's perimeter wall had been torn down and the area paved over for use as a parking lot, but it was no surprise when backhoes, shovels, trowels, and brushes turned up evidence of human remains. What was surprising was the actual number of "murderers'" skeletons the investigators managed to unearth — fifteen. Although not only hanged men died at the jail, none of the existing records seemed to indicate that inmates who died from other causes had been buried on site.

Back in 1872, the first person hanged, and buried, at the Toronto Jail was twenty-year-old John Traviss of East Gwillimbury, Ontario. He had shot and killed a local farmer, either, depending on which newspaper you happened to pick up, in a fit of cold rage directed against a rival in love or against a neighbour who had given him a bad name with the family of his beloved. Court records describing the victim, John Johnson, as an older man with a family suggest that the latter was the correct version. According to a witness, all that Traviss would say on his arrest was: "I am satisfied. I have had my revenge." The last man buried in the northeast yard was Edward Stewart, in March 1930. Stewart was a thirty-three-year-old labourer who murdered a Gerrard Street butcher during a bungled robbery attempt.

Originally, there had been a requirement that people executed for murder should be interred in the cemetery of the jail where they had been hanged. By 1930, however, this rule was no longer being rigorously adhered to. For the next thirty-two years, the bodies of men hanged at the Don Jail were generally claimed and buried by family or friends. An exception was the case of the last two men executed there in late 1962, Ronald Turpin and Arthur Lucas. Immediately after they were hanged back-to-back just after midnight on December 11, their bodies were hastily bundled into plain pine coffins and carted away to the Prospect Cemetery on St. Clair Avenue West in Toronto — not even embalmed, to the great sorrow and disgust of Salvation Army chaplain Cyril Everitt, their spiritual adviser, friend, and the officiant at their very early morning burial.

The archaeological investigators had an array of clues, tools, and techniques to aid them in their efforts to identify exactly who was buried in each of the unmarked graves. Historical research (much of it gleaned from archival news items), based on factors such as age, physical appearance, and descriptions of what the individuals were wearing at the time of death, was used to build up as comprehensive a profile as possible for each person hanged at the jail. These profiles were then systematically compared with data obtained in the field, both biological (stature, dental decay or missing teeth, soft tissue, and hair) and archaeological (bone or shell buttons, remnants of socks, a copper cross). The investigators were particularly interested in whether the men — pubic and cranial morphology confirmed that they were, indeed, all men — had actually been executed, so they looked for injuries to the cervical vertebrae that would point to judicial hanging.

The site report noted that historical records were often incomplete, vague, or simply incorrect. A newspaper report possibly from the early 1900s, for example, stated that a certain Robert Coulter was buried at the Don Jail. His execution took place in 1862; the construction of the jail was only completed a couple of years later. It seems highly unlikely that anyone would have been buried in the exercise yard before the jail was actually up and running. As it turned out, Coulter's body had been laid to rest in Toronto's St. James Cemetery. The lack of any kind of chronological arrangement in the location of the burials also complicated exact identification. And where were the graves of John Traviss, John Williams, and George Bennett, all known to have been buried there, in relation to one another? Rival newspapers gave conflicting reports. "Given these kinds of limitations, the personal identification of the remains should be considered provisional with only a few exceptions," warned the report.

So, for example, it was "possible" that Burial 10 was George Bennett, the bitter and resentful former *Globe* employee who took a gun to his ex-boss, George Brown, and was, as a result, hanged on July 23, 1880. He was described as being thirty-two years old at the time of death; he was wearing a suit and leather shoes; and his coffin had "silver ornaments." There seems to be a strong link in this case between the archival descriptions on the one hand, and, on the other, factors in Burial 10 such as the age range of the skeletal remains, the style of the clothing, and the presence of silver ornaments in the coffin.

It was also "possible" that Burial 14 was Frank McCullough, the charismatic and wildly popular folk hero doomed for shooting a Toronto policeman in 1918. He was in his midtwenties when he went to the gallows on June 13, 1919, which fits the age range established for Burial 14. McCullough was reportedly wearing "high black shoes" and buried in a "nice casket." Remnants of blunt-toed leather uppers and leather laces that were dated to the early twentieth century and six stamped-tin coffin studs seem to back up this supposition.

There were, however, absolutely no possibles or probables when it came to Burial 8. This individual was "almost certainly" Frederick L. Davis, the man hanged on May 9, 1922, for the rape and brutal murder of eight-year-old Philip Goldberg. There were so many positive pointers. Court documents put his age at forty-six, which matched the estimated age range of the skeleton. Archival newspapers reported that Davis had a gold tooth, wore a wig, walked with a cane, and was suffering from a terminal disease that would have killed him within two years. The excavation of Burial 8 turned up a gold-and-enamel dental bridge and remains bearing signs of advanced tertiary venereal syphilis. Symptoms of this disease include difficulty in coordinating muscle movements, bone loss, and, grimly, dementia. This would explain the cane, the missing teeth, the dental work, and the kind of mental deterioration that may have been a contributing factor in so savage a crime.

The site investigation concluded that, unless separately claimed for reburial by family members, the fifteen individuals should be "disinterred and re-interred in a proper cemetery." No one stepped forward to claim any of the bodies, and they have all now been laid to rest, still in unmarked graves, on a grassy slope framed by majestic old trees in St. James Cemetery on the west side of the Don River. A simple brass plaque announces that "Here lie the remains of 15 men, executed and buried at the Don Jail between 1871 [sic] and 1930 prior to the abolition of the death penalty in Canada. Their remains were moved to this plot in 2008."

But there must be at least one person who sometimes spares a thought for these lost souls. On a warm July day, a small, crumpled bouquet lies beside the marker — its flowers, once blue, now dry and faded.

Brass memorial plaque, dated 2008, at St. James Cemetery in Toronto. It commemorates the reinterment of fifteen bodies found in the "Murderer's Graveyard" at the Don Jail.

CHAPTER 26

Makeover

On the last Saturday in May 2019, a long line of people wearing coats and clutching umbrellas snaked around the side of a building just east of the Don River. Darkening skies and the menace of rain would not deter them from doggedly waiting their turn to go inside.

The occasion was the annual Doors Open Toronto, which, since the year 2000, has invited the public to explore city structures of architectural, historical, cultural, and social significance. Since 2014, one of the most eagerly visited buildings to throw its "doors open" has been the Bridgepoint Administration Building, better known as the Old Don Jail. The irony, of course, is that after all the years people spent trying desperately to get *out* of that infamous place, people are now eager to get *in*.

Once inside, visitors craned their necks in the soaring central rotunda to marvel at the skylight and clerestory windows, before walking down an old staircase and filing past a row of impossibly narrow cells in the basement.

The undeniable highlight of the tour, however, was the execution chamber on the second floor. Folks clustered in the corridor as a volunteer delivered a brief background blurb, then they stepped past the heavy steel door to peer around the grim two-level space where twenty-six men were hanged between 1908 and 1962.

What would Frank McCullough or the Boyd Gang have thought of this strange turn of events? They spent hours sawing away at the iron bars of their cell window to make their successful escapes from the forbidding jail. Or the acrobatic Polka Dotter Kenneth Green and his human pyramid, all of whom failed in their attempt to jump over the perimeter wall to freedom?

No need to speculate what Ontario Correctional Services Minister Frank Drea's opinion would have been. The man who presided over what he hoped was the final closing of the Don Jail doors in 1978, intending to invite in wrecking crews ASAP to smash the whole toxic place to smithereens, made his views blazingly (and presciently) clear at the time: preservation of the building "would mean that the curious would line up" to tour it, which, to him, was totally "repugnant."

To be fair, the old pile is in very different shape nowadays from the one that Drea walloped with his silvery sledgehammer on the last day of December 1977. With the participation of a slew of architectural firms and historical restoration experts, it has undergone a full makeover.

The process began in the early 2000s, when Michael McClelland, principal at ERA Architects, was invited to participate in the development of a conservation strategy for the historic building in keeping with the general changes Bridgepoint was planning for the site. The big challenge was how to turn a highly stigmatized space into the administrative centre of a new hospital devoted to complex care and rehabilitation. A series of heritage reports and applications submitted by ERA to the City of Toronto and to the city's Heritage Preservation Services stressed that the aim was "to encourage the evolution and growth of the site, while protecting the unique cultural and historical value of the site." This, then, would entail a reconfiguration of the building to fit its new purpose as well as an inside-and-out heritage restoration.

In 2008, ERA organized a review of the building's exterior to evaluate the installation and condition of the security bars, as well as the general state of the window frames, the glazing, the surrounding masonry, the roof, and the outer walls above grade. In spite of the Don's age and scanty maintenance over the years, the investigators found that the exterior was in surprisingly good condition. Their main concern was the deterioration caused to the window surrounds by the iron security bars.

In fact, what to do with the bars, those very visible reminders of the jail's dark past, caused much controversy. Bridgepoint would have liked to get rid of them all, citing "concerns regarding the impact of retained jail bars on patient and staff well being," but heritage considerations won through, and an agreement was reached to keep the bars on basement windows, and at least some of them on the other floors. This proved to be no easy task. As Andrew Pruss, principal architect at ERA, points out, the iron bars "were actually embedded in the stone frames and the windows were built around them." In most cases, the only way to remove the bars was to cut them out and reinstall them in the designated locations after the window masonry had been repaired. Without replacing the ugly mesh that covered many of the windows, of course. In stark contrast to the hours it took would-be escapers to painstakingly saw their way through the bars, the recommended removal procedure using oxyacetylene cutting torches would make short work of both vertical and horizontal bars — under two minutes apiece.

In 2008, ERA also undertook a "Bridgepoint Health Don Jail Prisoner Cell Survey." Interestingly, the survey noted that none of the cell doors still had locks — a reminder that thirty years previously, Frank Drea's staff had done a very good job of cutting them all away. To give a representation of the various types of cells existing in the jail, ERA identified four unique kinds to keep as examples. These consisted of a group of six one-person cells with their adjacent corridor or day room in the west wing of the basement; one solitary confinement cell in the same area; eight partly modified punishment cells in the central block, also in the basement; and, on the fourth floor on the east side of the central block, a couple of the 1888 Willmot-designed iron cells with their doors and stencilled numbering still intact. These iron cells occupy the space previously filled by the governor's residence. It was decided to retain the cells numbered 4 and 5, but conceal them in an office behind a large swing door.

The four steel-clad death-row cells on the second floor, so reviled by Drea, would emphatically *not* be retained. However, the small east-facing window with its multiple sets of bars, through which McCullough and the Boyd Gang had escaped, would remain.

Other must-haves in the heritage restoration were a rebuild of the rooftop ventilation towers (the west tower had been removed in the 1940s and the east tower in the 1970s), and the restoration of two chimneys in the central pavilion. The clerestory windows and the skylight in the rotunda would be restored and the glass floor reinstated. The annex on the west side, alias the Laundry Building, would be demolished and replaced by a new bridge link with Bridgepoint Health. Other amenities would include washrooms (an immense improvement over the night pails used by the previous occupants in their skinny cells and the single toilet and cold-water tap eventually installed in the overcrowded corridors), an elevator, and a new, glass, entry vestibule on the north side.

The final piece of the restoration puzzle was the "Bridgepoint Health Heritage Interpretation Plan" of 2008. Both the province and the city had identified the Old Don Jail as being of historical and architectural significance, and among their requirements was the development of a permanent public interpretation display. Additionally, one of the guiding principles established by the city was to present the jail in "a positive light as a progressive penal institution for its time." What a fine line the developers would have to tread between acknowledging "important heritage features ... such as the window bars, death row or gallows" and providing "sensitive interpretation for elements ... which may have negative associative values including the gallows or death row." Visitors may stroll through the building and the grounds today to discover whether the interpretive displays on the architecture and development of the jail, penal reform in Canada, and prisoner history succeed in achieving this delicate balance.

Between 2010 and 2013, multiple challenges and surprises awaited the teams of architects and heritage restoration experts involved in wrestling what Andrew Pruss calls that "large and derelict building" into its present shape.

As part of the redevelopment of the Bridgepoint Health site, the annex on the west side of the jail, which had originally served as the Laundry Building, was demolished in December 2009.

One of their dilemmas was the extent to which the building's exterior should be stripped of the ingrained grime and soot that had built up over the one-hundred-and-fifty-odd years of its existence. It ended up getting a light cleaning. As Michael McClelland notes, they wanted to keep some of the patina, so that it "looked as if it had age to it."

Even the surrounding garden area was the subject of some debate: one proposal was to install coffin-shaped features in the former northeast exercise yard or "Murderers' Graveyard" where the bodies of hanged inmates had originally been interred. Understandably, that suggestion did not fly.

Inside the building, one of the most extensive problems was the configuration of the tiny cells, which, as McClelland explains, were all "structural"; that is, the walls of each cell supported three stone ceiling slabs, and, just "like a house of cards," another identical cell was stacked on top. The slabs had to be gingerly removed one by one, making for great difficulty in opening up the spaces for their new and more expansive use as administrative offices.

And then there were the surprises.

During the course of the project, for example, workers discovered original finishes, such as remnants of wallpaper, hidden behind walls and ceilings. One of these fragments has been preserved and left in place for public viewing just below ceiling level in what was formerly the governor's apartment. Closed to the public for obvious reasons is a small room bristling with pipes and cables where two charming paintings, one of a waterfall and the other of a lake, adorn the walls. The landscapes, probably from the hand of a single inmate, are now carefully protected behind glass.

The restorers kept many fascinating features — the corridors or day rooms are there, as well as the railings and balconies in the rotunda, still supported by their coiled cast-iron serpents and griffins. Generally, however, the building is quite different now — a bright, white space with stone and blond wood floors, red accent walls, and glass and iron gates and balustrades. It is peopled during the day by hospital administrators, clinical experts, and their clients, as well as the odd interested member of the public wandering through on a self-guided tour. One staff member who often works late at night remarks that "for the history it has, it has a good feeling. You'd think it would be creepy, but it feels warm."

Described as a "wooden nickel," this disc was produced by a former correctional officer to commemorate the closure of the Don Jail in 2013.

But its sound and fury have been muted. And that is supremely ironic. As Pruss observes, "It was crowded for most of its history. That intensity is missing."

To the great delight of property owners in bustling Riverdale on the east side of the Don River, there is no longer a jail at the corner of Broadview Avenue and Gerrard Street East — for the first time in more than a hundred and fifty tumultuous years. The Old Don Jail has been transformed and its toxic neighbour, the New Don Jail, demolished.

It is the end of an era.

CHAPTER 27

Remember the Don

The west building was completed in 1865 [*sic*]. Ironically, it suffered a fire in 1858 [the actual date was 1862] prior to its completion. From the condemnation it received from grand juries in later years, as well as from criticism it has received from other quarters from time to time, we may consider it unfortunate that Phoenix ever rose from the ashes on Gerrard Street.

— His Honour Judge B. Barry Shapiro, commissioner of the 1978 *Report of the Royal Commission on the Toronto Jail and Custodial Services*

This particular phoenix, however, had succeeded in rising from the ashes back in 1862.

And the Don Jail had so much going for it. It was conceived during a period of great penal optimism, built in accordance with the most modern architectural principles, and run on a system based on the progressive Auburn philosophy. In spite of a series of bitter controversies during the construction period and grumblings about massive cost overruns, the final product was a huge improvement over its three hellish predecessors. The people of Toronto regarded it as the pride of their flourishing city.

So what went wrong?

From the outset, the basic Auburn model with its miniscule separate cells proved to be disastrously flawed. With no toilet facilities in the cells, it was impossible to maintain any decent standards of sanitation. And, as penal practices shifted, inmates spent less time outdoors or engaged in productive work. Instead, they were confined with little classification or separation of offenders in the corridors or day rooms, each of which was eventually fitted with just one toilet and one cold-water tap to serve the needs of dozens of inmates.

Perhaps the situation might not have deteriorated so rapidly if the jail had not been challenged by the vigorous growth of the city that had spawned it. As early as the 1880s, commentators noted that the Don, built for a city of around fifty thousand people, was no longer able to cope with a population now more than three times that size. The construction of other correctional facilities made little difference. Within a very short space of time, the "palace for prisoners" degenerated into a dysfunctional, understaffed, and "overcrowded dungeon," lurching from crisis to crisis.

Once the imminent closure of the jail loomed in the 1970s, the debate heated up as to what to do with this toxic "insult to humanity." There were a number of possible outcomes. Tearing it down was a popular choice, as had befallen the more-or-less contemporaneous Queen Street Mental Health Centre at 999 Queen Street West. Advocates of heritage conservation won the day, and the jail remained standing. For more than twenty years, however, it looked as though the building would simply be left to moulder with minimal maintenance, perhaps to meet its end destroyed, as had so nearly happened in 1862, by the wilful or negligent act of an "incendiary."

With the much-lauded heritage restoration of the Don and its incorporation into Bridgepoint Active Healthcare, the wheel, in a sense, has come full circle.

The players who were active in bringing about this transformation are all in agreement. In the words of Marian Walsh, who was president and CEO of Bridgepoint at the time, they renewed the site, changed "a place of incarceration to a place of healing," and thus returned it to its reformist roots.

Most of the ghostly signs of lives lived in the Don Jail have now been taken down or painted over, including this record of his life of crime reportedly scrawled on the wall of Cell 14 by one former occupant: "John Mucumber is here for stealing two flamingos from the Toronto Riverdale Zoo."

Gone, too, is the annex and its exit door, where, in the old days, released "cons" would scratch their names ("WILLIE T," "JOHN CLARKE") or sentence ("30 DYS") before moving out to face the world again.

There is the faintest vertical strip visible on the rear east side of the central building indicating the place where a wall, long since torn down, once stood, and along which five men scampered in their quest for freedom.

But some signs and symbols are still there, preserved as poignant reminders of past suffering. Steps away from the execution chamber on the second floor are black marks burned into the wooden floor boards, where condemned men would pause to stub out their last cigarette on their way to the gallows. The gallows are no more. Frank Drea saw to

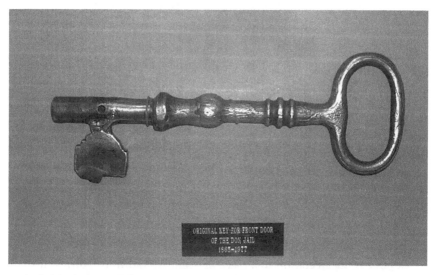

ORIGINAL KEY FOR FRONT DOOR
OF THE DON JAIL
1865-1977

Probably fashioned from steel and reportedly around fourteen inches in length, the original front-door key of the Old Don Jail took pride of place on the wall of the superintendent's office in the New Don. The key was removed during the decommissioning of the jail and has been archived with other items of historical significance.

that — making sure at the end of December 1977, to cries of "vandalism" from the City of Toronto's Historical Board, that the steel and wooden structure was spirited away to an undisclosed location where it would eventually be destroyed. Within the former latrine itself, however, the grey geometric shapes of the scaffold ghosted into the walls still mark the spot where twenty-six men, sentenced to death for murder, met their fates in the infamous jail before the abolition of capital punishment in Canada.

Between 1864 and 1978, according to some estimates, around one million people — old and young, sick and healthy, male and female, guilty and painfully innocent — passed beneath the grim visage of Father Time at the portal to the Old Don Jail.

These ghosts have not left the building.

"The energy of that place is still present," says Evan Tsitsias, artistic director of the Eclipse Theatre Company and director of *Kiss of the Spider Woman*, the musical theatre classic that was performed in the rotunda in early 2019. Based on the 1976 novel by Manuel Puig, *Kiss* conveys in words and music the touching story of a gay window dresser incarcerated with a Marxist revolutionary during Argentina's Dirty War of the 1970s and 1980s.

The production was nearly three years in the making, including meetings with Bridgepoint (they were "super helpful") and the Ontario Heritage Trust. And for five days in March, unsettling sounds of anguish and brutality once again rang out in the darkened rotunda.

"I was sometimes overwhelmed by the darkness of the space," says Tsitsias, adding that the jail takes on its own personality, particularly at night. He used its history to infuse and inform his piece with the aim of honouring the people who died there.

This desire for respectful recognition extended to the poetic land acknowledgement developed by cast member Kelsi James, which she delivered during a short tour of the jail prior to the performance. "I researched the history of the land and its people, and spoke with [assistant director] Joe [Recinos] and with my castmates, and wrote this poem as a thank you, and a call to action," says James.

Before we begin, I ask myself to look around
To notice my breath and my feet on this ground
And acknowledge the land that allows me to flourish
The waters and plants that sustain me and nourish.

The poem gracefully recognizes all those who have "cared for these lands and waterways," and, in particular, the Indigenous Peoples who were the "first storytellers here."

And what of the Don River, which has threaded its way, both literally and symbolically, through the story of the jail that shares its name? Sadly, it will never regain the pristine beauty that had early visitors and historians exclaiming with awe and delight. It is not doing too badly, though, considering the abuse it has been subjected to since British colonists first set up their tiny, ten-block hamlet of Muddy York in 1793. It is doing a lot better than when, anecdotally, it caught fire several times in the first half of the twentieth century. Or when, in 1969, an environmental group calling itself Pollution Probe held a solemn funeral for the Don, complete with hearse, coffin, flowers, weeping widow dressed in black, and the villain of the piece — a "greedy capitalist" in a top hat. Some of the wildlife is back — including birds, beavers, and turtles — and even the odd brave salmon has made a cautious reappearance. In May 2019, hundreds of conservationists, business people, and nature lovers canoed and kayaked along the river in the twenty-sixth annual "Paddle the Don" fundraiser.

Committed supporters of the Don welcomed the announcement in September 2019 that a $1.25 billion flood-protection project in Toronto's concrete-covered Port Lands district, just about the most contaminated area of all, is finally underway. As it feeds into the lake, the reconstructed river will meander through a new valley ecosystem. And, irony of ironies, an essential part of the plan is to recreate the much-reviled wetlands that were drained and paved over all those years ago.

ACKNOWLEDGEMENTS

There are great advantages to writing about your own city. Many of the places that feature largely in my book are situated within a few kilometres of where I live — among them, the sites of Toronto's three earliest jails, the Don Valley, Riverdale Park, and St. James Cemetery. The historic Don Jail itself is a brisk forty-minute walk from my home.

I undertook research trips to Ottawa and elsewhere in Canada, but, generally, the libraries and archives I haunted in the course of writing *The Don* are within extremely easy reach. Even the offices of Dundurn Press are just a short ride away.

And that is where my thank yous begin — with Kathryn Lane, Dundurn's associate publisher, who responded with great enthusiasm to my proposal for a book about Toronto's infamous jail. Thanks, too, to Elena Radic and the rest of the Dundurn team who shepherded *The Don* through the various stages of its production. And the book has benefitted immensely from the skill and professionalism of editors Dominic Farrell and Laurie Miller.

Writing is a very solitary pursuit, but I am most fortunate to be surrounded by a vibrant and supportive community of family, friends, fellow writers, and experts in a variety of disciplines. Present at every step of the way were Tuhin Giri and Cathy Landolt. I have Tuhin to thank for coming up with the book title and much, much more — he reviewed every chapter, pinpointing with great accuracy flaws in the logic and holes in the narrative. Cathy's skills in both website design and social media and digital marketing management have been invaluable. Catherine Rondina and fellow members of the #9 writing group offered early feedback, and folks like Sheryl Danilowitz, Lin Judelman, and Ruthie Swartzman were always ready to lend an ear to my stories and offer helpful (or sympathetic) comment when needed. Leah Daniels, Greg Judelman, and Lewis Poplak helped out with excellent introductions, and Jane Cobden generously sent me the precious originals of a series of newspaper articles about Canadian prisons written in 1971 by her late husband, Michael.

On the research side, kudos to Alan Walker and the outstanding Special Collections Department at the Toronto Reference Library, who provided me with information and access to many of the evocative images from Toronto's past that grace the pages of this book. Thanks, too, to the friendly and efficient staff at the City of Toronto Archives, the Archives of Ontario Library, and Library and Archives Canada in Ottawa, as well as to the Bank of Canada Museum and the Toronto Police Museum and Discovery Centre.

Patricia Petruga of Bridgepoint Health Science Library offered cheery and exceptionally efficient assistance, and the city and Bridgepoint Doors Open Toronto teams very kindly welcomed my participation in the event in 2019. I am also indebted to the people associated with the adaptive reuse of the heritage jail who gave so generously of their time and expertise, especially Frank Lewinberg and Amanda McCabe of Urban Strategies; Michael McClelland and Andrew Pruss of ERA Architects; and Bridgepoint's former president and CEO Marian Walsh.

I was fortunate in being able to connect with many other individuals who have been active in one way or another in the evolving saga of the two Don jails. Prominent among them is Paul McMaster, the Don's unofficial historian, who provided me with information, introductions, artifacts, and many outstanding photographs. Thanks to those who graciously agreed to speak with me, including Louie Aldaba,

Lee Chapelle, the late Gail Desabrais, Edward Hertrich, Steven Green, Kelsi James, John Minarik, Kari Niemi, John Sewell, the late Ian Starkie, Evan Tsitsias, and Peter Vronsky. A number of those I interviewed did not wish to be identified, and I have, of course, respected their wishes.

I also extend my grateful appreciation to Carolyn Poplak, Richard Poplak, Keith Pownall, Victor Russell, and Morris Zbar, whose impressive range of expertise as first readers of the manuscript improved it immeasurably. Thanks, too, to Valda Poplak for her meticulous attention to the bibliography.

Finally, as always, my very special gratitude to my husband, Phillip Poplak. Not only did he provide support and encouragement but also, with great culinary flair, many delicious meals to sustain us both as I worked my way through the book.

SELECTED BIBLIOGRAPHY

NEWSPAPERS

Canadian Illustrated News
Canadian Review
Globe, The (Toronto)
Globe and Mail
Guelph Mercury
Inside Toronto
Leader, The (Toronto)
Morning Chronicle
National Post
Ottawa Citizen
Quebec Daily Telegraph
Toronto Evening Telegram (also called the *Telegram*)
Toronto Star (earlier called the *Toronto Daily Star*)
Toronto Sun

REPORTS AND OTHER DOCUMENTS

Architectural drawings, studies, and reports
By-laws (Toronto)
Capital Case Files, RG 13, Department of Justice (Canada), Library
    and Archives Canada, Ottawa
Commissions of Inquiry (Ontario)

Grand jury reports
Official rules and regulations (Ontario)
Royal commission reports
Staff reports (Toronto)
Statutes (Ontario)
Toronto and Metropolitan Toronto Police memos, reports and other documents
Toronto city council minutes and committee reports

OTHER SOURCES

Arthur, Eric Ross. *Toronto: No Mean City*. 3rd ed. Toronto: University of Toronto Press, 1986.

Bateman, Chris. "A Short and Violent History of Toronto's Central Prison." *blogTO*. October 20, 2012. Accessed July 16, 2019. blogto.com/city/2012/10/a_short_and_violent_history_of_torontos_central_prison/.

———. "The Rise and Fall and Rise of St. Lawrence Hall." *Spacing Toronto*. December 29, 2018. spacing.ca/toronto/2016/12/09/rise-fall-st-lawrence-hall/.

Batten, Jack. *Judges*. Toronto: Macmillan of Canada, 1986.

Bonnell, Jennifer Leigh. *Imagined Futures and Unintended Consequences: An Environmental History of Toronto's Don River Valley*. PhD thesis. Dept. of Theory and Policy Study in Education. OISE, University of Toronto, 2010.

———. *Reclaiming the Don: An Environmental History of Toronto's Don River Valley*. Toronto: University of Toronto Press, 2014.

Boyer, J. Patrick. *A Passion for Justice: How "Vinegar Jim" McRuer Became Canada's Greatest Law Reformer*. Toronto: Blue Butterfly Books, 2008.

Boyle, Terry. *Fit to Be Tied: Ontario's Murderous Past*. Toronto: Polar Bear Press, 2001.

Bradburn, Jamie. "Historicist: What To Do With the Don Jail?" *Torontoist*. August 3, 2013. Accessed September 16, 2019. torontoist.com/2013/08/historicist-what-to-do-with-the-don-jail/.

Brown, Ron. *Behind Bars: Inside Ontario's Heritage Gaols.* Toronto: Natural Heritage Books, 2006.

Butts, Edward. *Line of Fire: Heroism, Tragedy, and Canada's Police.* Toronto: Dundurn Press, 2009.

———. "Recalling the Polka Dot Gang's Time in Guelph." *Guelph Mercury.* December 29, 2015. Accessed July 28, 2019. guelphmercury.com/news-story/6211246-recalling-the-polka-dot-gang-s-time-in-guelph/.

———. *Wrong Side of the Law: True Stories of Crime.* Toronto: Dundurn Press, 2013.

Careless, J.M.S. (James Maurice Stockford). *Toronto to 1918: An Illustrated History.* Toronto: James Lorimer, 1984.

Chandler, David B. *Capital Punishment in Canada: A Sociological Study of Repressive Law.* The Carleton Library, no.94. Toronto: McClelland and Stewart, in association with The Institute of Canadian Studies, Carleton University, 1976.

Dendy, William. *Lost Toronto.* Toronto: Oxford University Press, 1978.

Dickens, Charles. *American Notes for General Circulation.* London: Chapman & Hall, 1913.

"Eastern State Penitentiary Historic Site." Accessed March 20, 2019. easternstate.org/.

Einarson, Neil. "Thomas, William." In *Dictionary of Canadian Biography*, vol. 8. Accessed December 23, 2018. biographi.ca/en/bio/thomas_william_8E.html.

Ekstedt, John W. and Curt T. Griffiths. *Corrections in Canada: Policy and Practice.* 2nd ed. Toronto: Butterworths, 1988.

Filey Mike. *A Toronto Album: Glimpses of the City That Was.* 2nd ed. Toronto: Dundurn Press, 2001.

———. *A Toronto Album 2: More Glimpses of the City That Was.* Toronto: Dundurn Press, 2002.

Finlayson, George D. *John J. Robinette: Peerless Mentor: An Appreciation.* Toronto: Osgoode Society for Canadian Legal History, 2003.

Firth, Edith G. "Scadding, Henry." In *Dictionary of Canadian Biography*, vol. 13. Accessed February 04, 2019. biographi.ca/en/bio/scadding_henry_13E.html.

————. *The Town of York, 1793–1815: A Collection of Documents of Early Toronto*. The Publications of the Champlain Society. Ontario Series, V. Toronto: The Champlain Society for the Government of Ontario, University of Toronto Press, 1962.

Fletcher, Ron. *Over the Don*. Toronto: R. Fletcher, 2002.

Freeman, Victoria Jane. *"Toronto Has No History!" Indigeneity, Settler Colonialism and Historical Memory in Canada's Largest City*. Ph.D. thesis, Dept. of History, University of Toronto, 2010.

Gadoury, Lorraine, and Antonio Lechasseur. *Persons Sentenced to Death in Canada, 1867–1976: An Inventory of Case Files in the Fonds of the Department of Justice*. Accessed October 23, 2014. Ottawa: National Archives of Canada,1994. data2.archives.ca/pdf/pdf001/p000001052.pdf.

Gray, Charlotte. *The Massey Murder: A Maid, Her Master and the Trial That Shocked a Country*. Toronto: HarperCollins Canada, 2013.

Greenwood, F. Murray, and Beverley Boissery. *Uncertain Justice: Canadian Women and Capital Punishment 1754–1953*. Toronto: Dundurn Press, 2000.

Guillet, Edwin C. *Pioneer Settlements in Upper Canada*. Toronto: University of Toronto Press, 1969.

Hangman's Graveyard. Documentary. Directed by Mick Grogan and produced by Daniel Thomson. Toronto: Ballinran Entertainment, 2009.

Hay, Gordon. "Biography of John Howard." The John Howard Society of Canada. Accessed March 20, 2019. johnhoward.ca/about-us/history/biography-john-howard/.

Hibbert, Christopher. *The English: A Social History, 1066–1945*. London: Grafton, 1987.

Hoshowsky, Robert J. *The Last to Die: Ronald Turpin, Arthur Lucas, and the End of Capital Punishment in Canada*. Toronto: Dundurn Press, 2007.

Howard, John. *The State of the Prisons in England and Wales: With Preliminary Observations, and an Account of Some Foreign Prisons*. Printed by William Eyres, and sold by T. Cadell in the Strand, and N. Conant in Fleet Street. London: Warrington, 1777.

Hune-Brown, Nicholas. "Hell House: Why the Don Jail Is a Wretched, Dangerous Dungeon That Should Have Been Shut Down Ages Ago." *Toronto Life.* December 6, 2010. Accessed September 5, 2019. torontolife.com/city/hell-house/.

Johnson, Dana. "Prison Architecture." In *The Canadian Encyclopedia.* Accessed June 4, 2019. thecanadianencyclopedia.ca/en/article/prison-architecture.

Johnson, Mark D. *No Tears to the Gallows: The Strange Case of Frank McCullough.* Toronto: McClelland & Stewart, 2000.

Johnston, Norman Bruce. *The Human Cage: A Brief History of Prison Architecture.* New York: Published for the American Foundation, Institute of Corrections by Walker, 1973.

Jones, James Edmund. *Pioneer Crimes and Punishments in Toronto and the Home District: An Account of the Many Activities of the Magistrates Both in Criminal and Civil Matters, Drawn Largely from Records Hitherto for the Most Part Unpublished.* Toronto: G.N. Morang, 1924.

Lamb, Marjorie, and Barry Pearson. *The Boyd Gang.* Toronto: P. Martin Associates, 1976.

Lamport, Allan A. "What the Boyd Gang Fiasco Can Teach Us." *Maclean's.* December 1, 1952. Accessed September 10, 2018. archive. macleans.ca/article/1952/12/1/what-the-boyd-gang-fiasco-can-teach-us.

Levine, Allan Gerald. *Toronto: Biography of a City.* Madeira Park, BC: Douglas & McIntyre, 2014.

Leyton-Brown, Ken. *The Practice of Execution in Canada.* Vancouver: UBC Press, 2010.

McArthur, Glenn, and Annie Szamosi. *William Thomas, Architect: 1799-1860.* Ottawa: Archives of Canadian Art, 1996.

McNicoll, Susan. *Toronto Murders: Mysteries, Crime, and Scandals.* Canmore, AB: Altitude Publishing Canada Ltd., 2005.

Morriss, Shirley G. "Young, Thomas." In *Dictionary of Canadian Biography,* vol. 8. Accessed February 25, 2019. biographi.ca/en/bio/young_thomas_1860_8E.html.

Muir, Elizabeth Gillan, and Elizabeth Abbott. *Riverdale: East of the Don*. Toronto: Dundurn, 2014.

Ng, Nathan. "Explore Toronto's Past Through Maps ..." *Historical Maps of Toronto* (blog). Accessed December 15, 2019. oldtoronto-maps.blogspot.com/.

———. "Goad's Atlas of Toronto — Online!" *Goad's Atlas of Toronto — Online!* (blog), April 4, 2012. Accessed December 15, 2019. skritch.blogspot.com/2012/04/goads-atlas-of-toronto-on-line.html.

Nickerson, Janice. *Crime and Punishment in Upper Canada*. Toronto: Dundurn Press, 2010.

Ontario Cemeteries Act Site Investigation: The Old Don Jail Burial Area. Toronto: Archaeological Services, 2008.

Pfeifer, Jeffrey E., and Kenneth Bryan Leyton-Brown. *Death by Rope: An Anthology of Canadian Executions*. Regina: Vanity Press, 2007.

Plummer, Kevin. "Historicist: Titillating and Terrorizing Toronto." *Torontoist*. September 8, 2012. Accessed December 19, 2019. torontoist.com/2012/09/historicist_titillating_and_terrori/.

Pullen, Charles. *The Life and Times of Arthur Maloney: The Last of the Tribunes*. Toronto: Dundurn Press, 1994.

Raible, Chris. "999 Queen Street West: The Toronto Asylum Scandal." *Canada's History*. Accessed January 4, 2019. canadashistory.ca/explore/science-technology/999-queen-street-west-the-toronto-asylum-scandal.

Reed, Thomas Arthur. *The Scaddings: A Pioneer Family in York*. Toronto: 1944. Reprinted from the papers and records of the Ontario Historical Society, vol. 36.

Robertson, J. Ross (John Ross). *Landmarks of Toronto; a Collection of Historical Sketches of the Old Town of York from 1792 until 1833, and of Toronto from 1834 to 1893 Volume 1*. Toronto: J. Ross Robertson, 1894. Published from the *Toronto Evening Telegram*.

Ross, Alexander. "The Final Hours of the Last Two Men Executed in Canada." *Maclean's*. September 18, 1965. Accessed October 24, 2018.

macleans.ca/archives/the-final-hours-of-the-last-two-men-executed-in-Canada/.

Rust-D'Eye, George. *Cabbagetown Remembered*. Erin, ON: Boston Mills Press, 1984.

Sauriol, Charles. *Remembering the Don: A Rare Record of Earlier Times within the Don River Valley*. Scarborough, ON: Consolidated Amethyst Communications, 1981.

Scadding, Henry. *Toronto of Old*, edited by Frederick H. Armstrong. Toronto & Oxford: Dundurn Press, 1987.

Sewell, John. *How We Changed Toronto: The Inside Story of Twelve Creative, Tumultuous Years in Civic Life, 1969–1980*. Toronto: James Lorimer, 2015.

Simcoe, Elizabeth, and J. Ross Robertson. *The Diary of Mrs. John Graves Simcoe, Wife of the First Lieutenant-Governor of the Province of Upper Canada, 1792–6*. Toronto: Ontario Publishing Co. Ltd, 1934.

Strange, Carolyn. "Wounded Womanhood and Dead Men: Chivalry and the Trials of Clara Ford and Carrie Davies." In *Gender Conflicts: New Essays in Women's History*, edited by Franca Iacovetta and Mariana Valverde, 149–88. Toronto: University of Toronto Press, 1992.

Talbot, Edward Allen. *Five Years' Residence in the Canadas: Including a Tour through Part of the United States of America, in the Year 1823*. London: Printed for Longman, Hurst, Rees, Orme, Brown and Green, 1824.

The Riverdale Hospital: 140 Years of Breaking New Ground: 1860–2000. Toronto: Riverdale Hospital, 2000.

Thomas, Jocko. *From Police Headquarters: True Tales from the Big City Crime Beat*. Toronto: Stoddart, 1990.

Vallée, Brian. *Edwin Alonzo Boyd: The Story of the Notorious Boyd Gang*. Toronto: Doubleday Canada, 1997.

Wencer, David. "Historicist: Sticky Business." *Torontoist*. March 28, 2015. Accessed June 11, 2019. torontoist.com/2015/03/historicist-sticky-business/.

IMAGE CREDITS

91   Picture by W.H. Paget. Courtesy of Toronto Public Library.

103   Photograph by author. Library and Archives Canada/
RG13-B-1, vol. 1497, file no. cc 101 part 1.1 and Library and
Archives Canada/RG13-B-1, vol. 1499, file no. cc 101 part
8.3.

111   Sketch from the *Canadian Illustrated News*, attributed to
William Armstrong. Courtesy of Toronto Public Library.

119   *Toronto Star* Photograph Archive. Courtesy of Toronto Public
Library.

136   City of Toronto Archives, *Globe and Mail* fonds. Fonds 1266,
Item 148252.

146   © Government of Canada. Reproduced with the permission
of Library and Archives Canada (2019). Library and Archives
Canada/RG13-B-1, vol. 1709, file no. cc 749, part 1–3.

154   © Government of Canada. Reproduced with the permission
of Library and Archives Canada (2019). Library and Archives
Canada/RG13-B-1, vol. 1709, file no. cc 749, part 1–3.

155   © Government of Canada. Reproduced with the permission
of Library and Archives Canada (2019). Library and Archives
Canada/RG13-B-1, vol. 1709, file no. cc 749, part 1–3.

162   Photograph by Herbert J. Holtom. City of Toronto Archives.

169   Illustrated by Urban Strategies. Courtesy of Bridgepoint
Health.

179   Photograph by Paul McMaster.

189   Photograph by the Toronto Historical Board. Courtesy of
John Sewell.

208   Illustrated by Urban Strategies. Courtesy of Bridgepoint
Health.

214   Photograph by the *Toronto Star*. Public Domain.

218   Photograph by author.

223   Photograph by Paul McMaster.

224   Photographs by author.

228   Photograph by Paul McMaster.

INDEX

Page numbers in italics refer to illustrations.

ABOUT THE AUTHOR

Lorna Poplak is a writer, editor, and researcher drawn to the people and stories behind historical facts. Her background is in law, literature, information technology, and technical communications. Lorna's written work includes children's literature, travel pieces, medical and scientific articles, blog posts, and a radio play. Other professional activities have included editing, fact checking, and proofreading works of fiction, non-fiction, and graphic literature. Lorna has lived in Toronto since emigrating to Canada from her native South Africa in 1989. She has served on the council of the Society for Technical Communication Toronto and on the board of the Canadian Society of Children's Authors, Illustrators and Performers. Lorna is a member of Crime Writers of Canada and Sisters in Crime. Her debut non-fiction book, *Drop Dead: A Horrible History of Hanging in Canada*, was published by Dundurn in July 2017.